REQUIEM FOR AN ARMY

REQUIEM FOR AN ARMY

The Demise of the
East German Military

Dale R. Herspring

ROWMAN & LITTLEFIELD PUBLISHERS, INC.
Lanham • Boulder • New York • Oxford

ROWMAN & LITTLEFIELD PUBLISHERS, INC.

Published in the United States of America
by Rowman & Littlefield Publishers, Inc.
4720 Boston Way, Lanham, Maryland 20706

12 Hid's Copse Road
Cumnor Hill, Oxford OX2 9JJ, England

British Library Cataloguing in Publication Information Available

Library of Congress Cataloging-in-Publication Data
Herspring, Dale R. (Dale Roy)
    Requiem for an army : the demise of the East German military /
Dale R. Herspring.
        p.   cm.
    Includes bibliographical references and index.
    ISBN 0-8476-8718-X (hardcover : alk. paper)—ISBN 0-8476-8719-8
(pbk. : alk. paper)
        1. Germany (East).   Nationale Volksarmee—Demobilization.
    2. Germany (East)—Military policy.   3. Germany—History—
Unification, 1990.   I. Title.
    UA719.3.H6424   1998
    355'.009431—dc21   98-25249
                                                                              CIP

Printed in the United States of America

∞ ™ The paper used in this publication meets the minimum requirements of
American National Standard for Information Sciences—Permanence of Paper
for Printed Library Materials, ANSI Z39.48-1984.

To those members of the NVA who, through their support of the peaceful transition to democracy at a time of great stress, helped make German unification a reality.

In my opinion, if blood had flowed, we would have never
achieved unification.

Wolfgang Schäuble

You get the impression that some people would very much like
to remove the NVA from history so that it is forgotten. . . .

Admiral Theodor Hoffmann

Contents

Preface

The purpose of this book is neither to praise nor to condemn the NVA. Rather, it is to provide a better understanding of the events that led to its collapse and the factors that motivated those who filled its ranks and served so faithfully in it over the years.

Some of my friends suggested that the NVA was not a particularly important military—"and besides it doesn't exist anymore." Others spoke of an army made up of "a bunch of thugs," who deserved to be consigned to the ash heap of history. Still others argued that I would be better advised to devote my efforts to analyzing the situation within the Bundeswehr, a military that will be important to the future of Europe.

Being stubborn, however, I refused to accept their advice. The more I worked on this project, the more convinced I became that writing this book was the right decision. First, for good or ill, I have spent a lifetime studying the NVA. I wrote the first book in English on the subject,[1] and I followed the organization over subsequent years. I was always amazed at how much a small country, with limited population and economic resources, was able to accomplish in the military domain. Indeed, it is no exaggeration to say that by the mid-1980s the NVA was the second most powerful and feared armed force in the Warsaw Pact. As a political scientist, I also was impressed to see how the political leadership used the military as part of its effort to make the GDR indispensable to the Soviets—and thereby block any attempts by the West Germans to make a deal with Moscow at East Berlin's expense.

But then the NVA began to fall apart. And what was more interesting to me, both as a scholar and a former policymaker, was that the East German officer corps not only did not resist the transition toward democracy, it actually supported it. While my own lengthy experience with Western militaries convinced me that every military has its share of thugs, and perhaps the NVA had more than others, I could not reconcile that perception with the actions of NVA professionals during 1989–90. Too often I think we in the West stereotyped security organs in the GDR—especially the border troops and the secret police. While the former were part of the NVA, the latter were much different. Many in the NVA disliked the Stasi as much if not more than those of us in the West who had a Stasi "shadow" every time we visited the GDR. In short, a distinction had to be made between those who were Stasi and those who were part of the highly efficient, highly competent NVA. The response of the NVA—including the border troops—to the changes in 1989–90 was very different from that of the Stasi.

I also wanted to illuminate the role played by the NVA in reuniting Germany. Reading major works on the fall of communism in East Germany, one could easily gain the impression that the NVA played a minimal role. Fortunately, the NVA did not become directly involved as the two Germanies moved closer to reunification. But that was no accident: it was a result of leadership at the top and a commitment on the part of the GDR's professional officers not to use force against their own people. Even then, the situation was very precarious and on several occasions could have been disastrous. In short, the more I looked at the events of 1989–90 the more convinced I became that there was a serious gap in the literature—especially in English.

Then there was the issue of ideology. Based on our understanding of the role of ideology in a party-army like the NVA, one would have assumed that the military would have been the strongest supporter of the old regime. But it wasn't. Why not? I decided that learning more about the end of the NVA would help shed light on the role that ideology played in the lives of the NVA's professionals.

Finally, there was the question of the kind of people who made up this military that I had observed for more than thirty years. What sorts of individuals chose to spend a lifetime in the NVA? What impact did their environment have on them? In contrast to other former communist armies, this was an especially interesting question, because we have the West German experience of dealing with more than 3,000 former NVA professionals who subsequently joined the Bundeswehr. Basic behavior characteristics became very clear as the Bundeswehr went through the process of reeducating these individuals—teaching them how to function in a Western, democratic military.

The NVA has been consigned to history. Only parts of its uniforms and other paraphernalia remain to be hawked around the Brandenburger Tor. Nevertheless, it would be both wrong and silly to ignore it; not only because its behavior during those critical days raises questions about our understanding of how communist militaries functioned, but also because it helps shed light on why some of the key decisions were taken by policymakers, both East and West. It also assists us in better understanding the kind of individuals who wore the uniform of the NVA, what they thought and how they responded at critical points.

A Note on the Names in This Text

Throughout this book, I have followed normal German spelling. Thus instead of *ss*, the German letter ß has been employed, e.g., *Keßler* instead of *Kessler*. Also I have used an umlaut in place of the English letter *e*, e.g., *Brünner* instead of *Bruenner*.

Acknowledgments

When I first mentioned to several of my friends and colleagues that I planned, sitting in the middle of Kansas, to write a book about the collapse of the East German military and its absorption into the Bundeswehr, a number of them suggested that I lacked common sense. "How can you hope to write a book of this kind unless you are on the spot in Germany?" was the typical reaction. What these individuals did not know was that I would be the recipient of extraordinary assistance from a number of sources, both in Kansas and abroad.

First, I would like to thank the staff of the library here at Kansas State University. Their help, and especially the support I received from the library's director, Brice Hobrock, was invaluable. On many occasions, the staff was asked to find obscure journals or books—none of which were present in our library. In many cases, obtaining this material required incredible persistence and creativity. I could never even have begun work on this book if it had not been for the conscientious and dedicated work of these individuals.

Second, I want to thank the sixty-nine former East German officers who filled out questionnaires concerning their experience during that fatal period from 1989 to 1990. The fact that I was able to obtain so many completed questionnaires added significantly to the value of this book. When it comes to individuals who played a key role in Germany, I cannot fail to mention Professor Dr. Egbert Fischer and the Deutscher Bundeswehrverband, who distributed the questionnaires, collected them, and sent them to me. Most of all, however, I want to thank Colonel Hans-Werner Weber, who played a very important role during the last days of the NVA. I have written a number of books, but never have I received such unselfish assistance from anyone. Colonel Weber not only provided his own views on many of these events—he also helped me obtain a number of the pictures included in this volume and was invaluable in assisting me in myriad other ways. It is no exaggeration to suggest that his assistance significantly increased the value and authoritativeness of this book. I would also like to thank Lt. Col. (GS) Reinhard Panin, a former member of the NVA who now serves in the Bundeswehr.

I am also indebted to Jürgen Eike, who provided me with copies of the interviews he conducted with a number of key players in this drama in preparation for his TV documentary film, "Die Verschwundene Armee." Mr. Eike also provided me with a copy of the film itself, which gave a useful insight into the events of 1989–90. Former Minister Rainer Eppelmann provided me with three of the pictures included in this volume. Finally, I want to express my thanks to my graduate student, Mr. Christian Ahlert, who helped me read some of the more indecipherable handwriting in some of the questionnaires.

Over the years I have worked with a number of editors, and all of them have been good. I would be remiss, however, if I did not single out Ms. Susan McEachern of Rowman and Littlefield. Her assistance in making this book readable as well as her many suggestions on how to improve it went far beyond what I have received in the past.

Finally, as was the case with other books I have written, I must acknowledge the role played by my family and in particular my younger son Kyle. Because of his father's deep interest in Germany, Kyle has endured the expectations of teachers who assume he is not only fluent in German, but also has an encyclopedic knowledge of German history and politics. Someday when he has learned German and sees just how exciting and interesting German history and politics can be, I think he will begin to understand why his father has devoted so much of his life to studying this intriguing country.

Acronyms and Abbreviations

BBC	British Broadcasting Corporation
CSCE	Conference on Security and Cooperation in Europe
CDU	Christian Democratic Union
CNN	Cable News Network
CPSU	Communist Party of the Soviet Union
CSU	Christian Socialist Union
DA	Democratic Awakening
DBP	Democratic Peasant's Party
DM	deutsche mark
EW	*Europäische Wehrkunde*
FAZ	*Frankfurter Allgemeine Zeitung*
FDJ	Free German Youth (Freie Deutsche Jugend)
FRG	Federal Republic of Germany
GDR	German Democratic Republic
GS	General Staff
GSU	German Social Union
HVA	Main Administration for Training (*Hauptverwaltung für Ausbildung*)
KVP	People's Police Quartered in Barracks (*Kasernierte Volkspolizei*)
LDPD	Liberal Democratic Party of Germany
MOD	Ministry of Defense
NATO	North Atlantic Treaty Organization
NCO	Non-Commissioned Officer
ND	*Neues Deutschland*
NDPD	National Democratic Party of Germany
NVA	*Nationale Volksarmee* or *National People's Army*
NYT	New York Times
PDS	Party of Democratic Socialism
SED	Socialist Unity Party

SPD	Social Democratic Party of Germany
Stasi	*Staatsicherheitsdienst* (State Security Service)
UPI	United Press International
USSR	Union of Soviet Socialist Republics
VP	*Volkspolizei* (People's Police)
WP	Washington Post

Introduction

Nothing plays out the way one's imaginary logic suggests it will.
Günter Schabowski

The National People's Army (Nationale Volksarmee or NVA) of the former German Democratic Republic is almost unique in the annals of military history. Unlike the Imperial Russian Army, the German Wehrmacht, the Nationalist Chinese Army, or the South Vietnamese military, it did not collapse as a result of long and bloody internal or external wars. Instead, the NVA did something unprecedented: it supported the introduction of democracy in the GDR and in the process it helped dig its own grave. A few—very few—former members of the NVA were absorbed into the West German Bundeswehr. The rest were thrown out of the military after lengthy careers and, with minimal help from Bonn, expected to fend for themselves.

The experience of the NVA raises two key questions which will be the focus of this book. First, why did the political leadership choose not to use the NVA against the populace? Similarly, once it became clear that the old system was collapsing, why did the NVA not resort to the use of arms to protect the polity it was sworn to serve and from which it received so many benefits? Most Western models would suggest that in the face of open threats to the military's core interests, the generals would have responded by fighting to keep the old regime in power. Yet this did not happen in the GDR. Why not?

A second purpose of this book is to understand the process of integrating these former NVA officers and NCOs into the Bundeswehr. This was not an easy task. While most of them were competent military specialists, their attitudes, ideas, and approaches to dealing with military issues were heavily influenced by two factors: first, their tendency to copy the Prussian/Russian idea of total obedience, even to the point of using brute force on occasion in dealing with subordinates; and second, as a result of their isolation from society and extensive indoctrina-

1

tion in the principles of Marxism-Leninism, their lack of understanding of how a military operates in a democratic polity.

Why No Military Intervention?

This question is of more than academic interest. Most observers agreed that if serious violence had accompanied the fall of communism in the GDR, German unification would never have occurred. To quote one senior NVA officer, "What would have happened if only one tank had appeared in Berlin, or if only one shot had been fired at a politician?"[1] There were acts of violence to be sure—some by the populace, most by the security organs—but almost none by the military. What is most important, however, is that a Chinese solution comparable to the Tiananmen Square massacre was avoided. Such a development would have had the most serious implications for internal politics in both the GDR and the former Soviet Union (at a minimum it would have strengthened the hands of the hard-liners in both countries). In addition, it would have seriously undermined East-West relations, which were the key to German unification. Without the "honeymoon" of 1990, German unification would never have taken place.

It is of course true that some troops were mobilized at the time of the demonstrations in early October 1989 and that there were a few moments surrounding the opening of the Berlin Wall on November 9 when it looked like some of the border troops (at that time a part of the NVA) might resort to the use of force, but in the end, they avoided violence.

This is not to say that everyone in the NVA welcomed the changes that occurred in the GDR in 1989. Indeed, many of the officers would have happily retained the old system. The important point is that by remaining neutral during the struggle against Erich Honecker, the NVA ensured that change would be peaceful. As the country began its slide into systemic collapse, first under Egon Krenz and later under Hans Modrow, there were repeated expressions of concern about what the officers and men of the NVA would do. Would they permit the country to fall apart? After all, not only was the state (and party) they were sworn to defend disintegrating, chaos was haunting all parts of society—including the military. NVA professionals had a lot to lose—their careers, their benefits, and their prestigious positions in society.[2] However, they made no attempt to turn back the clock. They marched into the new democratic polity in step with the rest of society.

As it became increasingly clear that East Germany would be taken over by Bonn, attention shifted to the efforts by the NVA—under the leadership of its "pacifist" defense minister—to continue its existence as a territorial force. When it was decided that the NVA would cease to exist after October 3, 1990—the day Germany was formally united—the officers and NCOs of the NVA meekly accepted that situation. Indeed, while some left voluntarily and others, especially political officers and senior officers, were given their walking papers, the primary concern for many was how to continue their military careers in the Bundeswehr.

There were obvious signs of bitterness among these professionals directed only in part against Bonn and the Bundeswehr. It was also focused on the former GDR government and the Russians. Defense Minister Rainer Eppelmann had repeatedly assured NVA professionals that they would have a future military career—even after unification. However, when Soviet leader Mikhail Gorbachev informed West German Chancellor Helmut Kohl at their meeting on July 15–16, 1990, that the USSR would not object if a reunited Germany became a member of NATO, the bottom dropped out of the world of the NVA professionals. Not only would the NVA be disolved, the Bundeswehr would have to reduce its numbers from close to 500,000 to 370,000—not an especially hospitable environment for those seeking to join its ranks. It was clear that Eppelmann would not be able to keep his promise. It was also obvious that reunification would come very quickly. It came so fast, in fact, that NVA professionals hardly had time to make any plans for the future. In a word, the future was now.

Yet anger directed at Eppelmann was no greater than the sense of betrayal felt toward the Russians. For years NVA officers and NCOs had devoted their lives to the maintenance of the Soviet-imposed system. The NVA had worked closely with the Soviets, and many officers spoke Russian and had studied in the USSR. In addition, almost all of the military's equipment and doctrine was Russian, and within the Warsaw Pact they were more thoroughly subordinate to Russian control than other pact members. A significant part of the East German population also despised the NVA professionals for their loyalty to the Russians and the communist regime they served. In short, they had spent their lives defending not only the GDR, but the USSR as well. In return, they expected loyalty from Moscow, and Gorbachev had repeatedly promised he would never cast them adrift. Consequently, when Gorbachev did cut them loose, they felt like ships without rudders. The Russians had assured the East Germans that they were Moscow's most important allies. Now with the stroke of a pen everything they had worked and sacrificed for was gone.

In spite of these feelings of bitterness and betrayal, there is no record of any effort by any NVA officer to reverse history by the use of force. They did not like the future fate had willed them, but they accepted it.

The East German experience raises a number of important theoretical questions. For example, if one were to list the key factors that characterized civil-military relations in the GDR, they would include the following:

—The military was isolated from politics and civil society. First, military officers were told that participation in the political process was not a legitimate pursuit. Senior officers could lobby for resources and the defense minister was part of the political leadership, but for the majority of NVA members, the military was a "subject" organization. It received its orders from its political masters. Second, in order for the process of politicization/indoctrination to work, it was important that the military be kept separate from the rest of civil society. In this way the party-state was better able to make the army immune from "unhealthy" external influences. If, for example, the civilian world was infected with antisystemic attitudes but the military was sufficiently isolated, the impact of the anti-regime attitudes could be minimized.

—The military was cohesive. In order for a party-state to retain control over its armed forces, the latter must be cohesive enough to maintain strict discipline that a party-state expects. Needless to say, a cohesive, albeit subservient military organization would be much easier to discipline than one that was constantly involved in the political process—the way the Russian military has been in recent years.

—Finally, as a way of helping ensure its subordination, the military focused its efforts on one special goal: defending the country from external threats. This is not to suggest that it could not be used for other purposes, e.g., harvesting potatoes or supporting the police in the case of demonstrations. However, the greater the degree to which the military was used for these other purposes, the less effective it would be in carrying out its primary function. Additionally, if it became involved in such extraneous matters, factors such as unit cohesion and isolation would be affected adversely.

As a consequence, civil-military relations in the GDR were quite different from what one would have expected in the West. The civilians and military were more isolated from each other, cohesion played a very important role, and its primary focus was against external (as opposed to internal) enemies.

The Process of Integration

What was the difference between those who adapted and those who found it impossible to function in a military under the new conditions?

In the long run, those who opted to serve in the Bundeswehr—and were accepted by Bonn—did a credible job adjusting to their new environment, but it was not easy. Understanding some of the problems involved in assisting these individuals to adapt to the rules and procedures of a democratic military should help us understand the type of professional soldier produced by a unitary party-state. This latter factor is especially important as we find ourselves confronted with the many problems involved in creating a new, democratic form of civil-military relations in transitional polities. It also has considerable importance for our efforts to compare civil-military relations in these states with the democratizing process in areas such as Latin America. Is there a mind-set common to party-states that may help us better understand some of the difficulties faced by those transitioning from autocratic to democratic political systems? Can we construct an ideal type of an East German military officer (probably the closest to a model communist) and then compare that officer with those in other polities?

The NVA and Civil-Military Relations

Of all the former communist militaries of Eastern Europe, the NVA is the most important in helping us understand the differences between the Soviet and East European experience. To begin with, change in the GDR was more radical and complete than anywhere else in Eastern Europe. Why do I say that?

First, unlike the rest of the communist world (including Russia), the GDR found its military as well as the rest of its society absorbed into the Federal Republic. All the armies of Eastern Europe—and Russia for that matter—went through a process of departization and democratization. The leadership purged those in the military who were unable to adapt to a democratic political environment, and made a considerable effort to replace communist values with democratic ones. But none of them were dissolved and forced to become part of another, preexisting army.

In practice this meant that the Russians and the other East Europeans relied on cadre from the communist period. For example, in the case of Poland, Warsaw did not attempt to purify its armed forces by bringing in individuals from the outside, nor did it try to set up a new military structure. In contrast, the NVA disappeared—it ceased to exist! A few former members of the NVA were permitted to join the Bundeswehr; most, however, were sent packing.

Second, the regimentation, isolation, and intense politicization[3] to which the East German military was subjected meant that the type of individual who wore the uniform of the NVA was different from most other East European officers. For example, in contrast to the Polish military, East Germans were more regimented, less understanding and tolerant of the pluralistic influences inherent in a democratic polity, and less sensitive to the need to treat subordinate personnel in what the West would consider a humane fashion.

The reason for this very rigid and extensive politicization process was simple: East Berlin went farther than its communist neighbors to convince Moscow that the GDR, including the NVA, was the most reliable of its East European allies.[4] Throughout the GDR's existence, East Berlin was haunted by the fear—which turned out to be valid in the end—that Moscow would make a deal with the West Germans at its expense. To counter this danger, East Berlin did everything possible, especially in the military sphere, to prove to the Kremlin that the NVA was better prepared for combat, that it was more likely to stand by the Soviets, and that it was less susceptible to Western influences than other East European militaries.

Available evidence suggests that the East Germans were successful in this endeavor—at least for most of the NVA's existence. Of all the militaries of Eastern Europe, the NVA was considered by Russian military officers to be the best disciplined, best organized, and best prepared to wage war if the need arose. After all, according to one former NVA officer, 85 percent of the men and officers were on the base near their equipment and weapons at any time. He estimated that his mechanized battalion could have been in the field ready to fight in forty-five minutes. "No mechanized unit in all of NATO could have matched that."[5] It could also be argued that the NVA was most like the Red Army in terms of structure, personnel policy, doctrine, weapons, and so forth.

Third, the NVA relied more on the USSR than other East European militaries. As the dominant power in the relationship, the Soviet Army was only minimally dependent on the NVA. By contrast, the NVA relied almost totally on the Russians for all its needs including equipment, doctrine, a personnel system, and training. In addition, East Berlin went to great lengths to inculcate within its members the same value system held by the Russians. This extreme dependency relationship—pushed by the East German leadership for political reasons—had a major impact on East German civil-military relations.

One result was that the East German military was less involved than the Soviet military in the political process. For example, when it came to a struggle for resources, the East German military leadership was only peripherally engaged. It was Moscow and not East Berlin which set requirements for the GDR's military. At the same time, since political leaders were primarily interested in pleasing the Russians by maintaining a strong military, they were also more willing to part with money for the military. As a consequence, there was seldom a major battle over resource allocation. Yet as the GDR moved into the post-Honecker era it became clear that having avoided political participation for so many years, East German military officers were ill-equipped to understand and deal with the new, more competitive and more ambiguous political environment.

Because of its unique status, a careful analysis of the NVA's experience may help us better understand recent developments in both the former USSR and other Eastern European states. This is especially true when assessing the latter. Too often there has been a tendency to look at Eastern Europe as a political monolith simply because all the states shared the same communist ideology and in most cases were members of the Warsaw Pact. In fact, there were major differences among them. The more extreme nature of communism in the former GDR provides a good vantage point from which to view events elsewhere in the region.

All of these states are undergoing a transition from a highly centralized, politicized structure to a more decentralized, democratic one. However, each has a different foundation from which to build, as the East German experience highlights. Furthermore, because of the more rigid nature of the East German party-state, understanding the problems faced by the Bundeswehr in changing a totalitarian value structure into a set of values supportive of a democratic polity may help shed light on some of the problems confronting other transitional systems—not only those from Eastern Europe and the former Soviet Union, but from other highly centralized political systems as well.

The NVA and the End of Communism

A number of factors characterized civil-military relations during the 1989–90 period. To begin with, one is struck by the fact that so little mention was made of the NVA by most of the leading participants in the East German political process.[6] Did they assume the military would do whatever Moscow or East Berlin told it to do? Did they assume that the NVA was unimportant from a political standpoint? How could one ignore such a potentially powerful political force? Comments on the Stasi, the East German secret police, abound throughout the memoirs of East German politicians and in the analyses of Western specialists. The absence of much in the way of detailed comment about the NVA is particularly significant when one considers that it was also undergoing major changes.

Like the rest of East German society, by the beginning of 1990, the NVA was a paradigm of instability, if not chaos. Strikes and a lack of discipline were rampant throughout the armed forces. One would think that the temptation on the part of East German military officers to impose some sort of order on the NVA, and through it the rest of society, must have been almost unbearable.

In fact, as one reads the memoirs of the main participants it is clear that although they paid little attention to it publicly, they feared that the widening instability and insecurity could lead the military to become a political actor—i.e., take matters into its own hands. For example, Horst Teltschik, the West German official probably most responsible for overseeing the reunification of the two Germanies, expressed his and his government's concern over attitudes within the military. Lothar de Maiziere said that he feared that if he dissolved the NVA, those released would become a security risk.[7] Given the prominent place of the Soviet experience in German thinking, the worry that the military could tip the scales in one direction or another was not unreasonable.

As Gorbachev moved further and further toward reordering priorities, and as it became increasingly clear to Soviet military leaders that he was intruding into what they considered their bureaucratic prerogative, they complained publicly. Given the similarity between the Russian and East German polities, one would have expected a similar response by the GDR's generals. In fact, the leaders of the NVA never attempted to duplicate the actions of their Russian sponsors. Public complaints abounded, but they were made almost exclusively by low-ranking officers and NCOs. Indeed, what was most surprising in light of the Russian experience was the failure of the military leadership to adopt an assertive leadership role. They seemed to wait for directions—even if those orders went against what they believed to be the good of the institution they represented.

Sources

To this point, the vast majority of Western scholarship dealing with civil-military relations in communist polities has looked through a glass darkly. We were handicapped by a lack of information—although more was available than often acknowledged even by experts. We thought we understood how the process worked, but as we have discovered in recent years, things were not always as they seemed.

The experience of the NVA opens up a whole new chapter when it comes to understanding how civil-military relations function both within a communist political system and in one that is heavily dependent on outside support and undergoing a transition to a democratic polity. There are a variety of reasons for this situation. To begin with, we have numerous studies both in English and in German available on how the collapse of East Germany occurred.[8] There are few secrets about what happened.

A second advantage for those working on the collapse of the GDR and the NVA is that we now have the memoirs of most of the key players. In fact, it is almost as if everyone involved had an irresistible urge to put in writing their view of what happened and what role they played in it. In this sense, our knowledge of what happened to the NVA is far richer and more extensive than it is with regard to both the former Soviet Union and the other East European states. For example, we have the memoirs of Adm. Theodor Hoffmann, the last commander of the NVA; Rainer Eppelmann, the last Minister for Defense and Disarmament; Werner Ablaß, a deputy defense minister under Eppelmann; former East German Defense Minister Heinz Keßler; and most of the key East German political figures.[9] Among this group are former party chiefs Erich Honecker, Egon Krenz, and Hans Modrow; Politburo members Günter Schabowski and Günter Mittag; and SED party leader Gregor Gysi and former economics expert Christa Luft.[10] On the West German side, we have the memoirs of General Jörg Schönbohm, the commander of Kommando-Ost (the Bundeswehr unit set up in the former GDR that included former NVA professionals); Chancellor Helmut Kohl; and Horst Teltschik and Wolfgang Schäuble, both senior West German officials involved in the unification process.[11] Some of the statements in the various memoirs are contradictory, and all are self-serving. Nevertheless, taken together, they go a long way toward shining light on the events associated with the collapse of the NVA and its absorption into the Bundeswehr.

Third, we are fortunate to have a number of West German analyses that focus on the process of integrating NVA professionals into the Bundeswehr. What is most useful about these sources is that for the first time they provide us with a good understanding of not only the structure of life in the NVA, but equally important, we begin to see what kinds of personalities were produced by one of the most rigorous Marxist-Leninist regimes extant in the world prior to 1990.[12] Based on these analyses, it is clear that a number of the former NVA professionals experienced very serious problems in coming to grips with the new world of democracy and "innere Führung."[13]

Fourth, there is the press. From October 1989 until the unification of Germany a year later, the East German press became an increasingly valuable source of information. I have in mind newspapers such as

Neues Deutschland, the party paper. As East Germany went through the process of transformation from a totalitarian to a democratic state, this newspaper became increasingly useful. Equally important was the East German military press, and particularly the military paper *Volksarmee* (the name was changed to *Trend* in mid-1990). In addition, journals such as *Militärwesen* and *Militärgeschichte* were also valuable sources of information.

Not surprisingly, the Western media followed developments in the former GDR closely. In addition to German newspapers such as the *Frankfurter Allgemeine Zeitung*, the *New York Times*, the *Washington Post*, the *Chicago Tribune*, *Reuters*, and the BBC were very useful. For a brief period of time, the world's attention was focused on the GDR and the process of transition that was taking place within the NVA.

Fifth, as a result of the efforts of several former NVA officers, I was able to obtain answers to a number of questions concerning the end of the NVA from those who were the direct participants—some of whom now serve in the Bundeswehr. A total of sixty-nine questionnaires were returned (including twelve from individuals who also served in the Bundeswehr after the two militaries were combined).

All of these former NVA officers received the same open-ended questionnaire and took the time to answer my questions (a copy of the questionnaire is located at the end of this book). The questionnaire was translated into German and administered after I had completed a first draft of the book. Its primary purpose was to ask some fundamental questions concerning my findings. Was it true, for example, that the strike at Beelitz marked a fundamental turning point? What about the role played by the military in the events surrounding the October 6 confrontation between the police and demonstrators? The same was true for the assumption of the NVA officers into the Bundeswehr. How did they view the process? What were the most difficult problems they encountered? I did not make any attempt to establish statistical correlations because the nature of the questions precluded such an approach.

As far as those who filled out the questionnaire are concerned, the majority were between the ages of 50 and 60, although a number of responses were received from younger individuals. The majority were also at the O-5 (lieutenant colonel) or O-6 (colonel) level. One response was from a former major general, and a few responses also came from more junior officers. Almost all were from the army, and the positions they occupied ran the gamut from academics to individuals in combat positions. All were involved to one degree or another in the events of 1989–90.

Finally, I was also able to obtain copies of the interviews which Jürgen Eike completed after the collapse of East Germany with many of the main actors—especially on the East German side—for his TV documentary, "The Disappearing Army." These interviews provided another source of invaluable information.

Structure of the Study

Proceeding from the assumption that the military is a societal group like other similar organizations and thus is directly affected by what happens in the political sphere, chapters will look at both political events (internal and external) that are of direct relevance for developments within the NVA, and the military situation within the GDR.[14] For example, a decision to remove the party's privileged status from the constitution or the emergence of a new political leader (and ideas) cannot avoid influencing the armed forces.

Each of these chapters also will look at how these political events have affected developments within the NVA itself. Did the change in leadership impact on procedures within the NVA? If so, how? For example, what effect did the appointment of a pacifist clergyman (in the person of Rainer Eppelmann) as minister of disarmament and defense have on how the NVA functioned? What did it mean for organizational cohesion? What about elements such as discipline, political reliability, and combat readiness?

The concluding section of each chapter will focus on the meaning of developments during the time period covered for civil-military relations in the GDR as a whole. How—if at all—did they change? My assumption is that it was change in society as a whole that influenced change within the NVA (i.e., that the political world at large was the independent variable and that change in the NVA was a dependent variable). Was the relationship between civilians and military officers more stable or less stable as a result of these changes?

The exception to this structure comes in the last two chapters. The focus of chapters 6 and 7 is on the nature of an NVA officer as well as the West German experience in integrating former NVA types into the Bundeswehr. Accordingly, chapter 6 is devoted to a discussion of the type of individual created by the NVA. My purpose is to understand the kind of soldiers the Bundeswehr was dealing with as it attempted to retrain or reeducate them. Understanding the personality characteristics of those desiring to transfer into the Bundeswehr is crucial in defining the kind of officer and NCO the communist system produced.

Chapter 7 is devoted to understanding the techniques utilized by the Bundeswehr to teach these officers the fundamentals of democracy and democratic leadership or "Innere Führung" as they call it. Indeed, it is worth noting that Bonn went to great lengths to design programs that would help professionals from the NVA to change completely their understanding of how a military operates, how it treats its personnel, and what its place in society should be.

The last section of this final chapter focuses on the future. How successful was the Bundeswehr in integrating (and reeducating) these former members of the NVA into the Bundeswehr? What does this process tell us about the adaptation process in a much different military organization? Just how difficult is it to reeducate a professional trained in a totalitarian military to accept the precepts of a democratic one?

The conclusion of the book returns to the questions raised in the introduction. What does the East German experience tell us about civil-military relations in communist systems, especially those having a dependent relationship with a larger outside power? What does it tell us about the personality traits of those who have served in communist militaries? Is there a lesson for our larger understanding of civil-military relations in noncommunist polities as well? What does the East German experience do to help us understand the process of civil-military relations in larger countries such as the USSR? What factors led to the different reactions by Russian and East German officers in the face of state disintegration? In both cases, the systems they were sworn to protect collapsed, but the responses were different. In addition, is there something in this experience that will help us better understand some of the problems being experienced by Russian and other East European officers as they attempt to make the transition from communism to democracy?

Finally, and perhaps most important, what does the East German experience tell us about the transition from a highly centralized, ideological party-state to a more democratic polity? Are there aspects of the East German case that will help us better understand developments in Africa, Latin America, the Middle East or Asia? After all, many of these polities are also attempting to introduce more democratic political systems. Without a military that is prepared to support democracy, such efforts are doomed to failure.

Part I

Background to Crisis

1

The NVA: The Key to the GDR's Soviet Policy

I became a soldier in the firm conviction that I was serving a good and just cause.

Adm. Theodor Hoffmann

The NVA was an instrument of the state that created it, gave it its orders, outfitted it and paid it. It existed as long as that state existed and disappeared with it.

Col. Gen. Joachim Goldbach

The National People's Army (Nationale Volksarmee or NVA) was not created overnight. Rather, it evolved in accordance with Soviet policy toward Europe. After World War II, when Moscow still held out hope that Germany could be neutralized or perhaps united under its control, the country's military was nothing more than a police force. As time went on and the Kremlin became increasingly convinced that the division of Germany would last for the indefinite future, East Germany's armed forces took on an increasingly permanent and military cast. More and more effort was put into building them up, and by the mid-1980s the East German army had become Moscow's most important military ally and one of Europe's more impressive and feared armies.

Creating a Police Force

East Germany's first police units were established on October 31, 1945, in the immediate aftermath of World War II in what was then the Soviet Occupation Zone of Germany. At that time, this force was called the People's Police (Volkspolizei or VP). As one East German leader recalled:

On October 31, 1945, the Soviet Military Administration in Germany approved the creation of the People's Police. That was the birthday of the armed forces of the German working class, the birthday of the armed forces of the first Worker and Peasant force in Germany.[1]

By December 1945, the Volkspolizei had been placed under the control of the Ministry of the Interior.

The East Germans were in something of a quandary. On the one hand, East Berlin wanted stronger military or semimilitary forces as a sign of the new system's sovereignty. On the other hand, its Russian masters preferred to avoid any action that would help the West justify a division of Germany or legitimate the creation of a West German military. As a consequence, for the next few years, training was primarily devoted to domestic, police-related matters.

As time passed and the Russians decided that the division of Germany was irreversible, they gradually moved to create an army to protect the new state. Even at this point, Moscow went to great efforts to hide the fact that military training was under way. By 1949, however, there was no doubt of the ultimate goal among those who were undergoing training. Joachim Goldbach, who was later to play a key role in the NVA, observed that his training was almost entirely military. When he began, he used World War II-vintage German weapons and was subject to the kind of German regulations that had existed in the Wehrmacht. A short time later, however, these German weapons and regulations were replaced with Soviet ones.[2]

The next step in the buildup of the GDR's military forces came on April 26, 1950, when General Heinz Hoffmann, who would later head the NVA, was appointed chief of the newly created Main Administration for Training (Hauptverwaltung für Ausbildung or HVA) within the Ministry of the Interior.[3] The creation of the HVA meant that police instruction would be separated from the more militarily oriented training necessary for an army. Primary emphasis would be on training soldiers, not police officers.

The effort to develop a military force "behind the scenes" was soon successful. By mid-1951, some 78,000 men were serving in the HVA.[4] In 1952 the so-called Kampfgruppen were set up at East German factories. The idea was that these forces—comprising workers at a particular site, organized along factory lines—could be called to service in support of the country's regular military forces when needed. In fact, they were employed twice in support of the regime: once during civil unrest at the time of the Hungarian Revolution in 1956 and later in 1961 when the Berlin Wall was built.

By the end of 1952, the construction of an East German army moved to the next stage as the Second Party Conference of the SED (Socialist Unity Party) called for the formal establishment of an armed force.[5] As a result, the name of the East German military was changed to KVP (Kasernierte Volkspolizei). The German term is difficult to translate into English, but in essence it refers to police or military forces that are quartered in barracks as military or semi-military units, not on the street enforcing laws. It is worth noting that despite the name change, and the greater willingness of the East Germans to discuss openly their emerging military forces, publicly East Berlin continued to keep up the subterfuge that these forces were police, rather than military in the sense that the term is normally understood. At the same time, a tremendous recruiting effort led by the FDJ (Free German Youth) was undertaken to convince young Germans to join the military.

Another indication of the East German intention to use these forces for military purposes came in August of 1952, when an army corps with seven divisions was set up. A year later, military ranks were introduced in place of the police ranks that had been utilized up to that time. By 1954 the KVP's manpower strength stood at 90,000.[6] Despite its limited size, the KVP had everything it needed to build a much larger and effective military. The political leadership was only waiting for an excuse in order to build the KVP into a full-blown military. That excuse came in 1955.

In September 1954, the London Conference invited West Germany to join the NATO alliance. A few days later the Bundestag approved the invitation and the following May, the Federal Republic officially became a member.

The East German leadership seized on the decision to justify what it had been planning to do all along: to proclaim openly the existence of its armed forces and to build them into a modern fighting force. A meeting of the Central Committee of the SED in April 1955 decided that in response to "West German remilitarization," the German Democratic Republic had no alternative but to strengthen its own armed forces.

At the same time, East Berlin began discussions with other communist states concerning the creation of a military alliance in response to NATO's action. The result was the Warsaw Pact, which was signed on May 5, 1955. The East German legislature, the Volkskammer, ratified the agreement just a week later.

While the GDR had been discussing the creation of a military pact, the Russians had been supplying it with heavy weapons. As a result, by the first part of 1955 the East German military possessed six armored regiments, eighteen motorized infantry regiments, and five artillery regiments.[7] The bottom line, from a military point of view, was that by the time East Germany joined the Warsaw Pact, "at least with regard to its organization and weapons it was a combat-capable mechanized army."[8]

Nevertheless, from East Germany's perspective, much remained to be done. To begin with, many of its officers had very little education because of the disruption caused by the war and the GDR's conscious effort to select those who were most reliable politically to staff its armed forces. Significantly, only five percent of officers in the NVA had served previously in the Wehrmacht. By contrast, the newly created Bundeswehr relied on veterans of the Wehrmacht. Similarly, the Red Army in its early days had made widespread use of officers from the Imperial Army.[9] From a political standpoint, it is worth noting that in 1951 more than 85 percent of officers came from the working class.[10] Indeed, a strong impression that emerges from reading the autobiographies as well as from interviewing individuals who served during this period was that almost all of them came from very humble beginnings. They recognized that they owed their officer status to the new system, and as a result they developed a strong sense of loyalty to it from the beginning. This would make the refusal of those whose existence had been dedicated to this system, and who owed so much to it, to use force against the East German people one of the more surprising aspects of the tumultuous days of 1989 and 1990.

By relying upon this more politically reliable, but technically and educationally deficient group of individuals, the new regime was forced into a major effort to raise the educational standards of its officer corps. Otherwise, they would never be able to operate an increasingly technical military. As the main East German history of the country's armed forces described:

> New demands were soon made in the schools and the higher schools of the KVP. Above all these demands called for higher quality in teaching and training. The cadets had to be given the knowledge and capability which would enable them to lead military collectives. In some cases, above all in the higher schools of the KVP, new educational fields were introduced.[11]

Creating a Soviet Bond

By 1949 major efforts were under way to Sovietize the East German military. First, a number of future NVA officers were sent in great secrecy to the USSR to study. As a young lieutenant, Klaus-Jürgen Baarß, who was later to head East Germany's air force, spent thirteen months learning to fly in the Soviet Union.[12] In addition to such basic courses, other officers were sent to the USSR to study at higher levels. Theodor Hoffmann, who was to become the GDR's defense minister, spent three and a half years in Leningrad at the Naval Academy.[13]

In fact, it would be hard to find many senior members of the East German military who, at some point in their career, did not study at a Soviet military institution of higher education. Between 1950 and 1989 a total of 13,500 officers were trained in the USSR. Three hundred eighty five of these officers finished the prestigous Voroshilov General Staff Academy.[14] For most NVA officers, the experience appears to have been constructive. As one officer who studied at the Frunze Academy recalled, "I remember positively my experience in Moscow and my relationship to our Soviet colleagues."[15]

Soviet advisors also were present at all levels in the NVA. As Gen. Fritz Streletz observed:

> Until the middle or the end of the fifties we had Soviet advisors every-where. From the beginning there were advisors from the minister down to regimental commander. Let me give an example. During the beginning phase, a regiment had twenty-five to thirty advisors. That meant that every company commander had a Soviet officer as an advisor at his side.[16]

Gradually, as the percentage of officers trained in the USSR increased, the size of Moscow's advisory group decreased proportionately. The task of those who remained was twofold: first, to coordinate between divisions and the Group of Soviet Forces in Germany; second, to assist in transmitting information and lessons from the Soviet armed forces to units in the NVA.[17]

For those at lower levels, contacts with Soviet forces stationed in the GDR were organized on a regular basis. Political lectures emphasized the Soviet system's "achievements," while almost all of the NVA's equipment, its doctrine, and its training procedures came from the USSR. As a former transport officer observed, "For the whole opera-tional area of the NVA, that is, the troops that would operate jointly, the Soviet Army was the absolute model."[18]

Although the NVA followed Moscow's lead in most areas, it did not do so blindly, and when it could it exerted its own German individual-ity. For example, the question of march procedure was raised early on. Russian advisers suggested that the East Germans adopt the Soviet style of 120 steps per minute. The normal German march tempo is 114; thus, stepping to a 120 tempo was awkward with German march music. Gen. Horst Stechbarth raised the issue with then-defense minis-ter Willi Stoph. The latter opted for the German tempo, remarking that "the parade will take place in Berlin and not in Moscow."[19]

Given the close connections between the NVA and the Russian military, and the fact that the majority of senior officers had studied in the USSR and spoke Russian, it was not surprising that NVA officers had good ties with their Russian colleagues. Almost all comments in interviews and memoirs concerning NVA–Russian military contacts were positive. NVA officers seem to have genuinely enjoyed working and socializing with Russian officers. Over time, they began to forge a strong bond of collegiality. NVA officers trusted their Russian counterparts and felt they were all part of one team. Consequently, when the Russians later decided to abandon the NVA there would be deep feelings of betrayal on the part of many East German officers.

Before discussing the specific steps the East German leadership took to build up a strong, cohesive, combat-capable military, it should be noted that the NVA played a critical role in East Berlin's policy vis-à-vis the Russians. The East German leadership's recurring political nightmare was to wake up one day and find that Moscow had made a deal at its expense with the more economically attractive Federal Republic. After all, as the West German *Wirtschaftswunder* grew increasingly strong, the attraction of the West German deutsche mark became almost irresistible. Meanwhile, West Germany's primary concern was to break down the wall of isolation that the GDR was trying to build by getting Moscow to push East Berlin toward closer and more open ties with the FRG.

In the end, this concern would turn out to be well founded as Gorbachev sold the East Germans down the river in return for some desperately needed economic assistance from the West Germans. In the meantime, however, East Germany's political leadership was determined to do everything possible to make its country attractive to the Russians. On foreign policy issues, the East Germans often were more supportive of Russian policy than were the Russians themselves. In the economic sphere they worked overtime to create a technological infrastructure that would be indispensable.

Military issues were similarly motivated. The East Germans set out to create the most advanced, reliable, and dependable military leadership imaginable. As a consequence, the GDR was prepared to pay any cost to build a military force that would become critical to the Russians and the Warsaw Pact.[20]

Building a Modern Combat-Capable Army

In order to mark a break between the old "paramilitary" forces and the newly emerging East German military, the Volkskammer passed a law on January 18, 1956, authorizing the creation of a National People's Army to be set up from the cadre of the KVP, and the establishment of a Ministry of National Defense (thus taking the military away from the Interior Ministry). To quote Willi Stoph, the first minister of national defense:

> In accordance with the elementary right that belongs to every sovereign, independent state it is time to create a National People's Army. The National People's Army will consist of ground, air and naval forces, which are necessary for the defense of the German Democratic Republic. . . . This People's Army—whose members come out of the ranks of the people, must guarantee the military defense of the homeland and its democratic achievements in the interest of the working class.[21]

The constitution was changed to make it clear that every East German male had an obligation to serve in the military. According to article 5, "Service in defense of the Fatherland and the achievements of socialism is an honorable national duty for the citizens of the GDR."[22] There was, however, no draft at this time.

On October 2, 1956, General Hoffmann issued Order No. 1/1956 creating the NVA with a personnel strength of 120,000. New uniforms were issued, which not only contrasted with the Soviet style worn by the KVP but that were strongly reminiscent of the old Wehrmacht.[23] Most members of the KVP "spontaneously" declared their readiness to serve in the NVA. Service began on March 1, 1956, and a headquarters was established at Strausberg, not far from Berlin.[24]

Despite the preparatory work done during the days of the KVP, the East Germans had a number of problems to overcome before their military could be considered formidable by Warsaw Pact standards. What was most impressive about their approach was the systematic—one might even say Prussian—way in which East Berlin went about trying to solve the problems.

The first issue was the low level of education attained by most NVA officers. The majority had served in the KVP and simply changed their uniforms when the NVA was established. Some had been in the communist underground during the thirties and forties; others had fought in the Spanish Civil War. The NVA also included a number of former members of the country's youth organization who had attended an officers school, as well as older individuals who had attended Soviet schools. Unfortunately, many if not most lacked the necessary technical background. For example, in discussing his experience as a cadet during the late forties, a former NVA officer noted that few of the cadets in his unit had finished school, and that "only two had an Abitur (a high school diploma permitting a student to attend a university)."[25]

The reason for this low level of education was simple: As far as the political leadership was concerned, the key criterion was that "high leadership and director positions in the NVA were always bound up with a significant political mandate."[26] Because East Berlin had the luxury of relying on Soviet forces for protection, it could afford to put political considerations first. As in the Soviet Union, even those few military experts the military had utilized during its early days "were more and more pushed aside," to be replaced by those who had strong party credentials and had been trained in the Soviet Union, as well as by those who had been trained in the new GDR.[27]

Recognizing the educational deficit on the part of its officers, the East German military launched a major effort to educate them. For example, in 1956 only thirty-four percent of all officers had the equivalent of a technical education. As a consequence, until the end of the 1960s, the NVA was forced to provide additional training for those wishing to become officers. East German efforts paid off; by 1972 the number was up to 88 percent, and by 1981 it was over 90 percent. Similarly, in 1956 only 2 percent of all officers had an academic education (the equivalent of a master's degree); by 1974 this figure was up to 22 percent and by 1981 it stood at 25 percent. Finally, the educational level of soldiers and NCOs also increased significantly. In 1956, the percentage that had finished the tenth or twelfth class stood at 4 percent. By 1972 it was up to 75 percent and by 1981 it was over 80 percent.[28] This increase in technical education not only produced an officer better able to deal with the challenges of the modern military, it also permitted the East Germans to get rid of the Wehrmacht holdovers. According to one senior East German officer the issue came to a head in 1959. As a result, the vast majority (those serving in academic institutions and on staffs were an exception) were gradually forced out.[29] By the mid-1960s, only sixty-four officers from the former Wehrmacht were still in the NVA.[30]

The second major challenge confronting the NVA was to make its forces operational. The first fully operational unit was the 1st Mechanized Division, which was stationed in Potsdam. It became part of the NVA in April 1956 and participated in the May Day parade. By the end of 1956, the NVA possessed four mechanized infantry divisions and three armored divisions. On December 1, the last units of the KVP were dissolved. Thus, within ten months, the NVA was ready to assume its role within the Warsaw Pact. All the preparation done under the auspices of the HVA and the KVP had paid off. No one could accuse the East Germans of not doing their homework.

Yet, the technical level of the NVA's equipment and weapons was modest. The main battle tank was the World War II vintage T-34. By the end of 1956, the East Germans had begun to introduce the more modern T-54. Similarly, by September of the same year, the East Germans began introducing the MiG-19 into their air force. In spite of these new weapons systems, the overall technological level of the NVA remained far behind the Soviets. It was only during the mid-sixties that more modern weapons systems began to appear. In 1963–64 the MiG-21 was introduced, followed two years later by the T-55.[31]

One measure of the improving technological capabilities of the NVA was the level of horsepower equivalent present in an East German unit.[32] The higher it is, the more mechanized and technically proficient it will be in a combat situation. By 1958 this number was up to 25.4, by 1964 to 29.1,[33] and by 1971 to 30.5.[34] However one measured the technological sophistication of the NVA at this time, one point was clear: the political leadership was making the armed forces a high priority. The East Germans would soon find themselves on a par with the best of the other East European militaries.

Exercises are another key to military preparedness. With their desire to convince the Russians that they were an indispensable part of the Warsaw Pact, the East Germans felt it was critical to play a meaningful role as soon as possible. Working hard to improve further their operational capabilities, the East Germans in 1962 held two large-scale maneuvers: "Vitr" in the south under Soviet leadership, and "Baltyk-Odra" in the north under Polish leadership. This was the first time that the NVA had participated in such a large Pact maneuver. Also in 1962 for the first time the East German air force took part in Pact air defense exercises.

The year 1968 was a turning point for the NVA as well as for the Pact itself. For the first time, the armed forces showed they were ready to participate in the invasion of another country as Czechoslovakia's freedom movement was crushed. Parts of the 11th Motorized Division were subordinated to the First Soviet Guards Armored Army while segments of the Seventh Armored Division were placed under the control of the 20th Guards Army. Contrary to popular myth, neither of these East German army units participated directly in the invasion, although both were moved toward the Czechoslovak border and certainly were prepared to take part had they received the appropriate orders.[35] Small numbers of East German military personnel (e.g., liaison officers, communicators, and reconnaissance personnel) did enter Czechoslovakia. They returned to their bases in the GDR during August and September.[36]

The year 1980 was another significant period in the development of the NVA. Most of the first generation of military officers—those who had fought in Spain, or who had been "old communists"—began to retire. For example, Adm. Waldemar Verner, the long-time head of the

Main Political Administration, left the service. It was also at this time that a new personality emerged on the scene—one who was to play a very important role in the hectic days of October 1989. In contrast to other senior military officers, the new chief of the main staff, Gen. Fritz Streletz, had spent his entire career in the NVA or its predecessor the KVP.[37] His technical competence and military qualifications marked the passing of the torch to a new generation among senior officers in the NVA. Indeed, when Minister of Defense Heinz Hoffmann died in 1985, the last of the old generation was gone.

The importance of the passing of the old generation and the emergence of this new, more professional and technically competent group of officers was not that they suddenly stopped believing in the state's Marxist ideology. Rather, it was that ideological factors receded into the background. Although they were certainly affected by the ideological world they lived in, their support was more for general concepts than for actual ideological policies.

Meanwhile, the quality of the NVA as a military force continued to rise. In December 1973 a new "combat document" had been issued that made the East Germans even more interoperable with the Group of Soviet Forces in Germany. A year later the rank of warrant officer had been introduced.[38] By October 1977, the strength of the NVA stood at 143,000. There were 98,000 in the army, 28,000 in the air force, and 17,000 in the navy.[39] In 1979, new weapons systems such as the MiG-23, the Mi-24 Hind helicopter gunship, and the T-72 main battle tank were introduced. By 1987 the NVA was playing a critical part in the Warsaw Pact's "Strategic Defensive Operations."[40]

However, throughout the eighties economic problems came increasingly to the fore. Economic difficulties not only made the GDR increasingly dependent on Bonn for credits, they also meant that the NVA would find it more difficult to purchase the latest weapons it needed to play the role of *prima inter pares* among the other East European military forces.

For example, East Berlin could not purchase Moscow's newest tank, the T-80. As a result, the NVA was forced to modernize its existing stock of T-72s and in some cases even T-55s. The air force received only twenty MiG-29s. In the mid-1980s an additional fifty-four Su-22s were purchased. The rest of the country's air wing was composed of the older MiG-23s and MiG-21s.

Political Control of the NVA

To ensure the reliability of the NVA, the leadership set up an elaborate system of political controls modeled on the Soviet experience—although with some important differences. This control system included political officers and a political apparatus to oversee not only the work of the political officers, but of the whole military structure as well. In addition, this system contained part-time ideological training courses for officers as well as ideological indoctrination courses for enlisted personnel. A party organization also was active throughout the military. Indeed, by 1962, 98.1 percent of all officers were party members.[41] Political officers also were permitted to evaluate regular officers and a network of secret police officers ensured that everyone behaved.

This network of controls[42] meant that all officers were subject to two levels of discipline. First, there was the standard military hierarchy, even more pronounced in the NVA than in most militaries. Second, there was party discipline. In practice, if an individual—however good his military record—was not considered politically reliable by his political masters, his career would be short indeed. For example, let us assume that Major Schmidt was asked by his party secretary to "volunteer" to lead a group of soldiers working to beautify the city on his day off. Technically, he could refuse. After all, military officers get very few days off as it is, and one might expect that he would want to spend it with his family. If he did, however, the party secretary would be in a position to criticize him for his lack of zeal or dedication to the party. Such a comment would certainly not help him in his career. In any case, in the majority of instances an order from the party had the same validity as one from a military superior. Exceptions were few and far between.

The one critical difference between the East German and the Soviet military political structures was that NVA political officers were never called upon to play the role of "commissars." Werner Rothe, a senior member of the NVA's political apparatus, defined the difference:

> The political officer as the Commander's Deputy was constantly portrayed as a commissar (even if only as a form of speech). . . . The concept "Commissar" really comes from the French Revolution. In that instance, commissars, for example in the Battle by Vlamy and later, played a significant role as a mobilizing force. . . . We never had such commissars.[43]

Closely related to the issue of political control was the NVA's effort to find a historical identity. The East German military was in a unique position within the Warsaw Pact. The Poles or the Hungarians or the Rumanians had only one army, while Germany had two. And although Germany had two armies, it had only one language, and at least during the early years, only one history and culture. East Berlin set out to break this all-German mold and create a separate identity. Nowhere was this attempt more evident than in the NVA itself.

In essence, the East Germans had to create a completely new historical identity, while in the process convincing members of the NVA that
they were just as German as their cousins to the west—and that unlike
the Bundeswehr, they belonged to a military that was not imperialistic
and that was part of the "progressive" world. As one former East German officer put it:

> From the totality of the inheritance of German military history, events,
> personalities, behavior, and achievements, only those which had a lasting
> impact and which speeded up social progress during that period were
> selected.[44]

This meant looking for positive aspects of the German past—ones
that would underscore the worker-and-peasant nature of the new German state. Toward this end, those in East Germany who had fought on
the side of the Russians or against Franco in the Spanish Civil War
were held up as heroes worthy of emulation. The East Germans placed
a premium on events like the Peasants War (arguing that it was primarily an uprising against the Prussian Junkers), the War of Liberation
fought by the Freikorps against Napoleon in 1813–14, and the Revolution of 1849. On the military side, heroes were created out of individuals such as Gen. Gerhard von Scharnhorst (because of the military reforms he introduced) and Gen. Neidhardt von Gneisenau (because of
his reformist views).

Germany's role in World War II was discussed in very negative
terms. In East German mythology, it was the capitalistic and imperialistic nature of the Hitler regime that was responsible for the war. The
task of the new East German regime was to create an army that was
no longer a tool of imperialism, but rather one that served the new
workers and peasants' state.

This attachment to East Berlin's special reading of the past was emphasized further by the decision to change the name of the navy from
Seestreitkräfte to Volksmarine (People's Navy) in 1960. In addition, a
number of ships and military objects were named to reflect the NVA's
close ties to ideologically acceptable figures such as Karl Marx, Friedrich Engels, Karl Liebknecht, and Rosa Luxemburg. To emphasize further the close ties between the NVA and its special tradition, a military
museum was opened in Potsdam, and in February 1966 a new medal
called the "Scharnhorst Orden" was introduced "for outstanding leadership and special service in leading troops."[45]

Civilian Work

Unlike most Western militaries, the NVA was soon called upon to
assist the state in developing the civilian economy. Beginning in 1963,

massive numbers of soldiers were ordered to help with the harvest. Then in 1964, the army began sending conscripts to work in civilian companies such as the petrochemical works in Schwedt.

Although few paid much attention to the military's decision (under strong political pressure) to send soldiers and officers to help in the civilian economy, in time the policy would have disastrous effects. It was as if once the decision had been made, the floodgates were opened. Whenever problems arose in the civilian sector, the military was called upon to help. Not only did such actions damage the civilian economy by removing an incentive to make needed reforms, it also undermined military preparedness. Those individuals working in the fields or in factories were not training. According to Streletz, "On the one hand, they demanded 85 percent combat readiness from us, while on the other hand, we were sending 10,000 to 11,000 soldiers to industry. This made it doubly difficult for the soldiers who remained in the units who now had to maintain an 85 percent combat readiness."[46]

This policy also created two categories of conscription in the eyes of young East Germans. The first was primarily dedicated to civilian work while the other related to the military.[47] The problem for the NVA was that it would never be able to reconcile these two factors. It also led to the belief that "soldiers were the cheapest form of labor, since factories did not have to pay as much for them as regular workers"—a situation that inevitably had a negative impact on morale in the military.[48]

The Berlin Wall

The building of the Berlin Wall in 1961 was to have a major impact on the NVA. Prior to its construction one never knew on Monday morning who would show up for work, whether in the military or civilian sector. Because of the four-power arrangement governing Berlin, all a soldier (or a civilian) had to do was to reach East Berlin and then cross the unguarded border into the West. This hemorrhaging of manpower had a disastrous impact on the military. Not only was it difficult to keep military personnel in the country (officers never knew when they would lose a key individual), but there was also a problem with recruitment. In addition, it was hard for the East Germans to convince the Russians that the NVA was playing a key role when some of its soldiers were defecting to the West and presumably taking important military secrets with them. If a draft had been introduced prior to the construction of the wall, it probably would have only led to further defections to the West. The East Germans could and did employ all manner of propaganda in an effort to increase recruitment—but voluntarism went only so far.

The open border was effectively sealed by the wall. East Germany for the first time had some control over its population. The following year conscription was introduced, giving the NVA a predictable personnel pool. The military was now in a position to tighten the screws when it came to security and politicization. Those in the military had no alternative but to adapt.

Proletarian Internationalism

In January 1978, East Berlin introduced a new political concept. Earlier emphasis had been on the importance of a socialist German soldier. Now, however, in an effort to convince the Russians just how dedicated and reliable a partner the NVA was, the concept of "proletarian internationalism" took center stage. In essence, this new emphasis focused attention on the NVA's commitment to support the USSR and all that it stood for. Contacts between East German and Soviet forces became even closer, with common training programs that would make units eventually interchangeable.

Conclusion

East Berlin's efforts to demonstrate its support for Moscow constantly went beyond those of its Warsaw Pact allies. This was evident not only in its efforts to produce one of the best and most combat-capable militaries in Europe, but also in its support for Soviet policy in the Third World. By 1977, the East Germans were providing military assistance to some twenty-two African states.[49] Not only did this aid help the GDR win international recognition, it also demonstrated to Moscow that the NVA (and thereby the GDR) played a critical role in the Kremlin's Third World policy. Indeed, throughout the 1970s and the 1980s the East Germans seemed to be everywhere, thereby providing the Soviets with diplomatic cover.

By the end of the 1980s, despite a number of problems on the horizon (e.g., increased work by soldiers on civilian projects and the introduction of a new and ambiguous military doctrine in 1987), the NVA was still the best of the non-Soviet armies of the Warsaw Pact. The country's economy was deteriorating and political cynicism was becoming more widespread, while the country's political leadership seemed to be losing touch daily; nevertheless, within the NVA discipline was high, the officers and troops well trained, the equipment well maintained, and the ability to put troops in the field in a short amount of time unmatched. No other military in the world—East or West—

could have accomplished what the East Germans were capable of doing so quickly and so efficiently.

Yet, in a period of less than two years the East German military would no longer exist. One of the best and most professional party-armies would belong to history. Why? Not only would this army disintegrate, those who served in its ranks would play a critical role in the process of German reunification. They would not only do nothing to halt the process, many would work actively to ensure that the transition to democracy was peaceful. Had this highly trained, well-equipped army not acted in this manner, not only would the idea of German reunification have remained a dream, communism would not have collapsed throughout Russia and Eastern Europe when it did. The pressure for Soviet intervention would have been overwhelming. Needless to say, such an action would have undermined Gorbachev and his policy of *perestroika*. A hard-line coup could well have succeeded in the USSR—with all of the implications such an action would have had for Europe and the world.

October, 1948. Members of the Volkspolizei receive their weapons and take their oath of allegiance. Credit: Militärhistorisches Museum (cited hereafter as MHM)

May 1, 1949. Parade by the Volkspolizei in Berlin. Credit: MHM

1951. East German leader Wilhelm Pieck visits members of the Main Administration for Training. Future NVA head Heinz Hoffmann is on the far left. Credit: MHM

1963. Marshal of the Soviet Union Andrei Grechko, together with East German party leader Walter Ulbricht and NVA chief Gen. Heinz Hoffmann during the joint Warsaw Pact Maneuver Quartet. Credit: MHM

32

1970. East German leaders Walter Ulbricht, Heinz Hoffmann, and Erich Honecker during the Warsaw Pact Maneuver Waffenbrüderschaft 70. Credit: MHM

1980. East German landing craft participate in Waffenbrüderschaft 80. Credit: MHM

1980. East German tanks participate in Waffenbrüderschaft 80. Credit MHM

1984. East German soldiers clean their weapons during Schild 84. Credit: MHM

1984. East German armored vehicles clear a water obstacle. Credit: MHM

Circa 1986. East German trainers at an East German airfield. Credit: Filmstudio der NVA

Part II

The End of the NVA

2

The Beginning of the End: Honecker Is Ousted

The Germans in the East as well as the West have become Realists. Whatever they feel in the depth of their hearts about the reunification of their divided nation—they know only too well that German unity hardly stands in the cards for the current generation, and not even for the lifetime of the next generation.

Theo Sommer, Chief Editor, *Die Zeit*

If there was any time in modern history that showed just how much and how quickly the world could change, it was 1989. In Eastern Europe in general, and the GDR in particular, calm prevailed on January 1 of that year. There were certainly signs of discontent here and there, but most observers would have agreed with Theo Sommer. German reunification? Perhaps, but not in our lifetime. Yet only a few months later the world was watching the fall of the Berlin Wall, certainly one of the most dramatic and unexpected events of the second half of the twentieth century.

If the end of communism in the GDR was a surprise, the fact that the NVA did little or nothing to save the old regime was even more unexpected. For years the NVA—and especially its officer corps—had been viewed by people both within the GDR and abroad as one of the most pampered and reliable parts of East German society. Better pay, better housing, better access to consumer goods, all were believed to be things that would make them some of the regime's most ardent defenders. Yet during the events of October—which ultimately led to Communist party chief Erich Honecker's ouster—the NVA was notable for its noninvolvement in defending the regime from its opponents, the East German people. The NVA turned out to be what the party had long claimed it was—an army of the people: It was not prepared to turn its guns on the masses in order to keep Honecker and his aged cronies in power.

A close look at events during 1989 shows that the East German populace was becoming increasingly cynical about the party leadership—a feeling which had also begun to infect the NVA. In this context, it is important to keep in mind that the NVA, like any military, was not an independent entity. The party in a unitary party-state tries to isolate the military to the maximum degree possible, but when this sense of isolation begins to break down, the negative attitudes and views of the populace can have an important impact on the armed forces. This is especially true if military cohesion is being undermined by compelling the armed forces to perform functions unrelated to its main purpose: defending the state from external threats.

Everything Is Normal?

Despite signs of discontent, for the most part the GDR appeared to be one of the most stable of all of Moscow's East European military allies. The NVA's loyalty to the Honecker regime was unquestioned, and its key role within the Warsaw Pact was critical. As one analyst put it:

> For its size, the NVA had been regarded as the most effective East European armed force. It was equipped with the Warsaw Pact's most modern weaponry (over 2,000 tanks and 1,600 artillery pieces in six ready divisions, and some 400 combat aircraft), and an enormous scale of munitions. In addition, it occupied some 1,070 facilities in 532 separate locations.[1]

Defense Minister Heinz Keßler's 30th-anniversary speech to the Friedrich Engels Military Academy on January 4, 1989, conveyed the impression that nothing had changed for the last ten years. In addition to paying homage to all of the appropriate political symbols—the proletariat, the Communist party, the Soviet Union—Keßler assured his listeners that the NVA was prepared to do everything necessary "to protect reliably Worker and Peasant Power." His speech was full of the normal East German Cold War rhetoric, noting that military power remained one of the key elements in the "imperialists' " plan to bring socialism to its knees. Indeed, Keßler's speech could have been written five or ten years earlier. Furthermore, while Keßler spoke of the need to modify military doctrine—something that would become necessary as a result of Honecker's announcement on January 23 of a "unilateral" cut of NVA forces (including ten thousand troops, six armored regiments, six hundred tanks, and fifty combat aircraft), there was no sign of the "new thinking" that was playing such an important role within the Soviet military.[2]

A month later, the NVA was celebrating its ties to the USSR in a week of "Comrades in Arms" (Waffenbrüderschaft). East German speeches hailed the closeness of the ties between the NVA and the Soviet armed forces stationed in the GDR. For example, Keßler emphasized that no one would be able to undercut "our class and military ties." He went on to praise the building of the Berlin Wall, noting that Moscow stood solidly behind the GDR both in 1961 and in 1989. As usual, Keßler emphasized the role of the NVA, assuring his listeners that it remained ready to carry out any tasks assigned to it.[3]

The Honecker Regime on the Road to Collapse

Despite a calm outward appearance, subterranean change was already under way in the GDR. Gorbachev had introduced his policy of *peres-troika*, which threatened East Berlin's leaders. Indeed, as early as 1987, Kurt Hager, a member of the Politburo, had commented on changes in the USSR by noting that just because a neighbor refurbishes his apartment it does not mean that one should copy him.[4] Honecker and his colleagues were clearly concerned about the impact that liberalizing tendencies in Moscow would have on their tightly controlled East German polity. Insofar as the NVA was concerned, there was a conscious effort on the part of East German officials to isolate it from what was occurring. To quote one former NVA officer:

> At the time of *Perestroika*, I was at the Military Academy in Dresden. The isolation went to the point that we could no longer participate in the party meetings of Russian officers and the height of stupidity was that we ourselves could not speak on the issue of the Soviet Union in our party meetings—it was always an "internal affair" of the USSR.[5]

While this isolationist policy may have made some sense from the leadership's perspective, its major impact was to undercut the legitimacy and believability of SED ideology.

Whether it was caused by internal problems in the GDR or "infection" from the USSR, growing skepticism toward the leadership was evident by 1988 on the part of the East German populace. Primary public concerns were with the supply of goods (74 percent) and the state of the environment (84 percent). To make matters worse, only 23 percent believed that the future would bring improvement, while 65 percent doubted that the GDR would be able catch up to the world's leading industrial nations by the year 2000. In addition, alienation was at an all-time high among young people.[6] Other data suggest that this sense of alienation had important implications for the military. For example, one analyst noted that in 1987 only 46 percent of youth declared a readiness to give their lives in defense of socialism. This contrasted with 80 percent in 1980.[7]

This feeling of alienation was not limited to the youth, however. Colonel Hans-Werner Weber reports, for example, that by the beginning of 1989 there "was almost no agreement between the leadership and the membership."[8] The party leadership—and especially Erich Honecker—was becoming increasingly isolated from the rank and file and did not appear to understand what was happening. Indeed, Honecker and some of his colleagues seemed to be living in an artificial world of their own. As Markus Wolf put it with reference to members of the Politburo, "They had nothing to lose . . . and they dared not have another opinion."[9]

On May 2, the Hungarians opened their border and in the process permitted a limited number of East Germans to pass into Austria and thence into the FRG. While deeply shocked, the East German leadership attempted to put the best face on things. Keßler, for example, told the Politburo that he had spoken with the Hungarian defense minister and that while Budapest was reducing the number of border installations, Hungary would continue to honor its obligation to not permit East Germans to leave the country unless they had a valid exit permit from the GDR.[10] Günter Schabowski admitted that he, like others, "had preferred to ignore his foreboding. General Keßler's spirited explanation had provided a comfortable 'alibi.' "[11]

Another dose of reality was not long in coming. On May 7 the results of local elections were announced. That day's headline in *Neues Deutschland* trumpeted, "98.85 Voted for the Candidates of the National Front." In fact, the election results were anything but accurate. According to one source, "We now know that as much as 10% of the populace had voted against the SED." Indeed, Hager pointed out in a Politburo meeting that the percentage of votes against the SED was even higher at some universities.[12]

The public easily saw through the regime's falsification; the SED leadership had done the same thing in the past. What was different this time, however, was that significant numbers of citizens were no longer intimidated, and in spite of the presence of one of communism's most efficient and effective secret police networks, they began to demonstrate each month on the date of this election—the seventh. By the time October rolled around, these demonstrations would become so massive that Honecker himself would be forced out of office. What is probably most surprising about this electoral falsification and the public outcry that followed was that the Politburo did nothing to defuse the public outrage. It never entered anyone's mind to order a recount.

From the standpoint of the East German leadership, the world was being turned upside down. *Perestroika* in the USSR, open borders in Hungary, liberalism in other parts of Eastern Europe, and discontent at home were events this aging leadership could not understand. Worse, not understanding the seriousness of the situation, they did nothing to deal with it. Instead, they ignored it.

On June 4, the Chinese regime used troops to crack down on protesters occupying Tiananmen Square. The bloody action was televised on CNN throughout the world—including in the GDR. Despite widespread condemnation from other capitals around the world, the Volkskammer praised Beijing's suppression of "counterrevolutionary riots." In addition, East German Foreign Minister Oskar Fischer played up the closeness of Chinese-East German ties about a week later when the Chinese foreign minister visited East Berlin. This was followed by a series of visits to China by East German leaders: Hans Modrow in June, Günter Schabowski in July, and Egon Krenz in September.[13] The possibility that the East German leadership would consider a Chinese solution to deal with demonstrations concerned not only the populace, but the West and important segments of the political elite as well.

Meanwhile, despite Budapest's assurances to the contrary, East Germans were leaving through Hungary in record numbers. During the first eight months of 1989, some 80,000 left the GDR—and almost a third of these were illegal emigrants. To make matters worse, many of those who departed took critical skills with them. Over five hundred doctors and nurses left the East Berlin region alone. In addition, hundreds of East Germans crowded into the West German embassies in Prague and Budapest as well as Bonn's mission in East Berlin. Then Budapest informed East Berlin that beginning September 11, East Germans would be permitted to cross into Austria without a special exit permit approved by the GDR government.[14]

Some in the leadership had begun to realize that the challenge to the East German system was fundamental. As Keßler put it in his memoirs:

> The majority of Central Committee members knew for certain . . . that a difficult political crisis had developed in the GDR—in the economy, in the supply of necessary raw materials and consumer goods, in the Republic's financial balance sheet, and in the rapidly deteriorating attitude of a great part of the population, especially the youth.[15]

The problem, however, was Honecker, according to Keßler. He and the other "elderly" members of the Politburo would not or could not understand just how bad the situation was. Soon there would be a ring of reality to the old East German joke about Honecker returning to Berlin only to find the city deserted with a sign next to a hole in the wall reading, "Dear Erich, Remember the last one out must turn off the lights." The problem that faced the East German government seemed simple enough: maintaining control, a goal that would turn out to be more difficult than anyone realized.

The NVA and the Honecker Regime

Instability in the GDR inevitably raised the question of the military's role. What would the NVA do if called upon to help "normalize" the situation? In fact, the NVA was experiencing problems of its own. While it may have still have been combat-capable—able to put 85 percent of its forces in the field on 48 hours' notice, serious fissures were already evident.

First, let us look at the situation from the army's standpoint. One area that specialists in the West tended to ignore in evaluating the combat effectiveness of the NVA was the amount of effort and time it devoted to work in the civilian economy. Adm. Theodor Hoffmann, who would later become defense minister, reported in January 1987 that an average of ten thousand soldiers were doing civilian work during any two-week period. This was the result of an order (104/88) issued by the Minister of Defense in 1988, which called for the constant employment of that number of army and border troop personnel in some sixty-four industrial combines and factories. Taking so many men out of active service had an immediate impact on the armed forces. Hoffmann noted, for example, that of the fourteen active motorized infantry regiments, half were not in a state of combat readiness. In one military district, two out of three regiments were not combat-capable. And without these motorized infantry regiments, the two armored divisions were not combat-capable.

In February 1989, an additional 960 NVA and border troops were assigned to the state forestry service.[16] In his memoirs, Gen. Jörg Schönbohm (who was later to command Kommando-Ost, the combined German military contingent in what had been the GDR), commented that this use of military personnel in the civilian economy, which he claimed at some points included up to 55,000 troops, was the beginning of the end for the NVA as a military force.[17]

Morale within the NVA was also a problem as the drop in the party's authority increased. Hoffmann reported, for example, that during the summer of 1989 the majority of military party secretaries failed to report to their appropriate political structure the many "harsh, critical comments concerning the political and economic situation in the GDR as well as comments concerning the lack of a conception and alienation of the party leadership."[18] To a large degree, the party was the glue that held this tightly structured, party-state army together. Indeed, when it came to the officer corps, few in the NVA could conceive of anything taking place outside of the party structure. They had been raised to believe in the all-encompasing embrace of the SED, and few thought beyond its tenets for inspiration.

Even if the beginnings of this collapse in party authority was not visible at this time—even to those in the party leadership—the turmoil right under the surface was a clear sign that all was not well in the military. As the Russians, much to their chagrin, learned at about the same time, a unified Communist party was critical to the maintenance of organizational cohesion in the armed forces.[19]

Indeed, Hoffmann reported problems with military reliability as early as October 1988. At that time, doubts about the policies followed by the SED leadership were already emerging in opinion polls conducted by the army. In addition, there was a feeling on the part of many military officers that the party leadership was simply too old to deal with the problems it faced. In December 1988 it was reported to the defense minister that in the months of October and November alone, ninety-eight members of the border troops had to be moved to rear positions because of doubts about their reliability. That made a total of 422 for 1988. Pressure on junior officers was also extreme, especially given the absence of so many conscripts, who were off doing civilian chores. One analysis revealed that, for more than 30 percent of the young officers, the average workday was 11 hours long, Saturdays included.[20]

And the situation continued to deteriorate. Hoffmann reported an opinion poll conducted in 1989 among NVA personnel that revealed that 45 percent of the soldiers and 20 percent of the NCOs believed that conscription was unnecessary, and that 10 percent of the NCOs felt that any kind of military service was unnecessary.[21] Rainer Eppelmann, the Protestant clergyman who became the GDR's last defense minister, reported that as early as the summer of 1989 a number of colonels had come to him to express their concern over events in the GDR.[22]

Another development that could not avoid influencing the NVA was the exchange of visits by NVA and Bundeswehr delegations that occurred as a result of the CSCE (Conference on Security and Cooperation in Europe) negotiations. In 1989 a West German delegation led by Brig. Gen. Hermann Hagena visited the Friedrich Engels Military

Academy in Dresden from February 26 to March 1. This was followed by a visit to Hamburg by an NVA delegation led by Maj. Gen. Rolf Lehmann for discussions with West German military officers. The meetings focused on issues such as European security, reducing the offensive capabilities of both sides, and military doctrine—none of which were especially important from a substantive standpoint. Much more significant was the fact that they occurred and that proposals were made for continuing them in the future.[23] Although it could not be said that these visits had a major impact on the NVA, they did mark an important turning point: senior officers, many of whom had been as isolated as lower-ranking officers in the NVA, were beginning to look at the West in a slightly different, somewhat less dogmatic light.

Despite the turmoil within the NVA, few realized either the depth of the problems facing the GDR, or the magnitude of the changes that lay ahead. The new recruits who began their military service in May may have heard of concerns within the military, but few had any idea that soon not only the NVA but the GDR itself would be turned upside-down. Indeed, by the time they ended their term of service, there would no longer be either a GDR or an NVA.[24]

The Long Hot Summer—and Fall

It is usually the case that ignoring problems only tends to make them worse, and this is exactly what happened in the GDR. First, let us look at the civilian world.

During June there was a rock concert in West Berlin. The impact on East German youth was immediate and hostile to the authorities. They assembled and began chanting "Gorbachev! Gorbachev!"—a call for the introduction of the liberalizing reforms of *perestroika* that Soviet leader Mikhail Gorbachev had already made a part of Soviet life. Cries of "Away with the Wall!" soon followed, as East German security forces quickly moved in to restore order.[25] While this incident involved only a few hundred demonstrators, it showed that East Germans were growing bolder in their defiance of the government and were increasingly prepared to take on the GDR's security forces.

The rock concert incident was a harbinger of more serious things to come. On July 8 Honecker returned early from a Warsaw Pact meeting in Bucharest because of illness. Two days later he underwent a gall-bladder operation.[26] Egon Krenz was put in charge while Honecker recuperated. Indeed, Krenz claims that for a period of fourteen days there was no other senior party official in Berlin; all of the rest were on vacation. From a political standpoint, Honecker's sickness came at the worst possible time. As Krenz himself noted, this was the period when increasing numbers of East Germans were seeking to leave the country.[27] On August 1, several hundred GDR citizens stormed the FRG's offices in East Berlin, requesting permission to resettle in West Germany. Within two weeks, Bonn's embassy in Prague had to close because of the hundreds of GDR citizens seeking refuge there.

Krenz claims that he and some of his colleagues realized just how serious the situation was and asked Honecker to present a proposal to the Politburo for dealing with the underlying causes. Honecker responded by telling Krenz to go on vacation, even though the latter had offered to postpone his trip in order to deal with the current urgent situation.[28] As a consequence, Günter Mittag, the country's economic czar, took over while Honecker finished recuperating. Krenz claims that when he went on vacation, Mittag did nothing to deal with the situation. Indeed, on August 18 when Politburo member Herbert Krolikowski met with Chancellor Helmut Kohl's aide, Rudolf Seiters, to discuss the presence of East Germans in West German embassies and offices, Krolikowski took a typically hard-line stance by reiterating the standard GDR line: "Questions concerning the permanent exit of citizens of the GDR have been clearly stated in legal regulations."[29] Thus, at the moment when decisiveness was needed, there was a serious lack of leadership.

For its part, Bonn adopted a low-key approach. The West Germans obviously wanted the East German refugees out of their embassies, but at the same time they did not want to do anything to destabilize the situation in the GDR. The West German government wanted the East Germans to stay home and to push for liberalization—as had happened in most of the other East European states. Meanwhile, Kohl expressed his readiness to meet with Honecker to help resolve some of the problems facing East Germany.[30] Honecker refused.

Despite these ominous signs on the horizon, the East German leadership seemed oblivious to the danger represented by the mass flight of its citizens. On August 26, for example, *Neues Deutschland* published an article reminiscent of the worst days of the Cold War. It reiterated the point that the SED fully intended to keep its leading role in the country. Indeed, if anything, the article made it clear that any idea of compromise was out of the question as long as this political leadership remained in power.[31]

Finally, on August 29, the Politburo for the first time discussed the mass flight of its citizens. Rather than coming to grips with the problems facing the GDR, however, the Politburo placed the blame for everything on the West. For example, *Neues Deutschland* criticized the "Western media circus" for creating the problems facing the country.[32]

Meanwhile, the situation within the GDR was going from bad to worse. As one analyst put it:

> The unremitting manpower drain robbed the GDR of the equivalent of the work force of one medium-sized company per day. Bottlenecks developed, especially in medical services and other businesses requiring particular skills. The psychological results were even more debilitating. The departure of many of the best and brightest demoralized the remainder and engendered a pervasive loss of self-confidence. Dutiful citizens began to ponder whether it made any sense to stay behind. The political repercussions were most disastrous.[33]

In addition to the obvious political and psychological problems, this hemorrhage of humanity also would create very serious difficulties for the military. Not only would it be forced to fill increasingly large gaps in the civilian work force, it would also be affected seriously from a psychological standpoint and would face increasing difficulties in filling its own ranks.

In September, the protests against the falsification of the May elections took on new life. On September 4, for example, 1,200 people gathered for peace prayers in the Nikolai Church in Leipzig. They then marched to Market Square, chanting demands for the right to free assembly.

Then on September 10, the Hungarians completely opened their borders. Within 72 hours, 12,000 left Hungary for the West.[34] Needless to say, the East German leadership was outraged. Cries of betrayal were heard. The East Germans again turned to the Soviets for help. According to one source, Soviet Foreign Ministry spokesman Gennadi Gerasimov responded to public inquiries by noting that although Hungary's action had been unexpected, "it does not directly affect us."[35] The same source claims that Gorbachev told his aides that he was "disgusted" with Honecker's "inept" handling of problems in the GDR. It was becoming clear that if Honecker and his colleagues intended to maintain order and if it became necessary to use force, they would need to call upon the NVA, not Soviet forces.

The refugee question was discussed again in the Politburo on September 12. Schabowski claimed that his demand that the Politburo issue a public statement on the topic was denied. Those opposed contended that such basic questions could only be considered in the presence of the general secretary and Honecker was still recuperating from his operation. Furthermore, they argued that it would be better not to discuss such matters in public.[36] Schabowski wrote that he felt the Politburo was engaged in flights of fantasy:

The meetings of the Politburo and the Secretariat became ever more like a scene from the theater of the absurd. While the people deserted us, we were engaged in the art of social foresight, for example, how we could acknowledge the pioneering work of Otto Lilienthal in 1991.[37]

It was a case of the Politburo living in what Schabowski called "splendid isolation."

In mid-September a new force appeared on the East German scene, one that was to have a major impact on the future of the country. The New Forum, a loose grouping of opposition forces, asked to be accepted as a legitimate part of the country's political landscape. Not surprisingly, the Interior Ministry quickly ruled that it was illegal—and hostile to the state and the country's constitution.[38]

In the meantime, the domestic situation continued to deteriorate. On September 24, the first countrywide meeting of opposition groups took place in Leipzig, followed a day later by the largest protest demonstration to date. According to one observer, some 6,500 people took part. At the same time, security chief Erich Mielke routed one of his situation reports to Keßler, suggesting that he believed that developments were getting out of hand and that the party might have to call on the NVA to help keep order.[39]

Four days later the number of refugees in the West German Embassy in Prague exceeded 1,500. An additional 400 were in the West German Embassy in Warsaw. Within a week, the number in Prague would rise to over 10,000, and on October 4, East Berlin would decide to seal its border with Czechoslovakia to stop the flow.[40]

On September 29, the Politburo met. Despite the unsettled nature of events, Honecker's primary concern was the upcoming celebration of the fortieth anniversary of the GDR, scheduled for October 7. Everything he—and the GDR leadership—did during the next week or so was aimed at ensuring that these celebrations went smoothly. At the meeting, Honecker refused to deal with the issue of what to do as the country began to fall apart. Instead, he looked at the embassy occupation question only as a problem that could impact negatively on the celebrations.[41]

Honecker then came up with the idea of moving the East Germans who were occupying the West German Embassy in Prague to the FRG by first going through the GDR. For his part, Krenz called Honecker's plan "a senseless decision." It would not solve the underlying problem, and as Krenz noted in his memoirs, everyone soon knew that the trains would pass through East Germany on October 4. Others in the leadership (including Keßler, according to Krenz) also began to realize that the worsening situation demanded attention, but in the face of Honecker's opposition they were afraid to act.[42]

Meanwhile, the demonstrations continued. On October 2, around fifteen thousand people marched through the streets of Leipzig demanding that the government accept the existence of New Forum. In a call that was to become only too familiar in coming days, the crowd chanted "Gorby" and "Gorby, help us," in an obvious reference to the liberalizing measures that had been introduced in the USSR but strongly opposed by the old men running the GDR. This was by far the largest antigovernment demonstration to date in the country. The police responded by attacking small groups with clubs and electric cattle prods. Numerous people were hospitalized and more than a dozen were arrested.[43]

Publicly, the Honecker government continued to adopt a hard line. On October 2, for example, *Neues Deutschland* published an editorial with a statement added by Honecker that said good riddance to those who betrayed their country by leaving for the West. He wrote bitterly, "One should not shed any tears for them."[44] Unfortunately, the hardline approach taken by the Honecker government was not having its intended effect. The populace was becoming more restive and willing to take its grievances to the streets. Indeed, it is noteworthy that Mielke was sending out top secret memos to the leadership—including Keßler—in which he discussed in some detail actions the security organs were taking to control dissident political forces, including New Forum. Clearly the country's security services were very worried.[45]

The increasing instability again raised questions concerning the potential role of the NVA. After all, if the country's security forces were ineffective, the next obvious step was to call out the army. However, the news for those who might want to take such an action was not good. There would be serious problems if an effort was made to use the NVA to maintain internal order.

The NVA: Hidden Problems?

Morale problems were continuing to mount within the NVA. Hoffmann reported, for example, that between July and mid-October thirty members of the NVA deserted to the FRG and another fifty were captured as they tried to escape.[46]

One of the major reasons for this drop in morale was a lack of leadership. To begin with, the National Defense Council, which was the country's most senior military body, met for the last time on June 16. During July and August—when direction was most necessary, no meetings were held because Honecker was sick.[47] And Keßler was not much help either. Hoffmann claimed that for much of the time leading up to the

October period, Keßler did not understand the seriousness of what was happening. For example, he noted that on September 8 Keßler called senior East German military officers together to talk about problems in the GDR. Hoffmann said that Keßler's presentation was a serious disappointment.

> The Minister gave no explanation for the paralysis of the Party and State leadership. A desire for adventure and avoiding the consequences of one's personal actions (getting a girl pregnant) were listed as possible motives for the many young people leaving the country alongside anger at the difficult situation and hate of socialism. *The real, decisive causes were not recognized.*[48]

In the meantime, Keßler added, it was important to remain vigilant—some of those who had gone to the West, but later returned, probably were sent back by Western intelligence agencies. It was no wonder that senior military leaders like Hoffmann felt a sense of hopelessness in dealing with the country's political and military leaderships.

Keßler was not much more forthcoming when it came to dealing with the troops. For example, on September 13 he met with a group of four hundred reservists. He spoke of the threat from the West—especially the FRG—and the achievements of socialism, but he made no mention of the massive problems facing the GDR in light of the attempted and successful flight of thousands of its citizens, including members of the NVA.[49]

The first public admission by Keßler that things were not as they should be came in a visit he made to the Military Political Academy on September 21. During his meetings with students, he responded to comments on the importance of reforming the country by noting, "We naturally also know what has to be done to bring order in our country just as we know what we can do and what at the moment is not possible."[50]

In spite of his refusal to admit publicly the existence of problems within the NVA, it soon became clear that the military leadership was both aware of them and attempting to deal with them. For example, in a meeting with senior military officers on September 22, Keßler announced that, beginning December 1, a new set of internal regulations would be introduced. These regulations would permit greater freedom to NVA personnel. Career military would now be able to have their own private television sets, and wear civilian clothes when not on duty, while conscripts could travel in private vehicles, take leave three times a year, and so on.[51] While these actions may not appear especially forthcoming to someone used to Western military traditions, for the

tightly controlled NVA they represented a major breakthrough. Officers and NCOs could now wear civilian clothes—unthinkable in the
past!

Another problem facing the NVA, according to Hoffmann, was that
soldiers were not trained to deal with domestic unrest. Indeed, the
GDR's constitution said nothing about the use of NVA troops for domestic purposes. As a result, "for many years there was no plan for
the use of NVA troops in any type of armed conflict in internal affairs,
not even against 'counter-revolutionaries' or 'provocateurs' and that as
a result there were neither plans, nor training nor appropriate equipment." There were, however, legal provisions permitting the use of the
military to back up the police. For example, the National Defense
Council issued Orders 08/89 and 09/89, permitting the creation of
units to assist the police if the situation demanded it. This was followed by the issuance of Order Number 105/89 by the minister of
national defense which created "Hundertschaften" (units made up of
one hundred men) to support the police in an emergency. But the political training the soldiers had received, as well as their own self-image,
focused exclusively on protecting the country from external threats.[52]
In spite of the steps taken by Keßler and the National Defense Council,
it was still questionable whether the military would follow orders—or
be able to carry them out effectively in an emergency.

The NVA and the October Demonstrations

On October 4, trains carrying the East Germans who had occupied the
West German Embassy in Prague passed through Dresden. Not surprisingly, thousands of angry East Germans demonstrated against the
decision to permit some of their fellow citizens to leave the country
while they were forced to remain behind. The situation quickly grew
dangerous. To quote one analyst, "In Dresden about ten thousand protesters confronted the secret police with cobblestones against water
cannons in a pitched battle that damaged the main train station."[53] As
Krenz pointed out in his memoirs, the action had the opposite impact
from that which Honecker intended. "Once again ugly pictures went
around the world. This was three days before our national holiday."[54]
Hans Modrow, who was later to be given the task of trying to save
what was left of the GDR, reacted similarly, calling the idea of the trip
"nonsense."[55]

The role played by the NVA in this incident is now fairly clear. On
the basis of decisions taken by the National Defense Council, part of
the NVA was placed on alert for eventual support of the police. About

11:30 in the evening of October 4 there was a phone call between Keßler and Mielke. Based on this conversation, parts of the 7th Panzer Division, as well as officers from the Friedrich Engels Military Academy (located in Dresden) and cadets from the officer schools at Löbau, Kamenz, and Bautzen, were mobilized.[56] These units were placed under the command of Lieutenant General Manfred Gehmert, commander of the Military Academy. Weapons and ammunition were issued the following day. Thirty bullets were issued for machine pistols and six for pistols.[57] However, both Keßler and Hoffmann made the point that troops were prohibited from using their weapons.[58] Meanwhile, Mielke issued orders to security forces to stop "provocations" by all means.

Insofar as the use of NVA troops is concerned, the best evidence indicates that twenty-four Hundertschaften were deployed in Dresden. A number of senior officers worked to convince Keßler not to use loaded weapons, and to leave them on base. Keßler agreed and at 10:20, an order to that effect was issued. Ammunition was returned, and instead, nightsticks were given to the troops.

Only thirteen of these units actually left their barracks. By 9 p.m., five were deployed at the main train station. Their task was to block off access to the station itself. Twenty members of a long-range reconnaissance platoon (*Fernaufklärungszug*), together with their platoon leader, were ordered to seize "four or five individuals out of the crowd and to bring them behind the barriers erected by the police." It is not clear if that action was ever carried out. In addition, some of the soldiers were utilized to free two police vehicles that were surrounded by a crowd. So far as can be determined, this was the only instance in Dresden in which soldiers were utilized against GDR civilians. Five other units were utilized from 8 p.m. on October 7 to 1 a.m. on October 8 to guard buildings in Dresden. Three additional units were placed on call and brought to ready rooms in the city. On October 10, all of these units were returned to their bases.[59]

This is not to suggest that the situation in Dresden was a picnic. In fact, the police reacted viciously, attacking demonstrators and bystanders alike. Soldiers were both insulted and attacked with stones.[60]

The use of NVA troops was not limited to Dresden. In Leipzig, for example, twenty-seven Hundertschaften were created to guard strategic objects (e.g., the main train station, the post office, and the radio/TV station). Fifteen of these units were issued nightsticks. Additional units were prepared for possible duty and issued nightsticks and shields, but they were never utilized.

Between twenty and thirty Hundertschaften with nightsticks were used to support the police in Berlin. Two units were deployed near the Brandenburger Tor. For a short time on October 25, one unit guarded the Palast der Republik. Other NVA units also were put on alert for possible use in Berlin, Karl-Marx-Stadt, and other parts of the country. The 179 Hundertschaften were dissolved on 11 November around 6 p.m.[61]

Thus, with the exception of Dresden, the NVA played no role when it came to controlling crowds during the October demonstrations. Even in the case of Dresden, we know of only one instance in which soldiers actually came in contact with civilians. And this in spite of a thinly veiled warning by Keßler published on October 6 to the effect that the NVA would do everything possible to "fight" attempts at counterrevolution in the GDR.[62] While the behavior of these troops—had they been ordered to use force—must remain open to question, one participant claimed that in such a case, some would have refused to obey orders.[63]

Celebrating the GDR's Anniversary

October 7 was the day Erich Honecker had been living for, the crowning jewel in his long—and as he saw it—illustrious career. Indeed, one of the key purposes of the celebrations was to show the world that the GDR was the most advanced of all the socialist countries (including the USSR, in Honecker's mind). The events of the previous week would be dismissed as an aberration. Honecker was still in control and the country would continue its march toward socialism.

Soviet party chief Gorbachev arrived on October 6 at Berlin-Schönefeld. The afternoon festivities went as planned. Honecker welcomed Gorbachev to Berlin in a speech that suggested everything was going well in the GDR and included a none-too-subtle warning to Gorbachev concerning his liberal version of communism. As Honecker put it, "In any case, we will solve our problems ourselves with our socialist means." Needless to say, he made no mention of the refugees or the internal problems of the GDR. In contrast, Gorbachev's speech was, in Schabowski's opinion, "statesman-like, moderate." It focused on events in the USSR: "Our Party and our people are committed to see the reforms, which will radically renew Soviet society, to a successful conclusion."[64]

The celebrations began Saturday morning with a military parade on Karl-Marx Allee. From all outward appearances, everything was going smoothly. Honecker was animated, and Gorbachev also seemed to be interested in events. However, after the parade, Honecker and Gorbachev had a private meeting, which did not go well. Günter Mittag, who tried in vain to be included in it, noted that Honecker was not in a good mood when he returned.[65] Then came a meeting with the East

German Politburo, the course of which shocked even the most dedicated party leaders.

Gorbachev's speech to the Politburo included a warning aimed directly at Honecker: "Life punishes those who react too late. That is something we learned from our own experiences." Honecker listened to Gorbachev "with a flushed face, that reflected his internal tension." In response, Honecker spoke about the economic successes of the GDR, in particular in the area of microelectronics. He spoke of full shelves in GDR stores (in contrast to the USSR, one assumes).[66] Gorbachev's only response was a click of his tongue. This ended the meeting.

Next came a reception at the Palast der Republik, the most important governmental building in the GDR. While Honecker was toasting Gorbachev and proclaiming the GDR's many accomplishments, some 15,000 to 20,000 people had gathered at Alexander Platz, only a stone's throw away. The demonstrators dispersed peacefully, but some of those who were passing the palace on the opposite side of the Spree River began chanting, "Gorby, Gorby," "Gorby help us," and "We are the people."[67] Despite the peaceful nature of the crowd, once it reached the Prenzlauer District, the police attacked. Demonstrators and passersby alike were beaten.

Once the festivities concluded, Gorbachev returned to Moscow. Krenz claims that just prior to his departure from Schönefeld, Gorbachev advised a small group of Politburo members, "*Deistvuite*" (take action). This report is disputed by Schabowski, who doubts that Gorbachev would have said such a thing in front of Hermann Axen and Mittag, both close allies of Honecker.[68] In any case, both Schabowski and Krenz report that during the course of Gorbachev's visit both he and Krenz told Valentin Falin, a close advisor to Gorbachev on German matters, that they were embarrassed by Honecker's actions and that something would happen soon. From this point on, the die was cast—Honecker's time was limited. For his part, on his return to Moscow, Gorbachev told his staff that Honecker was not up to the job.[69]

The next morning, unaware of the violence that had taken place the night before, Krenz and Schabowski met with Mielke and other senior security officials. Schabowski said that he came away from this meeting, which focused on the importance of supplying propagandists to talk to future demonstrators, with the impression that Mielke, who was nothing more than a mouthpiece for Honecker, continued to believe in the possibility of a military solution to the country's problems.[70]

In an effort to calm the situation, Krenz drafted a memo that he planned to present to the Politburo for approval. In contrast to the statement published a week earlier, this proposed party decree stated that there were a number of reasons why people kept leaving the GDR and argued that existing problems must be solved in a "democratic" manner. Honecker was still incapable of understanding either the depth of the problems facing the country or the need for creative solutions, and called Krenz's suggestion a "personal affront."[71] As one writer put it,

> East German leaders largely lived in a make-believe world, unaware of either actual economic conditions or mounting popular discontent. The immobility of the SED stemmed not only from its post-Stalinist politics, but also from its aged leader's loss of touch with reality.[72]

Meanwhile, matters were heating up in Leipzig. Fearful that the planned demonstrations could quickly spin out of control—some 50,000 people were expected, which would make the October 9 demonstration the largest since the uprising on June 17, 1953—the three secretaries of the SED district leadership appealed directly to East Berlin to help avoid violence. Krenz, who was the Central Committee's secretary for security, called back at 7 p.m. to state that he agreed with their appeal for nonviolence. He somehow managed to get Keßler, Mielke, and Interior Minister Friedrich Dickel to go along. Whatever other sins he may have committed during his political life, when it came to the potential use of military force against GDR citizens, Krenz was opposed.

Much to Honecker's surprise, when the Politburo met on October 10, it agreed with Krenz's proposed party statement. It was published by the Politburo on October 11 and appeared in *Neues Deutschland* the following day.[73] Unfortunately, as Modrow pointed out, the statement was already behind the times when it was published. It was too little too late, and Honecker did little to build on it when he subsequently addressed a meeting of district secretaries. During his two-hour speech, Honecker ignored the country's problems—everything was NATO's fault.[74] Honecker thus succeeded in alienating both the East German populace and the party leadership. It was becoming increasingly clear that the only hope of salvation would come with his removal.

On October 13, Krenz again visited Leipzig. He was worried about the demonstrations planned for the 16th. What if they got out of hand? It was at this time that Col. Gen. Fritz Streletz, the secretary of the National Defense Council, took a leading role. He traveled with Krenz to Leipzig along with a number of other senior security officials. Krenz and the local authorities agreed that force would only be used if police or key buildings were directly attacked and that under no circumstances would weapons be utilized.

Based on this conversation, Streletz wrote Order 09, which stated very clearly that the use of force or weapons was "strictly forbidden."[75] Streletz and Krenz then took the order to Honecker for approval. Honecker still did not understand just how serious the situation was. He suggested that barriers should be constructed in the center of Leipzig to separate the demonstrators and that "a tank regiment should drive through the city," presumably to scare the inhabitants.[76] In the end, however, he signed the order.

On the 16th, Krenz, Mielke, Dickel, and Streletz (Keßler was on an official visit to Nicaragua), assembled in Dickel's office to keep an eye on events in Leipzig. Honecker soon joined them and according to Krenz was "exhausted and nervous." Several times Streletz tried to calm him down. As it turned out, the demonstration on the 16th was orderly—even if very large. The local security forces followed Streletz's instructions and did not use force.

If nothing else, Krenz said that Honecker's actions at that time convinced him that he had to raise the question of Honecker's ouster at the Politburo meeting scheduled for the next day.[77]

When the twenty-five member Politburo assembled at ten in the morning, Honecker asked if there were any additions to the agenda. In response, Willi Stoph suggested "the removal of Erich Honecker and the appointment of Egon Krenz as General Secretary." Both decisions were approved unanimously. In addition, Mittag, and Joachim Herrmann, who was responsible for the press, were also removed. The Honecker era was at an end and the Krenz interregnum—which would last for a far shorter period of time than anyone anticipated—had begun.

The Role of the NVA

According to Schabowski, Honecker and Mielke had spoken privately of the possibility of a military solution to the problem of popular demonstrations. Schabowski claims that while he and others knew that this conversation had taken place, they were excluded from discussions of it. "It was in the hands of others."[78]

Looking back at the events surrounding the difficult days of October, it was clear that the NVA continued to suffer from morale problems. For example, the public image of the NVA had sunk so low that soldiers ceased wearing their uniforms in public. This led Admiral Hoffmann, who was commander of the East German Navy at that time, to ask Keßler to permit him to talk to the media in the Baltic regions concerning the attitude of the armed forces toward change in the GDR. He hoped that this step would improve morale within the navy by demonstrating to the public that the military was also in favor of change. Keßler turned him down.

Meanwhile, there was a push within the NVA for more openness in dealing with military and military-related issues. In addition, soldiers began asking questions and expressing concerns over the existence of special stores for the elite. In short, NVA personnel were increasingly refusing to accept the party's official line.[79] Thus, while on the one hand it was clear that there was an aversion to the use of the military by civilians like Krenz and Schabowski, on the other, there was also some question of the willingness of NVA to be used in an effort to maintain internal order. As Hoffmann noted earlier, this was not something for which they were trained, either physically or psychologically. Furthermore, there is a consensus among most observers that "the generals and admirals made clear that the leadership was clearly trying to ensure that no weapon would be used against the people."[80]

At the time of the demonstrations in Dresden, there were reports in the West German media suggesting not only that the NVA was involved in putting down the demonstrations, but that the Red Army took part as well.[81] In fact, the Red Army played no role at all. When Gorbachev returned to Moscow after his visit to Berlin, he ordered Soviet troops to stay out of internal East German matters.[82] Indeed, there are reports that the Soviet military itself had urged the NVA to stay out of political matters and "not to use arms against its citizens." One source claims that the Russian military made it clear to East German authorities that "if they acted with military means against the people, the Russians would stay in their barracks."[83] This may well have been one of the reasons why the generals and admirals were opposed to the use of NVA troops against the populace: without Soviet support, the situation could quickly deteriorate into a civil war.

Conclusion

Looking at the evolution of the NVA during the first ten months of 1989, a number of factors stand out. First, the fact that it was forced to engage so heavily in civilian work even before things started falling apart not only damaged its combat readiness, it also undermined its sense of organizational cohesion and isolation. Having soldiers gone for weeks or months was bound to undercut not only discipline, but the military's ability to inculcate a unified *Weltanschauung* as well. How could it ensure that they did not watch or listen to Western radio and TV stations? Or guarantee that they did not pick up some of the negative civilian attitudes—especially after the miserable way in which the party handled the elections in May?

Indeed, one of the reasons why Honecker feared *perestroika* was that he believed—correctly—that factors such as increased contacts with the Bundeswehr would lead NVA officers to question many of the policies followed by the East German regime.

Second, the collapse of party authority meant that even those who were isolated in a military environment were beginning to turn against the very people who relied upon them—or who might want to rely upon them in a crisis. Similarly, the lack of leadership on the part of Keßler and his limited understanding of political trends did not help matters. Reading comments from senior East German military officers, one comes away with the sense that some felt disdain for him. This was certainly true of Hoffmann. While it is doubtful that even a dynamic Keßler could have saved the party's position in the military, a more vigorous approach on his part might have been able to slow down the disintegration process. For example, Hoffmann noted that when the Main Political Administration was asked for an explanation to pass on to the soldiers concerning what was happening in the civilian sector, none was forthcoming. A good leader would have ensured that even if the statement had to be incomplete, some sort of explanation would have been provided.[84]

Finally, one of the key elements in civil-military relations in a unitary party-state is the maintenance of a clear distinction between the military and the political elite. It is thus critical to create a situation in which the soldier—whether private or general—focuses solely on military matters, leaving all political decisions to the country's political authorities. In addition, although not critical, it is important that the military believe that political authorities are competent and capable—something that increasingly was not the case within the NVA.

As the NVA moved into the post-Honecker period, it still retained a considerable degree of cohesion in spite of what had happened in preceding months. Indeed, there were very few in the East or the West who believed that the government would eventually collapse on its own. After all, there was always the possibility that this army could be used against the East German populace, and then there was the question of a coup. Some in the West worried that, faced with chaos in the political sphere, some of the country's military officers might decide to take matters into their own hands. It was one thing for Honecker to be replaced by Krenz—it was still a communist government. But what if the communist regime itself fell? What would the NVA do in such a case?

3

Krenz Picks Up the Pieces: The NVA Is Depoliticized

In the first phase, the period up to the 8th Party Conference (November 8), we lived in the hope that it would be possible for us to build a better GDR.

Günter Schabowski

Günter Mittag probably described Egon Krenz best when he called him "the man without a conception."[1] Krenz was faced with a situation that up to that time was almost unique in the annals of communist history: what to do while the unitary party-state he headed was collapsing all around him. The task was made even more difficult as it became clear that Moscow would do nothing to help keep the SED regime in power. If it was to survive, it would have to do so on its own. As far as Krenz was concerned, he had no idea what to do.

On October 18, 1989, Krenz gave a major speech before a national TV audience. In contrast to Honecker, he admitted the existence of economic problems. But he argued against German reunification, maintaining that the GDR should remain a socialist state. He promised East German citizens that in addition to improving the country's economy, he would respect "socialist human rights," would grant greater freedom to travel abroad (one of the restrictions that upset GDR citizens the most), and was prepared for a dialogue with all of East German society, but especially with those who wanted an improved "socialist" system.[2] However, the speech did him little good. He managed to alienate everyone.

To begin with, Krenz sounded too much like Honecker, even if the content was more liberal. While he was more open-minded than Honecker, he did not go far enough toward opening up East German society to please the country's youth. On the other hand, the fact that he was prepared to make concessions at all upset many of the old-line party regulars. In short, he was caught between a rock and a hard place.

Instead of coming through with new ideas on how to turn the country around, Krenz defended the old system, arguing that all it needed was some fine tuning. The popular comment about Krenz going around the GDR at this time was, "One swallow does not make a spring."[3] East Germany had a new leader, but there was no sign that he had either the imagination, the intention, or the power needed to introduce the kind of fundamental changes that were required if the old system was to survive. Krenz's failure to come through in his speech was magnified by the fact that 120,000 people were marching through Leipzig that very day, demanding free elections and an end to communism.

Given this background, it should come as no surprise that groups like New Forum were skeptical about the new general secretary, who—as the man responsible for security matters in the upper ranks of the SED—had helped create the current repressive environment. As one East Berliner put it, "It's like replacing a lame white horse with a lame brown one."[4] If the past was any guide to the future, Krenz was simply making a tactical retreat until the party's control had improved.

To be fair to Krenz, however, he did take some long-needed positive steps. For example, he immediately met with representatives of the Evangelical Church who had played a key negotiating role in helping avoid violence in Dresden, and he agreed with them on the need to create a new law on elections. Then he ordered Interior Minister Friedrich Dickel to prepare a law on the freedom of travel. Krenz was at least trying to deal with the country's problems, even if he was taking a piecemeal approach.

To the degree that Krenz did have a plan, it was to follow the approach taken by Gorbachev and his colleagues in Moscow as he constantly reiterated the importance of ties between East Berlin and the USSR.[5] He would try—belatedly to be sure—to introduce a policy of *glasnost* and *perestroika* in the GDR. The real question facing Krenz was whether he could make the many concessions demanded by the East German public while at the same time maintaining control of the country and its communist political structure.

For his part, Gorbachev welcomed the change in political leadership in East Berlin. In a congratulatory telegram, Gorbachev wished Krenz success and stated that he was confident that together with the SED leadership, the GDR would follow a policy of "renewal and continuity" in dealing with the many problems facing the country.[6] Three days later Gorbachev spoke with Krenz on the telephone and invited him to visit Moscow.[7] There was no doubt in anyone's mind that Gorbachev was pleased with the leadership change in East Berlin, a view not shared by Marshal Dmitri Yazov, the Soviet defense minister.[8]

Another big change that occurred as a result of Erich Honecker's ouster was the opening up of a dialogue between East Berlin and Bonn. Whereas Honecker had summarily rejected Chancellor Helmut Kohl's overtures, Krenz spoke with Kohl by telephone on October 26. Krenz stated that the East German system would remain socialist, but he said that he would support the *"Wende"* (turning point) in GDR politics by pushing through specific reforms.[9] Krenz also agreed to receive Rudolf Seiters, a key official in Chancellor Kohl's office, to discuss the future of GDR-FRG relations.

The NVA Looks for Guidance

In the context of East German civil-military relations, Defense Minister Heinz Keßler continued to be a political nonentity. He was never perceived by his civilian colleagues as a political threat, nor did he attempt to assert himself when it came to key decisions—even on matters of national security. Other senior political officials were ousted, but he lasted well into the middle of November. Even then his ouster was related not to internal SED politics, but to a desire on the part of the political-military leadership to put an effective leader at the head of the NVA in an effort to stop the process of disintegration. However, his lack of leadership during the extra month he hung on contributed to an ever worsening climate within the army. On October 18, 1989, Keßler tried to convince participants at the Ninth Central Committee Plenum that NATO was the cause of all of the GDR's problems, but "he was shouted down."[10] Then on October 25, Keßler addressed a group of senior party secretaries from the Defense Ministry. He promised to do a better job of informing them of what was transpiring in the GDR and in particular in the NVA. However, Keßler's reception was not a warm one. "All of the speakers expressed their concerns about the existing situation, trying to find causes for it." In an effort to improve communication between Keßler, the Ministry of Defense, and the rest of the military, conference attendees proposed the creation of a central structure to lead party work. They also warned, "Party information must work in both directions so that every question, every hint, and every criticism is given a factual answer."[11]

A week later, Col. Gen. Horst Brünner, head of the Main Political Administration, published an article advocating the need to radically improve political work within the NVA. Anyone reading this essay could not help but conclude that without major changes, the NVA would continue to deteriorate. Despite this warning, however, Keßler did little to provide the guidance so desperately needed.[12]

Indeed, one of the main stumbling blocks was Keßler's inability to understand what was happening. Given his skewed view, he could hardly have been expected to provide the kind of leadership the NVA needed. A former East German general put it best:

> The minister at that time continued in November to insist that the Monday demonstrators in Leipzig were confused and that the rest—since the border was opened—are people from over there who have the task of changing our mood. Minister Keßler would not grasp the consequences—perhaps he couldn't.[13]

Stabilizing Efforts

Meanwhile, demonstrations continued. On October 23, 1989, some 300,000 people marched in Leipzig. A week later, similar crowds again marched in Leipzig and in other parts of the GDR, including Schwerin.[14] In an effort to pacify the increasingly restless East German public, Krenz made additional concessions that would have been unthinkable during Honecker's time. For example, on October 28 the State Council announced an amnesty for refugees and "peaceful demonstrators." This amnesty covered people who, prior to October 27, had tried to leave the GDR illegally, as well as those who had been charged with crimes related to the demonstrations—assuming they had not committed acts of violence.[15]

The new regime broke another political taboo when it began formal talks with New Forum. Before assessing the course of these discussions, it is important to note that New Forum was not a traditional political structure. It included representatives from a variety of parties or political persuasions. Indeed, the purpose of this organization was to create a structure in which alternative political actions could be discussed. Its biggest weakness was its lack of a vertical political structure. As Goertemaker put it, "Their idea was that a new, humane, and socialist East Germany could rise from the people's will without encumbering it with structures or preconceptions."

As nice-sounding and as well-intentioned as many of New Forum's leaders were, the group's days were numbered. Some members would go on to play important roles in the short-lived East German experiment with democracy, but as an organization it would quietly pass into history.[16] After the first discussion between the regime and New Forum, Schabowski said that he had "a positive feeling," but he also noted the party leadership was uncertain how to deal with this organization. A tightly knit political opposition group would have been easier to handle, but New Forum's loose structure and desire to propose new ideas made it difficult for old-time party bureaucrats to adjust.[17]

On October 31, Krenz and his colleagues received a shock that upset them almost more than the constant countrywide demonstrations. During a meeting of the Politburo, Planning Chief Gerhard Schürer revealed the full extent of economic deterioration of the East German economy. It was so bad, he said, that it "threatened the solvency of the GDR." Instead of the 4.8 percent increase in the national income that had been expected, the actual figure was only 3.8 percent. This left a deficit of 32 billion marks (East). This came as a complete surprise, according to Krenz. As he put it, "We were living at the expense of our children and grandchildren. This economic situation tied our political hands."[18]

In the same meeting, the Politburo also discussed a new draft travel law that was ready for circulation to senior government officials. Citizens of the GDR would be permitted to travel abroad for a maximum of one month per year without hard currency, provided they had a passport and a visa. Schabowski argued that the procedure was overly bureaucratic, maintaining that East Germans should simply be given passports and permitted to travel when and where they wanted.[19]

When this new law was published on November 6, it met with almost universal opposition. That same day, several hundred thousand people demonstrated, demanding "a travel law without restrictions." Why should East Germans have to go through police authorities to get permission to travel? It meant that the security services would still be able to restrict travel. As Hans Modrow put it, "It was completely unacceptable to the citizens."[20] Some members of the SED found it unacceptable as well.[21]

Even more important was the crowd's demand that "the Wall must go."[22] No matter how hard Krenz tried to move things in a positive direction, he seemed to be constantly behind—not only in terms of the actions he took, but also in understanding the mood of the populace. People were no longer talking about minor modifications to the system; the changes that East Germans were now demanding were systemic. Indeed, by this time the leadership's room for maneuver was very limited. Demonstrations were continuing and they were becoming increasingly radical. The nature of their demands was escalating—they had begun calling on the SED to share power through free elections! In addition, massive numbers of East Germans continued to leave the country every day for the FRG, which was a concern to Bonn as well.[23]

In an effort to strengthen his position, Krenz visited Moscow on November 1 to get Gorbachev's blessing. Following the meeting, he gave a press conference in which he stated that Gorbachev had emphasized that "all questions which concern the GDR must be decided in its capital city." The message was clear: Gorbachev supported the GDR's new leader, but he expected him to take care of East Germany's problems himself.[24] Speaking a day later in Poland, Krenz restated the essence of his position: The communist system would stay and the GDR would resolve its problems alone. The future would be determined by "the state sovereignty of the GDR in a socialist way with a human face."[25] Krenz argued repeatedly that the Communist party's leading role was enshrined in the constitution, and as a result it could not and would not be changed, regardless of public demands to the contrary.

Meanwhile, a number of particularly unpopular SED leaders were removed as the party attempted to project a new, more sympathetic image. On November 2 it was announced that labor leader Harry Tisch and Margot Honecker, the former party leader's unpopular wife who was in charge of education, were stepping down. That was followed the next day by Krenz's announcement on East German TV that Kurt Hager, Erich Mielke, Hermann Axen, Alfred Neumann, and Erich Mückenberger were all leaving the SED Politburo. In an effort to further solidify public support, Krenz proposed a political reform program that called for more accurate and truthful information, greater respect for human rights, educational renewal, and a restructuring of the country's desperate economy.[26]

Krenz's efforts were for naught. On November 4, over 500,000 people demonstrated in East Berlin. The government/party went to considerable efforts to keep the event peaceful. Both Schabowski and the famous spy master and sometime-dissident, Markus Wolf, tried to speak to the demonstrators but were jeered. The public did not want talk, they wanted action—specifically the repeal of article 1 of the constitution, as well as a rewriting of the country's criminal code to remove the bans on disseminating unauthorized information and holding unauthorized assemblies.

Among the most insightful observers of the East German scene was Horst Teltschik, the West German official who more than anyone else was to play a key role in bringing about German unification. Commenting on the November 4 demonstration, which he stated included a million people, Teltschik remarked, "It was obvious to anyone that the GDR leadership no longer had the situation under control."[27]

The reader should not get the impression that Krenz was unaware of how bad things were. In his memoirs, for example, he wrote that he received information that between November 4 and 6 some 23,200

GDR citizens had left the country, an average of more than 300 persons an hour.[28]

Recognizing the desperate situation, West German Chancellor Kohl mentioned East German events in his annual state of the nation speech. In it he called on the SED to abandon its privileged position as well as to permit independent parties and free elections. In addition, Kohl stated that Bonn would be prepared to consider a new form of economic assistance provided East Berlin made fundamental reforms in the country's economy. He also emphasized that the FRG remained committed to reunification.[29]

On November 7, the entire forty-one-person government resigned "in the interest of society and of the people."[30] Later that day the Central Committee elected a new eleven-person Executive Committee headed by Modrow. Surprisingly, given his inept performance within the NVA, Keßler was included among the eleven. Apparently, no one in the leadership either feared Keßler or realized that a change at the top was needed. The fact that Keßler continued to hang on for another week is surprising given the comments Krenz made about the situation in the military to a class of graduates from the Military Academy on November 1. Krenz told these graduates that the Politburo had permitted "criticism and self-criticism to be underdeveloped in the military" and noted that the situation in the armed forces was really worse than advertised.[31]

The Berlin Wall Opens

The opening of the Berlin Wall on the evening of November 9 was one of the more bizarre incidents surrounding the collapse of the GDR. It came as a complete surprise to the NVA and border troops who were on duty. At 6 p.m., Krenz gave Schabowski two papers, which Schabowski understood he was to read at a press conference scheduled for later that evening. The key document concerned travel, but unknown to Schabowski, it was not intended to be made public at that time. Reading from the text, Schabowski announced to a live TV audience that the GDR had opened its borders. When a journalist asked if that meant that any GDR citizen could now travel freely to the West, Schabowski responded affirmatively, and added that it became effective "at once" (*ab sofort*).

The cat was now out of the bag. Thousands of East Germans converged on the East Berlin/West Berlin border. Border guards had neither advance knowledge of the new regulations, nor had they been given orders to let people through. They had no idea what to do. In an earlier day, they would have opened fire. But now . . . ? Eventually, recognizing the seriousness of the situation, the high command ordered the border guards to open the gates and people streamed into West Berlin.[32]

With the wall now open, East Germans moved easily into the FRG. Movement from East to West increased not only as a result of natural curiosity, but because the prospect of good-paying jobs in the FRG was irresistible to most East Germans. In fact, the situation within the GDR was totally confused. On November 10, the Central Committee adjourned early because of the chaos caused by the unintended opening of the wall the night before. No one knew what to do. "We quickly decided to schedule the insufficiently discussed Action Program and the Party Conference for December 15–17."[33] On that same day, Krenz addressed a gathering of some 150,000 SED party members. He was faced with an impossible task. On the one hand, some party members continued to believe that his "liberalizing" tendencies were undermining the party's control over society. On the other, there were those who felt he was not going far enough. As one writer put it, "According to numerous reports, local leaders and members felt betrayed. 'The comrades' trust in the party erodes day by day.' "[34]

In retrospect, the danger of military intervention or the use of the military against civilians was higher on the evening of November 9 than it had been at any time during the October demonstrations.

From the military's standpoint, it was not only the border guards who were caught by surprise by the events of November 9. According to Adm. Theodor Hoffmann, that evening he and his colleagues— including Col. Gen. Klaus Dieter Baumgarten, the chief of border troops—were in Strausberg waiting for Keßler's arrival. Baumgarten was called out of the meeting for a phone call. He was told by his chief of staff that the government had issued a decree opening the borders and that thousands of people were converging on the border demanding permission to cross into West Berlin. Baumgarten's chief of staff asked for instructions. Baumgarten relayed the request to the other senior officers who were present. According to Hoffmann, "All members at the collegium meeting were taken by surprise."[35]

Once Keßler arrived, he spoke with Krenz, who instructed him that force was not to be used. He then called the commander of Soviet forces in Germany, who informed Keßler that he had just received an order from Moscow telling him that Soviet forces were to remain in their barracks and not become involved in what was happening in the GDR.[36]

Meanwhile, Keßler told Baumgarten to get further clarification concerning events at the border. At this point Baumgarten asked permission to leave the meeting, expressing concern that the situation could deteriorate to the point where the border troops, totally confused about what was going on, might use their weapons in a crisis. In fact, no one had any idea of the magnitude of the problem. If they had known, Hoffmann said, the meeting would have ended immediately in order to provide help to the border guards (who were subordinated to the military).

For their part, the soldiers at the border were confused and distraught. On the one hand, they were being told to uphold the laws of the GDR, which prohibited individuals from leaving the country without prior permission from the Interior Ministry. At the same time, they were confronted with thousands of East Germans who were telling them that the rules of the game had changed—anyone who wanted to could leave. This situation raised the question of the future of the border troops, some of whom had served for years under very difficult conditions and were despised by many of their fellow citizens. What should they do? According to one former border guard officer, "the greatest problem was to ensure that hotheads or fanatics" did not get out of control.

Based on the available information, the danger of conflict with civilians was greater than many realized. Border troops guarding the area around the Brandenburger Tor were placed on heightened alert and reserve forces were brought in to back them up. Weapons and ammunition were issued and some of these units reportedly were prepared to shoot.[37]

In the end, bloodshed was avoided. General Streletz hit the nail on the head when he observed, "We can be happy that the members of the border troops carried out their task in such a disciplined fashion, because the order read: 'In no case make use of weapons,' and this order was strictly observed."[38] But looking back, it is clear that had someone opened fire, the consequences could have been catastrophic.

One of the most intriguing aspects of this whole affair is the possibility that the leadership of the NVA overrode an attempt by the political leadership to impose a Tiananmen Square–type solution by using military force to reseal the country's borders with the West.[39] According to this thesis, senior political officials had planned to use the NVA to close the border immediately if it was opened and thereby save the old system.

There are indications that Keßler may indeed have considered using the military.[40] One well-informed source noted, for example, that the former commander of Artillery Regiment 1 had talked about an order he had received to put his men on alert and to issue ammunition for possible use in Berlin to reseal the Wall.[41]

It is clear that NVA troops, in particular those around Berlin, were placed on alert for possible use in "maintaining order."[42]According to General Stechbarth, Keßler called him on November 11 and asked if he was ready to send two regiments to Berlin. However, Stechbarth said he suggested that Keßler rethink matters and proposed that they look at other alternatives.[43] Generals Joachim Goldbach, Manfred Grätz, and Hans Süß pointed out that the troops were not in position to carry out such a mission and that it would be difficult for them to travel all the way around Berlin without causing further problems. To quote the commander of the First Motorized Infantry Division, "I believe that if we with our military units had traveled to Berlin, the danger of a bloodbath would have been great."[44] Fortunately, through the cooperation of the West Berlin police and the border troops, the Wall had been cleared of demonstrators, giving the situation a greater sense of normalcy.[45] The heightened state of combat readiness was canceled.

General Streletz has disputed these claims of possible military action, contending that "there was never any intention to close the Berlin border, but [only] to establish peace and order."[46] Streletz also maintained that although a heightened form of combat readiness had been ordered, the fact that the First Motorized Division was to move without armor or artillery made clear that there was no intention to use these forces to reseal the Wall. Furthermore, he argued, if the military had intended to seal up the Wall, everything would have been done in great secrecy. In fact, secrecy was not imposed, and Streletz added that such an attempt to reseal the Wall would have only been taken if ordered by senior political authorities. Finally, as Keßler observed, "If we had intended to close the border, we would not have asked the West Berlin police for assistance."[47]

So who is right? Based on the available data—and some speculation—this writer suspects that, given his conservative ideological leanings, Keßler would have used the military if he had thought such an option would have been effective. However, his subordinates (and especially Gen. Goldbach) made clear to him that for a variety of reasons use of the military was not realistic and would only lead to a bloodbath. In Streletz's case, it is hard to reconcile an effort to reclose the border by force with his successful effort to overturn Honecker's desire to use force in Leipzig only a month earlier. Regardless of what he might have secretly wished for the GDR, Streletz comes across as a very realistic, sober military officer. A massacre by an army that was disintegrating would have served no purpose other than to plunge the country into a disastrous civil war.

Transition at the Defense Ministry

On November 11, 1989, Keßler was sharply criticized at a meeting of party activists, who asked him to step down.[48] Then came a meeting on November 14 in which Keßler announced that Krenz had asked him to stay on as defense minister. In response, the majority of members of the Ministry of Defense's Collegium—including Hoffmann—reiterated their call for him to step down. As they put it, "Comrade Minister, if you want to keep the army together, then withdraw your candidateship."[49]

Another meeting was held the same day in which "neither Keßler nor any other participant in the meeting went into the most important problem"—which Hoffmann defined as the role of the Communist party in the GDR.[50] This is not to suggest that Keßler was oblivious to the fact that both the GDR and the NVA faced serious problems. He acknowledged his own responsibility for problems in the NVA, and he outlined a number of major changes he planned to make in an article published the day after the incidents at the Berlin Wall.[51] Bowing to the inevitable, however, Keßler resigned and on November 15, Hoffmann unexpectedly got the call to become defense minister.

Before discussing Hoffmann's role as defense minister, let us take a closer look at Keßler's role through the eyes of his subordinates. One of the questions asked of former NVA officers in researching this book was how they evaluated Keßler's actions during this period. There were several different responses. The majority remarked that he was "over-taxed" and that he was too closely tied to the past, and especially to his friend Erich Honecker, to understand the full extent of the changes taking place. As one respondent put it, "I see his personal tragedy in that he was not in a position to recognize the forthcoming collapse of the system and as a result, he was unable to make a constructive contribution."

Others commented that his most positive act in the fall of 1989 was that "he recognized that the NVA could not be used against the people," and therefore "did nothing." By doing nothing, such individuals meant that he could have tried to use force to restore order, but that he chose a different, more positive course.[52] Indeed, almost all respondents agreed that the use of force "would have inevitably led to a confrontation within the NVA." The consequences would have been catastrophic for the military and the country.

If there was one point upon which the respondents agreed, however, it was that the opening of the Wall had a disastrous effect on the NVA. Officers remarked that it ushered in a period of uncertainty and skepticism toward the regime. "There were many questions that no one could satisfactorily answer," noted a former major general. A former colonel said that it raised the question, "What would become of the NVA?" Or as another observed, "The NVA was no longer obligated to defend the country against the FRG." Discipline began to decline, according to several, and as a consquence the combat readiness of the armed forces dropped.

Once Vice Admiral Hoffmann arrived at the Strausberg headquarters of the NVA, he was ushered in to see Keßler, who told him that he was to become the new defense minister and would at the same time be promoted to colonel general in the army. Hoffmann wrote that, since the army was the largest service, it was assumed by everyone that he would want to switch services. However, he was shocked at the suggestion that after so many years wearing a blue navy uniform he should now put on an army uniform. Navy men are a different breed from the other services, and Hoffmann put his foot down. No one knew what to do. The idea of a Navy officer serving as defense minister was more than many senior army officers could bear. As a result, Hoffmann raised the question directly with Krenz. Noting that he was fortunate that Krenz also came from the "waterfront," Hoffmann said that he obtained Krenz's approval and was promoted instead to admiral.[53]

One of the first steps taken following Hoffmann's appointment was the issuance of an order separating the party organization from the leadership of the NVA. Party instructions from the SED for the NVA and the border troops were rescinded. The Secretaries of the Main Political Administration and the Political Sections for the forces were also dissolved. Not surprisingly, the worst of the criticism against the party and its mistakes fell on the shoulders of political officers. However, Hoffmann wrote that while he recognized that many political officers were themselves responsible for the "dogmatic" approach taken in political work in the NVA, there were many others who had worked hard to find answers to the problems facing the military. In any case, he noted, they were not the only ones guilty of creating the situation in which the NVA now found itself, and they should not be singled out for special criticism.[54]

The primary impact of this depoliticization was that the Main Political Administration lost its connection to any political party. But at the same time, there was also a feeling that some sort of a political structure would continue to be needed in the future. As the new chief of the Main Political Administration put it, "We are of the opinion that we will also need organs and personnel in the future which are concerned with political education, and especially for the training and information of army members—that means a structure which must be concerned with state and military-political tasks."[55] Political pluralism was becoming a reality in the NVA.

Modrow Emerges As a Political Force

Kohl and Krenz continued their private discussions in November. The two spoke on November 11 shortly after the East Germans had opened the Wall. Both agreed that everything should be done to avoid emotional and radical actions, and Krenz asked for Kohl's assistance in keeping the peace. In addition, Krenz pushed the need for West German financial help for the beleaguered East German economy. Kohl agreed to avoid doing or saying anything to inflame the situation, but as far as a formal meeting with Krenz was concerned, he saw no purpose for one until it became clear where the GDR regime was going.[56]

On November 13, Hans Modrow's authority increased significantly when he was elected president of the GDR's Council of Ministers—a key governmental post. Modrow, who had been the party boss in Dresden, had been a constant thorn in Honecker's and Mittag's sides. He had opposed Honecker's refusal to take liberalizing steps and had been blasted by the East Berlin party apparatus for his efforts. At this point, everyone in the party leadership, including Krenz, realized that Modrow was probably the only party official left with enough personal integrity to be credible to the East German populace. He was the regime's last hope.

Modrow played his new role well. He attacked the old SED officials, claiming that the very existence of socialism was at stake. He promised to overhaul the economy and stated that he was committed to reforms in other areas as well. Modrow's position was not an enviable one, however. His task was to keep the Communist party in power—yet he promised free elections. The difficulty was that no one seriously thought the Communists could win a free election. He had argued on several occasions that in the future the party should be separated from the state; in essence, the end of the party-state. Modrow also realized the enormity of the economic reformation facing the GDR, but he hoped that aid from the FRG would help soften that blow.

In an effort to win public support, a "Grand Coalition" was formed on November 17. The new government included twenty-eight ministers rather than the previous forty-one. The SED (Socialist Unity Party) was limited to seventeen ministries, while the LDPD (Liberal Democratic Party of Germany) had four, the CDU (Christian Democratic Union) three, and the DBP (Democratic Peasant's Party) and NDPD

(National Democratic Party of German) each had two. This new government also signaled the emergence of a new figure on the GDR political scene, one who was to play a pivotal role in coming months: Lothar de Maiziere, the new Chairman of the CDU, who was appointed head of the Ministry of Church Affairs.[57]

One of the first things the new Modrow government did was to convince the Politburo to endorse the idea of a "round table," a setting in which both government and nongovernmental representatives would meet to discuss and plan policy. Indeed, the SED leadership took the unusual step of calling for a "dialogue" between the government/ party and the round table. Subjects for discussion included issues such as a new electoral law, the holding of free elections, and reforming the constitution.[58] Only a few days later, Krenz came out in favor of eliminating Article 1, which enshrined the "leading role" of the SED in the East German constitution and was the instrument that had been used for so many years to silence the voices of those who called for the introduction of pluralistic democracy. At the same time, Krenz announced that the party's Control Commission had begun proceedings against Honecker, but that such proceedings would be held in abeyance, given the precarious state of Honecker's health.[59]

In spite of all of the "radical" actions taken by the Krenz/Modrow regime, there were few who had any idea just how fast the domestic scene would change. For example, upon his return to Bonn after a visit to East Berlin in mid-November, Seiters said that he doubted that a free election could take place prior to the fall of 1990 or even the spring of 1991.[60] One indication of how unrealistic this evaluation was came a day later when de Maiziere, the leader of the CDU, stated that his party favored a German "confederation" and that it wanted to vote on the issue by the middle of the following year at the latest.[61]

If Modrow, Krenz, and other SED leaders were united on one point, it was opposition to the idea of reunification—even if it came in the form of a confederation. For example, in discussing a proposed treaty between the GDR and the FRG, Modrow expressed support for it but added that he believed that "the existence of a sovereign GDR state is our departure point for questions of internal and external security." Or as he put it in another context, "Despite their different social orders, the two German states have a common history that is centuries long. Both sides should now seize the opportunity to give the relationship a good neighborly character."[62] Krenz made the same point when he and Modrow met with Seiters on November 21. According to Seiters, Krenz spoke of liberalizing the GDR, but he made it clear that the leadership believed that the GDR should remain a separate, sovereign country.[63]

This push for the continued existence of two separate Germanies was to be one of the linchpins of East German politics in coming months. At this point, everyone was primarily concerned about stability in the country. Mass demonstrations and even riots were possibilities. There was a danger that if too much emphasis was placed on reunification, it could further weaken the government's already fragile hold on East German society. Thus, German reunification still seemed a remote possibility at best.

It was at this point that Kohl entered the reunification debate when he announced a plan to help improve the GDR's economy. This plan, which was called the "Ten Point Program for German Unity," was to have a major influence on the course of events in the GDR.[64] The plan called for a staged approach to German unity. For example, Kohl offered immediate aid in the form of medical assistance and help with foreign currency for those who wished to travel. He offered to continue cooperating in areas such as the environment and the postal system, and he made it clear that he was prepared to give additional assistance—provided that the reforms planned by Krenz and Modrow became "irreversible." He also came out in favor of building common institutions between the two states, and in an effort to pacify other European states, which were worried about the power of a reunited Germany, he called for this process to take place within the framework of closer European and international cooperation.[65]

In fact, the situation in the GDR was so unstable that Kohl had to say and do something. Failure to act on his part would have made a bad situation even worse. His goal was "to provide a systematic, step-by-step approach to German unity."[66] If nothing else, he hoped to keep events from spinning out of control.

Kohl's speech changed the nature of the debate in the GDR. The East German regime would continue to call for two sovereign states, but the East German populace began to gradually realize that reunification was more than a grand theory. Nevertheless, Teltschik stated that the chancellor believed it would take five to ten years before a unified Germany became a reality. In fact, he told U.S. President George Bush that it would be an economic disaster if Germany were united within two years.[67]

At first, public opinion polls in the GDR seemed to support the chancellor's long-term view of reunification. For example, a poll conducted by West German TV and the magazine *Der Spiegel* showed 71 percent of those eligible to vote favored the continued existence of the GDR. Only 27 percent favored reunification.[68] In time, however, events would take on a momentum of their own and public opinion would change dramatically.

In the meantime, the East German regime liberalized further. On December 1, 1989 with no negative votes and only five abstentions, the Volkskammer voted to remove Article 1. No longer did the Communist party have a constitutionally guaranteed right to run the country. Originally, Article 1 of the constitution had read, "The German Democratic Republic is a socialist state of the workers and peasants. It is the political organization of the workers in the cities and the countryside under the leadership of the working class and its Marxist-Leninist party."[69] The last phrase beginning with "under" was dropped. The SED was now on the same playing field as other political parties. In addition, the Volkskammer issued a formal apology to the people of Czechoslovakia for East German participation in the 1968 invasion of that country.[70]

Despite Krenz's best efforts, it was becoming increasingly clear that he was more of a hindrance than a help to those trying to stabilize the situation in East Germany. Indeed, Krenz's authority had been especially hurt by the many corruption scandals that had become public knowledge. Stories of senior SED officials living in luxury—in houses with saunas and hot tubs—while the majority of the East German populace had to do without basic comforts, together with a feeling of disdain for individuals who proclaimed their adherence to an ideology that called for the equality of all while living in the lap of luxury, convinced the average East German that even more radical changes were needed. The situation had gotten to the point where "almost daily the newspapers print revelations about the sweet life of the Party and State leadership."[71] On November 18 the Volkskammer set up a committee to investigate official corruption, which issued an interim report in early December that spoke of shocking instances of misuse in building lavish homes, creating private hunting preserves, and similar luxurious styles of life.[72] Shortly thereafter, official investigations were under way.

The Military and Corruption

Although the public was disturbed by the extent of corruption among senior officials, members of the military were outraged. One source discussed the luxury villa (valued at 1.1 million marks) that was built for Defense Minister Keßler in Strausberg using military labor and supplies. Then there were reports of private hunting preserves reserved for senior members of the NVA—all paid for and maintained at state expense.[73] As Admiral Hoffmann put it, "Knowledge of cases of the misuse of office and corruption strengthened the already existing anger."[74] As another officer noted:

> Citizens of the GDR, including soldiers, were always trying to fill certain wishes, but could not because there was nothing available. But the next day they discovered through the media how one or another state functionary had lived. That created a sense of frustration.[75]

Beyond the general sense of anger over the revelations about widespread high-level corruption, professional soldiers were even more bitter about the impact of such actions on the army's public image. Such behavior focused attention on the military and the fact that officers were better paid than most civilians and were granted easier access to housing and some other amenities. Few civilians realized that the payoff was in exchange for incredibly long working hours as well as problems for spouses in finding jobs. The result was "increased mistrust against all high-ranking officers."[76] In response to these charges, Hoffmann created an Investigation Committee. The Committee considered a variety of reports and turned the material over to Hoffmann, who passed it on the relevant legal organs. According to Hoffmann, some were indicted and found guilty. By and large, however, Hoffmann felt that the NVA emerged relatively unscathed:

> The work of the Investigation Committee showed that professional soldiers in the NVA fulfilled their tasks with a high level of combat readiness and devotion as well as obedience to the law and military regulations and that they had carried out the hard, occasionally excessive demands of combat readiness under privations and stress—especially for the families.[77]

Needless to say, this discussion of corruption not only hurt NVA morale, but also raised serious questions about the willingness of soldiers, who were losing respect both for Krenz and the party he represented as well as their own military leadership, to carry out orders in a crisis.

Krenz Resigns

Krenz was faced with a hopeless situation. He was part of the old, the corrupt, the inept, the immoral. He had to go. One author said it well when he observed:

> The general secretary . . . could not even aspire to being a transitional leader. In demanding a thorough political house-cleaning, Krenz advanced the most cogent argument for his own departure. There was simply no denying that he had been as responsible for betraying the people's trust as had those he now so sternly attacked.[78]

On December 3, the SED's Politburo and the entire Central Committee resigned. Three days later Krenz resigned as chairman of the State Council and chairman of the National Defense Council of the GDR. After only fifty days, Krenz had gone from being the most powerful man in the GDR to an average citizen. Meanwhile, Honecker was put under house arrest at his home in Wandlitz. Indeed, it would not be long before Krenz, like Honecker and others, would face criminal charges because of their involvement with security issues—in particular, the infamous *Schießbefehl*, the "order to shoot," which resulted in a number of individuals trying to cross the inner-German border being shot and some killed.

Needless to say, the country's political and economic deterioration, not to mention its increasing instability, was bound to affect the NVA. Indeed, by the time Krenz resigned, it had become an army that simply was not capable of carrying out the missions assigned to it.

Given the radical nature and speed of the changes that the NVA was enduring, it should come as no surprise that morale was steadily declining. One of the first things Hoffmann did to deal with the many complaints and concerns within the NVA was to set up a Center for Consultation and Information at the MOD in Strausberg. The result was an avalanche of phone calls and telegrams. Within a week, the center had received 912 telephone calls, 600 telegrams and telexes, and 115 personal visits. The calls and letters dealt not only with complaints, but also made suggestions on what should be done to deal with the NVA in a period of major change.[79]

However, the new center was only a bandage on a hemorrhaging wound, and as Hoffmann noted, by the beginning of December it was becoming clear that something more had to be done quickly. Indeed, by this time demonstrations by reservists were taking place and the active duty NVA personnel desertion rate stood at ten to fifteen per day. In addition, Hoffmann estimated that 80 percent of officer candidates wanted to leave the officer schools.[80] At a meeting in a unit of one Mühlhausen, soldiers discussed "German unity"; a majority of these soldiers came out in support of reunification.[81] Meanwhile, the public image of the military was continuing to fall, and soldiers themselves were beginning to ask, Why are we here? Why should we have to serve in an army that is protecting a state that has no enemies and appears to be collapsing as well?

To make matters worse—if that were possible—pressures for work by military personnel in the civilian economy increased. Hoffmann personally opposed using the military to perform civilian jobs and argued that the military should only be used in such a fashion in catastrophic situations. Beginning December 1, an additional six thousand soldiers were sent to industry after receiving three months of military training. Indeed, when he met with members of the ground forces, Hoffmann was informed that the decision taken at the beginning of December to send soldiers to industry, forestry, and the health services, as well as to loan trucks to civilian organizations, meant that "there could not be any discussion of a systematic form of military training."[82]

Then an additional six hundred members of the border troops were sent to help in industry.

To understand the significance of the numbers, it is worth noting that during the 1988/89 training year, an average of 9,200 soldiers and some 322 vehicles were deployed each month in support of the civilian economy.[83] And these numbers were increasing. Indeed, on December 14, *Neues Deutschland* reported that a total of 19,100 soldiers were serving in the civilian economy.[84] The bottom line was that it was becoming impossible both to maintain discipline in the NVA and to unify it as a meaningful military machine. Three months of military training might be better than none, but not much.

In the minds of the leaders of the NVA, the only hope was some sort of military reform. A new structure had to be found to accommodate the military during a period of major political change. Almost all senior officers recognized that the old methods were clearly not working. However, as long as Keßler had been defense minister there was little that could have been done to change things. Given how bureaucratized the NVA was, structural change would only come if and when a man took over who was committed to making the kinds of changes that were needed.

The military took a number of steps. First, recognizing that there would be little chance of restoring confidence as long as the old cadre remained in place, a number of personnel changes were introduced. For example, Gen. Wolfgang Reinhold retired as head of the air force, and Gen. Horst Stechbarth left as head of the ground forces. In addition, Hoffmann set aside the requirement for early morning sports. Commanders were given greater flexibility to determine duty hours (which often ran ten hours a day or more, with little time off on the weekend). In addition, the MOD announced that a five day work week would go into effect after March 1, 1990.[85] Admiral Hoffmann was convinced that only through the introduction of a real and meaningful military reform could the NVA hope to win back both the support of its soldiers and that of an increasingly critical civilian population.

At Hoffmann's urging, a working group on military reform was set up under the chairmanship of Lt. Gen. Hans Süß. This reform had four major goals:

—dismantle the old political structure
—promote respect for democratic rights in the NVA
—stabilize the military in the face of personnel reductions
—determine the reason for and meaning of military service in the GDR[86]

To oversee the military reform movement, a government commission was created on December 12. Work continued on the reform plan, but within a short period of time, it became obvious that the problem was bigger than the NVA. As Hoffmann put it, "It soon became clear that it was not a question of a military reform of the NVA, but of a military reform of the GDR."[87] Indeed this would become one of the major problems faced by the NVA as it moved into the Modrow period: how to establish a military reform process at a time when the country—and the military—seemed to be falling apart.

Conclusion

Looking back at the NVA during the fifty days of the Krenz interregnum, a number of observations are in order. To begin with, it was clear that the lack of direction from Krenz and his associates hurt the NVA. One of the primary assumptions in any party-army relationship is that political authorities are firmly in charge and give clear (if not always wise or appropriate) directions to the military. This was certainly not the case with the NVA at this time. Neither the GDR's political nor military leaders knew where the country was going, nor did Krenz pay special attention to the military, as indicated by his asking Keßler to stay on as head of the NVA at a time when Krenz himself recognized that the military was in serious trouble.

Second, there was a lack of leadership. Neither Krenz nor Keßler was the type of individual who could seize hold during a crisis and pump new life into the armed forces. Both were psychologically married to the past. This meant that soldiers were expected to ignore events in the civilian world—an increasingly difficult demand. After all, not only was the Berlin Wall now open—and a number of NVA soldiers took advantage of the opportunity to visit the West—many of them were doing civilian work, which further opened them up to radicalizing civilian influences. Then there was the collapse of the SED. If nothing else, the existence of a unified, highly politicized party helped inculcate a single *Weltanschauung* into members of the military. Indeed, it was not surprising that soldiers and officers began to question the utility of having an army. What were they defending? Against what? Not only was the ideology bankrupt, it was turning out that the country's leaders and some of the senior military officers were corrupt. Disdain, if not outright contempt, for the country's senior party officials was evident everywhere—even among military officers. Furthermore, the ability of officers to maintain the high sense of discipline common to the NVA in the past also was gone, a situation made worse by the end of party hegemony. The best they could do was to try to maintain control, and as events in January 1990 were to show, there were cases when even that modest goal would prove impossible.

Finally, it was clear to everyone from Defense Minister Hoffmann down to the lowest private that the NVA was being transformed. Most understood where the NVA had come from, but few—if any—had any idea where the armed forces were going. Hoffmann did what any well-trained officer would do: He ordered his people to come up with a military reform plan. The problem with such a plan, however, was that to be meaningful, it had to be based on a number of assumptions. For example, what kind of financing would it receive? What kind of political structures would it serve? In a nutshell, the well-structured, unambiguous world that the NVA officers had known only a year before was crashing down around them. A party-army cannot survive when it loses direction.

The situation within the NVA and the GDR in general would only worsen. Modrow would do his best to breathe new life into the country, and Hoffmann and his colleagues would work overtime in an effort to salvage what was left of the NVA. But it would be a case of too little, too late. The train of disintegration had already left the station and there was nothing they could do to put things back together again.

19 October 1989. 150,000 East Germans demonstrate in Leipzig.
Credit: Deutsche Press Agentur (cited hereafter as DPA)

10 November 1989. Egon Krenz and Günter Schabowski try to discuss the current situation with a crowd of demonstrators.
Credit: DPA

4

Modrow Tries to Save Socialism: The Military on the Verge of Collapse

Because the leadership around Krenz had no concept and because it was not ready for a radical break with the past, the party had to fight for its existence.

Admiral Theodor Hoffmann

An Army cannot go into combat democratically.

Günter Schabowski

When he came to power, Hans Modrow was faced with an almost impossible task. He was committed to keeping the old communist/socialist system, albeit in a revised form. He believed that it would still be possible—even at this late date—to create a "democratic" Socialist/Communist party, one which would win the support of the East German people. The problem was that in spite of his efforts to remake the old SED, he was doing so at a time when the GDR was moving increasingly close to collapse.

Within the SED, there was consensus on one issue: the Stalinist past not only had to be repudiated, it had to be replaced by a new political structure. Unfortunately, there was considerable difference of opinion within the old party elite concerning what form this new party should take. What would be its goals? There were those who continued to mouth the standard communist slogans: Down with capitalism and imperialism! On the other hand, there were others who recognized that the old system had failed. Even the party newspaper *Neues Deutschland* noted, "The governmental and administrative socialism has definitely failed as a social system in our country."[1] For its part, the party leadership decided that it had to break with the past. To quote Gregor Gysi, Chairman of the new SED, "We need a complete break with the failed

Stalinist system, that is, the administrative-centralized system of social-ism in our country."[2]

Faced with the collapse of the old party, but unwilling to let go of the dreams of communism, there was another group that sincerely believed it would be possible to create a new type of party, one that would fall somewhere in between capitalism and old-style communism. Modrow belonged to this latter group and began calling for the SED (now called the SED-PDS after the Special Party Conference that met in December 1989) to become the party of the "third way." It would be neither capitalist nor communist. The problem, however, was that no one quite knew exactly what the "third way" meant in practice. As Gysi put it, "The Third Way exposes the democratic and humanitarian sources and content of our tradition in the German and international worker's movement and adopts it."[3] The leadership—including Modrow—did little to clarify its intentions. Indeed, it limited itself to clichés and denunciations of both the left and the right. The result was what one writer called a "hybrid party," which satisfied neither the old-time communists nor the reformers.[4]

Meanwhile, the government began to meet with representatives of other parts of society (including the New Forum) in a venue called the "Round Table." It is important to note that this structure exercised neither parliamentary nor executive powers. Rather, its purpose was to serve as a watchdog over the SED. It wanted to be informed of major economic, political, legal, financial, and security decisions and to be permitted to have its positions considered by those in power, but it did not want to participate in the governing process. From Modrow's point of view, the regime had no alternative but to meet with the Round Table. After all, the Communist party was crumbling. If nothing else, Modrow and his colleagues hoped that the fact that they were discussing important issues with members of the Round Table would help legitimize the regime.

One of the first demands made by New Forum was the dissolution of the Kampfgruppen—the paramilitary units, which were armed with light weapons, generally based at factories or other work places. They were viewed by the country's leadership—as well as its opponents—as an additional source of military support in a period of crisis. However, New Forum worried that such units could be used against regime opponents in a crunch. Furthermore, there was a feeling that the Kampfgruppen had outlived their usefulness. As one person put it, "In this period of disarmament in which we have come to know the parties better, we don't need the Kampfgruppen anymore."[5]

While Defense Minister Theodor Hoffmann didn't say so himself, abolishing the Kampfgruppen was also in the NVA's interest. After all, no professional military wants a "party army" around, especially at a time of serious political and social instability. Who could be sure what thousands of armed, undisciplined workers might do in a crisis?

As a consequence, on December 15, the Government's Press and Information Service stated that the Kampfgruppen would be disbanded as of June 30, 1990.[6] All of its weapons would be given to the NVA, a mixed blessing from the latter's standpoint. The military could ensure that weapons did not fall into the wrong hands, but this cache of weapons and munitions would have to be guarded, thereby further straining the resources—especially human—available to the military leadership.

If there was one thing that was clear to almost all observers at this time, it was that matters could get out of control. As Horst Teltschik noted, the Soviet leadership was "apparently concerned that the changes in Eastern Europe, and in the GDR, could get out of control."[7] This was one of the reasons why the FRG's defense minister, Gerhard Stoltenberg, called for discussions on defense issues with the GDR. Stoltenberg warned, "Defense policies cannot be excluded from the overall German-German dialogue." He went on to note that Bonn was prepared for discussions in this area, which as he argued, were one of the key elements of peace. After all, the revolution in Eastern Europe had resulted in major social and economic changes, a situation that required closer cooperation between the two Germanies.[8]

The defense commissioner of the Bundestag repeated Stoltenberg's call for more intense cooperation between the two German armies toward the end of 1989. He believed that a better understanding on the part of NVA personnel of the role played by individual soldiers in the Bundeswehr would have a positive impact in helping the two armies to grow together.[9] A Christmas celebration involving soldiers from both armies took place at an NVA air base,[10] but despite this positive beginning, contacts between the two armies would not develop as fast as first seemed likely.

Concern over instability in the GDR was not limited to official sources. For example, Stefan Heym, a noted German writer, warned that efforts to unite the two German states would lead to unrest and bloodshed in the GDR. He also expressed concern that weapons might be used if some in the GDR were to attack military targets.[11]

Recognizing how tenuous social and political stability were at this point, *Neues Deutschland* issued a call for the NVA to help maintain order. In particular, the newspaper warned about the possibility of "unauthorized access to weapons, munitions, and fuel."[12] At the same time, the military issued a statement making it clear that it would not permit attacks on military objects. "Illegal access to weapons, munitions, and fuel will be prevented."[13] The high command was aware of the danger of "creeping social anarchy," and the generals noted that they would do whatever was necessary to keep weapons out of unauthorized hands. As far as the leadership of the NVA was concerned, this revolution would continue to be a peaceful one.

For its part, Moscow maintained that it was committed to helping the new regime. Mikhail Gorbachev, for example, sent a special message noting that the future of *perestroika* was dependent upon the continued existence of the SED and the GDR.[14] And in one of his most memorable statements—one that would be repeated over and over especially by senior NVA officers—Gorbachev told a meeting of the Central Committee in Moscow that, "We declare with all decisiveness, that we will not leave the GDR in the lurch."[15] Members of the NVA had been raised to trust and believe in the USSR, and while some probably had their doubts, the fact that Moscow had publicly declared that it would stand by East Berlin in its time of trouble was taken very seriously.

The Modrow regime took another symbolically important step on December 13, when Modrow met with Bishop Werner Leich, chairman of the Evangelical Church Council, and Bishop Georg Sterzinsky, chairman of the Berlin Bishop's Conference. This was the first time in the history of the GDR that the country's leader had received church leaders in his office. Furthermore, for the first time, both church and state recognized their joint responsibility for a "peaceful Christmas."[16] For his part, Modrow was doing his best to build up public support for the regime.

For the military, Modrow's meeting with the GDR's church leaders had very important implications. Of all the communist militaries, the NVA had been one of the most strictly antireligious. The environment was dramatically opposed to that of, for example, the Polish army, where hostility toward religion was tempered by the presence of chaplains. When it came to individuals with strong religious convictions, believers often found themselves serving in *Bau Einheiten* or construction battalions—a very unattractive place for a young man to fulfill his military service. Now, however, the signals were clearly changing. Although the military did not openly advocate attendance at religious services, nor completely condone an officer's religious convictions, it was becoming more difficult to hold the line against religious participation. If the country's leader could meet with religious leaders and seek their cooperation in maintaining social calm, why couldn't members of the NVA attend church?

Efforts at Military Reform

The second meeting of the Round Table took place on December 18, 1989. The topic was military reform, an issue of major concern to the civilian participants. After all, no one could completely discount the possibility that an unreformed military would some day reverse the movement toward democracy and a market economy.

The country's military leaders were also concerned about reform. Hoffmann reports that Lt. Gen. Hans Süß had proposed holding a public forum on military reform on November 30.[17] It was clear to the military leadership that major changes in structure and procedure were necessary, and that to be effective, these changes had to both be transparent and involve all parts of GDR society. This was the purpose of the December 18 Round Table meeting at the Military Political University.

Some thirty-six individuals—from a variety of different parties and movements—gathered to discuss the issue of military reform. The military attendees expected the group to be strongly anti-military. They were surprised to learn that the Round Table also included individuals who had a rather sophisticated and sympathetic understanding of military issues, many of whom had spent long years in the NVA. They were not SED-PDS party members, but from the perspective of the NVA's leadership, their knowledge of military matters was very important. They understood the generals' logic and the admirals' comments. Hoffmann and his colleagues hoped this knowledge would lead to a more rational reform process.

At the meeting, Hoffmann was first asked by some of the participants if the meeting was being taped. (It wasn't.) They then raised questions about the utility of a discussion of military doctrine, given the unsettled nature of the GDR. Hoffmann was asked how the military would respond in the event of a putsch, and why those in charge of the NVA were all SED-PDS members. He was also asked if the armed forces accepted and would implement a progressive military reform. Hoffmann responded that on January 1, 1990, a major change in cadre would take place. He admitted that some in the NVA did not support reform, but he emphasized that they would be leaving the military. General Süß added that in the future, officers from other parties would be assuming leadership roles.[18]

In fact, major changes did occur. In an effort to show the troops that the military was attempting to bring in fresh blood, that is, officers more in tune with the current efforts at pluralism and military reform, changes in leadership were announced on December 29. Col. Gen. Fritz Streletz, the chief of staff, who had played such an important role in keeping the army out of the events of October, was replaced by Lt. Gen. Manfred Grätz, who had formerly been head of logistics. In addition, the ground forces' chief, Col. Gen. Horst Stechbarth, was replaced by Lt. Gen. Horst Skerra, and Col. Gen. Horst Brünner, who had been in charge of the Main Political Administration, announced his retirement.[19] These changes, together with those announced at the beginning of September, amounted to a major shakeup in the upper echelons of the NVA.

The important point was not that these changes signaled the arrival of "new blood." In fact, they didn't: All of the officers had served for many years in the NVA and had been long-time SED party members. Instead, these appointments represented a major turnover; all of the newly promoted officers could at least claim that they were in favor of the kinds of changes Admiral Hoffmann was trying to introduce.[20]

In the course of his December 18 speech at the Military Political University, Hoffmann declared that he foresaw the possibility of a civilian—one who was not a member of the SED—becoming defense minister. In addition, he announced that effective January 1, 1990, the SED's party organization in the NVA would be dissolved. He added that the Main Political Administration, which had responsibility for administering SED party matters in the military, would be disbanded in December. Matters such as "political education, cultural matters, work with the public, concern with social and youth problems would be the responsibility of a new structure." The nature and content of the latter would be discussed by the Round Table.

Hoffmann continued by noting that in the next year some ten thousand officers would be released from active duty and he made a plea for help in ensuring that they would be treated fairly. In the face of considerable opposition, Hoffmann and the then–finance minister, Christa Luft, later undertook a major effort to ensure that those NVA officers who were released from duty were given financial security. They pushed through a law which ensured that career soldiers who were fifty years old and were forced to leave the military would get at least 50 percent of their current salaries.[21]

Hoffmann concluded his December 18 speech by calling upon the Round Table to support convening a governmental commission on "military reform in the GDR." Its first meeting was scheduled for January 12, 1990. As a sign of just how unexpectedly fast events were moving, Hoffmann later noted that while January 12 didn't seem very far away at that time, "Until then a lot of water would flow down the Spree, the Havel and the Elbe."[22] He was right.

The latter part of 1989 marked an important milestone for the NVA. In spite of the many—and sometimes devastating—changes that it had gone through in the preceding four months, its leaders were making a serious effort to adapt to the new situation. This was especially true of efforts at military reform. Its leader, Lieutenant General Süß, publicly admitted that overcentralization had been a problem in the past. He stated that one of the NVA's major problems was that it had been an "army of the party." The task now, as Hoffmann had stated the previous month, was to make it an "army of the people." To be effective, Süß admitted that the NVA would have to do more to take into consideration the feelings and hopes of the average soldier. They could not simply be ignored as had been the case in the past. For the next several months, this meant that the idea of military reform would be openly discussed and debated in the GDR. This was something completely new—a military leadership that was prepared to discuss military doctrine with civilians in a transparent fashion. Indeed, the draft statement was made available to anyone who wanted to read it.[23]

Given the unstable situation in the GDR, attempts at military reform served only to worsen the situation.[24] When the reform plan was first announced toward the end of 1989, it raised the hopes of many in the NVA. However, the process of military reform would be a slow one. Not only was the military leadership unsure of what kind of a military the country would need in the future, it also worried that if it relaxed things too much, the situation would become chaotic. Controlled change is difficult to manage in any institution, but under the circumstances it was especially hard in a military that was based on the existence of a highly structured environment.

Despite the efforts of Süß and others, by mid-February the situation had deteriorated to the point where military reform no longer made sense. A former East German officer captured it best when he said, "There was too little attempt to change the nature of the army, and too much done to make its outward appearances more friendly."[25] Throughout this period, events were moving too fast and there was no clear idea of how the GDR would look in six months, let alone in six or ten years.

By mid-February, the end of the GDR was in sight. The focus shifted to the election campaigns, leaving serious military reform to wait until after the March 18 elections. The issue continued to be discussed both in the military and by the Round Table, which would adopt a ten-point position paper on military reform on February 26.[26] But for practical purposes, nothing of significance would happen until after the elections.

Depoliticizing the Military

Disbanding the political apparatus of the NVA was not an easy task. Overall, 96 percent of the officers, 94 percent of the warrant officers, and 60 percent of the career NCOs in the NVA were members of the SED—a total of 112,881 full members and 8,281 candidate members.[27]

By December, 1989, however, massive numbers of military and civilian party members were resigning from the party. In response, party leaders tried to inject greater democracy into the party structure. As far as the military was concerned, this meant that the "leading" role hitherto played by the political organs would become less important. After all, not only was it no longer necessary to spend time worrying about who would be appointed to key party positions (since this was now taking place in a democratic fashion), the need for the political organs to supervise activities within the military was almost nonexistent. This was particularly true in light of the decision to drop Article 1 of the constitution.

Indeed, a debate had been going on within the NVA for some time concerning the need for greater democracy and a less monopolistic position for the SED.[28] When he first took over as defense minister, Admiral Hoffmann himself had promised that the military would take a new look at the role of the both the party and political organs within the armed forces.[29]

The same was true of the party organization's privileged position within the military. In fact, members of the SED themselves recognized the need to end the party's monopolistic position in the army. One speaker at a military meeting pointed out, "We don't want to be an army of the party, but an army of the entire people. Therefore it is our wish that the party organization in the army and the border troops be dissolved."[30]

There was a feeling that no party had any more right to be represented in the military than another—indeed, the NVA's response to the changing situation was to prohibit party activity of any kind. If the NVA was not going to be the party-army of the past, then it would become completely apolitical in the sense that soldiers would avoid participation in partisan political activities. The alternative would have been political chaos, as the military was split among a variety of political persuasions.

Despite the pressure for disbandment of the Party structure by the rank and file, senior officers feared that such a development would contribute further to the disintegration of the military. The NVA was too close to collapse simply to ignore problems associated with both maintaining and building a sense of national consciousness. As a result, they decided to keep the existing political structures in order to provide "education and information for members of the military."[31]

Meanwhile, within the NVA, attention was focused on political education. The monopoly enjoyed by the SED and its corps of political officers and party structure had ended, but what was to replace it? Some officers argued that there should be no political work at all within the NVA. What passed for political work, they argued, should be carried out instead by "social forces."[32] Nevertheless, in mid-January, Order 6/90, "Concerning the Organization and Leadership of Civil Education in the National People's Army," was issued. According to this order, civil education was to be carried out by all officers under the direction of the Department of Civil Education Work. A regular military officer, Maj. Gen. Oliver Anders, who had been the commander of a motorized infantry division, was named to head the department. Political officers were to play a central role. To quote Hoffmann, "We consider it false to exclude individuals who have been political officers from civil education work—just because they were political officers."[33] After all, who knew better about inculcating ideas in the hearts and minds of NVA soldiers than former political officers. In fact, the majority of those employed in this capacity were former political officers.[34] In the meantime, Hoffmann announced that an Attestation Commission would review every officer. In evaluating his suitablity for future service, the key question would be whether or not he was competent. If he were—regardless of whether or not he had been a political officer—he would be permitted to stay in the NVA. If the opposite were the case, he would be asked to leave.

At the same time the attestation process was under way, the Military Political Academy was given the task of developing a concept for civil education. In April, a plan was published, which divided it into five categories: civil education, social work, furtherance of democratic participation, cultural activities, and work with the public.[35] Although civil education was very similar conceptually to the West German idea of *innere Führung*, it was more limited in scope. In the NVA, this kind of work was to be carried out by specially trained officers, while in the Bundeswehr, *innere Führung* was supposed to be part of the daily life of every officer and soldier. In any case, however, the institution of civil education, even if it was somewhat undefined and a bit bureaucratic in form, marked a considerable improvement over the old form of political education. Its biggest problem was that many believed the political officers were still married ideologically to the old political system.

As far as party membership was concerned, on January 18 all career personnel in the NVA were ordered to sign a document stating that they were renouncing membership in any political party, a situation that some members of the NVA found objectionable.[36] The biggest problem with the abolition of the key role played by the SED in the military was that it created a vacuum. The old ideas of patriotism were gone and the new concept of civil education was still being worked out. As a consequence, it further contributed to the sense of confusion and lack of direction evident in the NVA.

One of the most significant events of 1989 occurred on December 22. On that day, Chancellor Helmut Kohl crossed through the Brandenburg Gate—an area once reserved only for the kaiser and his family—to meet Hans Modrow as tens of thousands of Berliners on both sides cheered. Twenty-eight years of isolation between the two states had ended. Despite the joy involved in the ending of Germany's artificial division, the situation within the GDR was far from stable. This was especially true of the NVA.

Civilian Work for the Military

The departure of 330,000 of East Germany's 16.5 million people during 1989 further increased the need for the military to assist in the civilian economy. By December 22, the overall number of soldiers working in the civilian sector was up to 19,500, 12 percent of the NVA's total active duty strength.[37] By January the number had risen to 21,000.[38] Hoffmann complained bitterly, noting that those who served in hospitals and in industry were not in the units where they were needed. "This places even higher demands on those who remain with their units and who must carry out the tasks with an even greater amount of energy. This includes above all such undesirable tasks as guard duty."[39] The fact that so many soldiers (including reservists) were at work in the civilian economy undermined not only the ability of the NVA to carry out simple tasks, but also made the maintenance of discipline increasingly difficult. Furthermore, It had a devastating impact on morale as soldiers were paid far less than the workers they were supporting in the civilian economy. As General Streletz put it, "The soldiers noted with justification, We were called up to serve in the army, and we are serving in industry.'" The message to many of these young men was that the soldier was the "cheapest" form of labor in the country.[40]

Creating a Trade Union

Meanwhile, efforts were under way to create a Group of Professional Soldiers. This organization, modeled on a similar one in West Germany, would be similar to a trade union. Its purpose would be to protect the careers of the members of the NVA who were increasingly beginning to wonder about their own futures. And it was clear that East German military personnel had good reason to be concerned. There was the possibility that the NVA would cease to exist if Germany were reunited, and West German Defense Minister Stoltenberg had stated publicly that no professional military officer from the NVA would be given the option of joining the Bundeswehr.[41] A trade union might not solve all of the problems facing career soldiers, but it would at least give them a vehicle to express their views.[42]

For his part, Hoffmann ordered commanders to work with this new organization. "The Army Leadership and I myself have decided not only to accept this democratic organization, but to do everything possible to ensure its maximum affectivity and to include its representatives in important decisions."[43] For someone familiar with the Prussian-style discipline of the old NVA, such comments were not just blasphemy, they were almost incomprehensible. But the situation had changed so much in the previous three months that Hoffmann and his colleagues had no alternative.

In the beginning, this organization's efforts focused on trying to protect the social and political rights of those in the NVA who were fearful that they would be thrown into the civilian economy with little or no protection. Its second goal was to lobby for changes in the way things were done within the NVA, which in practice meant lobbying for shorter hours, more security, more freedom of action, and the like. An initial meeting was held in Leipzig on December 19 and attended by some two hundred delegates.[44] In a practical sense, the creation of a union of this type at this time (given the chaotic nature of events in the NVA) could not help but further undermine the leadership's already tenuous hold on discipline.

Why an NVA?

Meanwhile, serious questions were being raised about the purpose of the NVA. Why have a military if its primary purpose was to aid the civilian economy? After all, the Wall was gone and everyone was talking about creating closer ties between the two Germanies.

Admiral Hoffmann tried to answer this question in an interview in *Neues Deutschland*. He took the position that since there were two military blocs in Europe, any move by the GDR to get rid of its army would inevitably undermine this arrangement and lead to instability on the continent:

> As long as the two military blocs exist and their balance of forces represents one of the most important factors of European security, we will need to maintain the NVA as part of the Warsaw Pact at such a strength . . . which satisfies the principles of balance and mutuality.[45]

This argument that the NVA had to exist as long as the two blocs existed made sense in December, and the East Germans would continue to cite it like a mantra in coming months. The problem, however, was that it presumed the continued existence of the Pact as well as Russian support for the GDR. As long as Moscow was solidly behind East Berlin, Bonn and others in the West would be cautious about alienating the Russians, who held the keys to reunification. In fact, the East Germans had little else to hold onto except arguments for the continuing existence of the GDR. However, once Soviet support was withdrawn and the Warsaw Pact began to look like an institution of the past, this argument would ring hollow.

Hoffmann also touched on several other topics of interest in his interview. First, he noted that discussions were currently under way concerning the reduction of compulsory military service from eighteen to twelve months. In addition, he observed that alternate service was also under consideration. If introduced, he said it would last six months longer than military service. Furthermore, Hoffmann noted that the military parades that had taken place for years on Karl-Marx Allee would no longer be held, although in a concession to tradition, he said that parades after the conclusion of exercises and the weekly ceremony at the monument to the victims of fascism on Unter den Linden could continue.[46]

Strike in Beelitz

Despite the efforts of the leadership of the NVA to adapt to changing circumstances, it soon became obvious that the military was tottering on the brink of disaster if not full-scale collapse. According to Hoffmann, on January 1 he was called by General Grätz, who was serving his first day as head of the Main Staff of the NVA, as Hoffmann was driving from his home in Rostock back to Strausberg. Grätz informed Hoffmann that soldiers at the garrison in Beelitz had gone on strike.

The official report stated that at 1 a.m. on New Year's Day, 1990, some three hundred soldiers began a protest demonstration—the first time such a thing had happened in the NVA. They demanded that the military reform plan discussed by the Round Table be implemented immediately. The group put together a resolution signed by 378 individuals, which was released to the press about 1 p.m. that day.

Among the soldiers' demands were:

—The immediate transfer of military personnel to their home areas
—a shortening of military service to twelve months
—the creation of a law covering military service
—an improvement in living and service conditions
—public access to military bases

Grätz informed Hoffmann that General Skerra (who was also in his first day as chief of ground troops) was going to Beelitz. He also noted that the GDR TV program, "Aktuelle Kamera," was sending a team to cover events there. The latter revelation alone must have come as a bombshell to senior East German officers, who had been accustomed to dealing with such matters in secret. Now, not only were soldiers rebelling, but TV cameras would be there to record how they handled the matter. Even worse, it soon became obvious that the protests had spread to other military bases in the country. East Berlin was threatened with a nationwide mutiny. According to Hoffmann, this was his most critical and difficult moment as defense minister.[47]

The essence of the problem was that of the 120,000-odd members of the NVA, some 21,000 were working in the civilian sector. Soldiers found it hard to accept the fact that instead of reporting to factories near their homes, they were being sent all over the country to do civilian work. For military service work that would be understandable, but they were being treated as factory workers in uniform.

In an effort to defuse tensions, Hoffmann himself went to Beelitz and talked to the soldiers. He told them that he had "looked into your demands and I now ask you to fulfill one demand of mine—that you go back to your duties."[48] Insofar as their specific demands were concerned, he agreed to give conscripts greater freedom by permitting them to visit nightclubs past the normal curfew of 10 p.m. He also released them from the requirement of eating at their local military canteens. However, Hoffmann refused the soldier's demand that they be stationed near their homes.

Beyond the military implications of the Beelitz strike, the TV coverage of it was "catastrophic." The program gave the impression that all one had to do to get one's way was to demonstrate. After all, the soldiers in Beelitz had taken to the streets, and the government had immediately agreed to their demands. The party newspaper *Neues Deutschland* gave the same impression in its coverage of the strikes.[49]

On January 3, a number of military delegations visited Strausberg, "demanding to speak with the Defense Minister." Hoffmann met with them. He reported that during one meeting the behavior of the other side resembled what he called "lynch mob justice." The soldiers threatened that if he did not provide a clear answer to their questions, "tanks would begin to move in the direction of Berlin."[50]

Faced with the gravity of the situation, Hoffmann gave in. On January 4, the military announced that beginning that month military service would be reduced from eighteen months to one year and that soldiers on leave would be permitted to travel to the West. Another action that was to have major implications for the NVA was Hoffmann's decision (ratified by the parliament) to release all those who had served more than a year by January 26 from military service. As far as the NVA was concerned, this would mean a cut in the army's strength of between 25,000 and 30,000 men.[51] In addition, Hoffmann agreed that effective immediately a forty-five-hour Monday to Friday work week would be introduced, that 50 percent of all personnel would be permitted to go on leave at a time, that use of the term comrade (*Genoße*) would be dropped in favor of Mr. (*Herr*), that soldiers would be permitted to keep their personal identity cards with them, and that they would be allowed to travel beyond the city limits. Hoffmann then talked to senior government officials, who were visibly shaken. He advised them that additional steps would have to be taken to "stabilize" the situation.

Looking at the Beelitz episode in retrospect, Hoffmann's decision to talk to the strikers was the right one. Despite his pique at the media—not surprising given his lack of experience with it—he seems to have been genuinely sympathetic to the demands of the strikers. Nevertheless, he did his best to maintain as much authority as possible under the circumstances. Hoffmann, however, was smart enough to read the writing on the wall. In an interview with the West German publication *Stern*, he said that he had no intention of using weapons to control the situation. "What would have happened, if we had tried to clarify the situation by using weapons? These were men who were trained to use the weapons we had available to us. Of course we did not want to use weapons under the circumstances."[52]

As it turned out, the concessions he made as a result of the strike did little to calm the situation. For example, desertions—even by officers—increased.[53] Once again, it was a case of too little, too late. Morale was at an all-time low. As one writer from the Postdam garrison noted, "There are no motivated soldiers left here. Believe us, we no longer think that being a soldier makes sense and even our superiors agree with us unofficially."[54] And the problems did not stop there. According to the West German journal *Der Spiegel* a few days later East German soldiers in Potsdam—in front of cameras—refused to go on maneuvers with the Soviets. As one interviewee put it, "Not a single soldier stands morally behind the exercise." Faced with this, an officer said that in order to do anything, "We must find a consensus"—a statement that would not only have been unthinkable in the NVA six months earlier, but one that would be almost inconceivable in any army in the world, no matter how liberal its concept of command.[55]

When it came to Beelitz, Hoffmann admitted in his memoirs that it was a defeat. The generals had lost control. The mood within the ranks suggested that the situation would continue to worsen. Polls taken in the army at that time indicated that 84 percent of those questioned expressed concern about the security of the country, 75 percent feared the collapse of the NVA, 64 percent were concerned over the lack of any serious plans for the coming year, and 49 percent did not trust the leadership of the armed forces. In addition, only 26 percent of officers and warrant officers said they were prepared to serve any longer; 14 percent of these officers said they would be willing to serve until they reached age fifty, while 52 percent stated that they wanted to end their service in the NVA immediately. The percentage of soldiers who felt that their service was no longer needed rose from 65 percent in November 1989 to 75 percent by January 1990; the percentage among NCOs rose from 47 to 57 percent and among officers the percentage rose to 31 percent. Fully one-third of all members of the NVA said they expected the current situation to worsen. Even more important, more than half of all personnel favored either a confederation or unification with the FRG.[56]

Most of the sixty-nine former NVA officers who returned questionnaires considered the events at Beelitz a "moral turning point in the life of the army," as one officer put it. Or as another noted, "It signaled in all clarity that from a historical standpoint, the NVA had reached the end of the line." At the same time, it is important to note that other officers, especially those stationed in other parts of the country, argued that these events "were not decisive" or that they were "unimportant." Their point was that it did not immediately lead to a collapse of the units in which they were serving.

Nevertheless, discipline sank lower, there was less central control, political and job uncertainty increased—especially among regulars—and unit cohesion declined. The reality was that the army seemed to be melting away. Between December 1, 1989, and January 5, an additional 1,507 officers and soldiers deserted.[57] If the collapse of the Berlin Wall opened the door to dissolution, the events in Beelitz showed just how far deterioration had spread.

Defense Minister Hoffmann told Warsaw Pact Commander Gen. Pyotr Luschev that the situation was so bad that the NVA would have to reduce its obligations as well as its participation in the Pact's joint air defense program. Furthermore, he told Luschev that he could not say whether it would be possible to hold the next session of the Committee of Defense Ministers in Berlin in April or if such a meeting would even be worthwhile. On January 10, the two men decided that the NVA would participate in joint exercises, but at a reduced level.

On January 19, Hoffmann spoke before NVA officers and warned them that they had to do everything possible to avoid anarchy and to ensure that the NVA did not become a security problem. As far as

Beelitz was concerned, he said that as much as he hoped that such an event would not repeat itself, the possibility existed, and if it occurred, commanders must continue to avoid using force: "I must warn you that you must be prepared to deal with such mass protests by administrative means and methods."[58]

Problems within the NVA inevitably raised the question of whether or not the East German military had a future. What if the country were reunified? How would the question of the two armies be handled? In response to questions about the future of the NVA, Hoffmann responded as he had in the past: As long as the Warsaw Pact continued to exist, the NVA was critical to European stability. As he put it on January 17, "The immediate dissolution of the NVA prior to the confederation of both German states . . . would hinder rather than help the process of cooperation, of drawing closer together."[59]

Faced with all of these problems, Hoffmann informed Modrow that he wanted to retire. Modrow, however, believed that maintaining continuity within the upper ranks of the military was critical and he begged Hoffmann to stay. The latter agreed—albeit somewhat reluctantly.

Modrow Tries to Save the GDR

Instability was not a problem not only in the armed forces. On January 13–14, 1990, some 200,000 people demonstrated in Berlin for democratic renewal and against fascism, which many equated with the existing regime. Meanwhile, having already informed the Volkskammer that he was preparing to increase the importance of the Round Table, on January 15, Modrow raised it to the level of a cabinet. He believed that the country's only hope was to move moderate politicians into positions where they would be able to convince the bulk of East German society that supporting the existing system was in their own interest. In short, he had to broaden the base of support for the government to compensate for the disintegration of the SED-PDS.

In addressing the Round Table, Modrow went out of his way to stress his independence from any party. As he put it on January 22, "In my activity as Minister-President I see myself exclusively responsible to the people and not to a party. For that reason I need the advice . . . and the support of all parties and not only one party."[60]

On the same day, the West German newspaper *Bild Zeitung* proclaimed that units from the security service and the NVA were preparing a putsch against the Modrow government. Upon hearing these reports, Modrow immediately contacted both Hoffmann and the minister of the interior. It was quickly determined that all weapons were locked up and the actions that the *Bild Zeitung* had reported had not taken place. As a result, Modrow sharply denied these rumors. For his part, Hoffmann said that he informed the Round Table not only that such preparations had not occurred, but that members of the NVA were "outraged" at the illegal actions taken by members of the security services in the past.[61] Clearly, Hoffmann was attempting to distance the NVA from the Stasi, which was being attacked because of the contempt in which the East German populace—including many in the NVA—held it.

There has been a tendency on the part of some in both the East and West to lump the security services and the military in communist countries together. In fact, there were significant differences, a point Hoffmann tried to drive home. The security services might represent a potential risk to the new system, but in Hoffmann's mind that would never have been the case with the NVA.

Moscow and the GDR

January 24, 1990, marks an important date in the evolution of Soviet policy toward the GDR. On that day, Nikolai Portugalov, a senior official in the CPSU Central Committee, stated in an interview he gave to the West German newspaper *Bild*, "If the people of the GDR want reunification it will come. The USSR will not oppose such a decision." Or as he added elsewhere, "We will not intervene."[62] Needless to say, this statement had a major impact not only in Bonn and East Berlin, but within the NVA as well. As far as the West Germans were concerned, this marked a major change in Soviet policy. As Horst Teltschik put it, "I thought about my conversation with Portugalov in November and like the Chancellor I understood this interview as a fundamental change in the Soviet attitude toward unification."[63]

From that point on, the whole frame of reference would be different. No longer was reunification a question of *whether*, it had become one of *when*—a point Gorbachev made in a meeting with Modrow in Moscow on January 30. According to the press report, Gorbachev stated, "The Soviet Union has nothing in 'principle' against a unification of the two German states."[64] Modrow clearly understood Gorbachev's message and noted, "The unification of the two German states is the perspective that lies before us."[65] At the same time he stressed that it was important that the process take place slowly. Bonn and East Berlin now had the green light to begin the gradual movement toward unification. As it happened, unification was to come much faster than either Gorbachev or Modrow—not to mention Kohl—thought possible.

Few NVA members were aware of Portugalov's statement. These were professional military officers who were primarily concerned with keeping order in the armed forces—an increasingly difficult task—and who in any case were isolated from the rest of society and not trained to read such signals. From the standpoint of civil-military relations, this failure by the rank and file in the NVA to recognize the sea change that had occurred in Soviet policy would only make it more difficult to understand later developments.

The View from Bonn

On January 15, as the main headquarters of the East German security ministry was stormed, Chancellor Kohl began to realize how serious conditions were in the GDR. He was convinced that Modrow's go-slow approach would not work. Current circumstances threatened not only the reform process in East Germany, but that throughout Eastern Europe as well.

There was also concern over the situation within the NVA. According to Teltschik, the feeling in Bonn was that "the attitude in the Army and in the organs assigned the task of keeping order was getting worse"—not surprising given the events in Beelitz. Modrow himself reportedly told Kohl at this time that "he could no longer rely on some branches of the government to obey his orders."[66] The key obstacle was Modrow's refusal to give up his dream of a Communist party. He continued to believe that somehow he could combine the revived SED-PDS with a new, more democratic GDR.[67]

The West Germans decided that the best approach was to push the SED-PDS out of the government as quickly as possible. From Bonn's perspective, there was no sense in trying to salvage the existing governmental structure. In addition, there was the danger that staying in office would only legitimate Modrow in the eyes of the East German populace, something the anticommunist West wanted no part of. This was the heart of Kohl's opposition to a treaty between the two countries—it would only help Modrow stay in power.[68]

From a practical political standpoint, this meant postponing serious discussions with the East German government until after the upcoming elections. Unfortunately, Bonn never communicated this key change in policy to East Berlin. It was left to the East Germans to figure out. As a consequence, Modrow and his colleagues continued in their efforts to meet what they perceived to be Bonn's requirements for closer cooperation, unaware that regardless of what they did, the FRG was not prepared to engage. The result was a heightened sense of agitation vis-à-vis Bonn. For example, Modrow was distressed to learn during his meeting with Finance Minister Theodor Waigel that, despite Bonn's promise the previous year of financial assistance for the GDR's economy, the FRG would not be giving East Berlin any money.

From Bonn's point of view, this was a very delicate situation. On the one hand, Bonn wanted to present a public image of willingness to talk to and deal with the Modrow government—otherwise, the number of those leaving the GDR for the West would increase further. On the other hand, the West Germans believed that Modrow's replacement by a democratically elected government was the GDR's only hope for economic and political stability.

On January 25, Modrow and FRG Federal Minister Rudolf Seiters agreed on plans for a meeting in Bonn between Modrow and Chancellor Kohl. At the meeting, Modrow painted a very gloomy picture of the GDR's plight, arguing that the country was on the verge of collapse. The state's authority was disintegrating, and strikes were spreading throughout the country. In addition, he observed that the public was becoming increasingly aggressive in its demands. The only hope for control was immediate West German aid. He asked about the possibility of a "contractual community" and said that unless Bonn helped, the outlook for the GDR was catastrophic—a point he also made to the Volkskammer on January 29. According to Teltschik, Modrow said that even the Round Table was no longer effective as a vehicle for maintaining order.[69] Faced with this situation, Modrow announced that a vote on a new government would be moved up from May 6 to March 18. The country did not have the luxury of waiting an additional two months.

In order to deal with the many problems associated with reunification, Bonn set up a working group (*"Arbeitsgruppe Deutschlandpolitik"*). The group was located in the Chancellery, which meant that it was under the control of the chancellor, a good idea given the many differences of opinion that were to arise within the Bonn government. The working group met twice a week to coordinate the activities of the various branches of government. Under it, a number of committees were set up, including one that dealt with security issues.[70]

Manning the NVA

The decisions taken in early January to cut back on the time served by conscripts from eighteen months to twelve months and to release anyone who had served the required twelve months on January 26 created serious problems for the military. There simply were not enough soldiers to fill out the ranks. For example, in Halle prior to January 26, one regiment had 42 percent of its required conscripts and 48 percent of its NCOs. After January 26, the figures fell to 31 percent and 29 percent, respectively. When Hoffmann visited the 9th Panzer Division in Eggesin, he discovered that it was only 70 percent manned.[71]

In the air force, this manpower shortage meant that combat training could only be carried out in one or two companies per regiment. As a result, twelve to sixteen planes had to be taken out of service. The situation was no better in the navy, where forty-one out of a total of eighty ships had to be tied up because of personnel shortages. The Rear Services warned Hoffmann that lack of personnel and the decision not to call up reserves made it impossible to guarantee the country's mobilization potential or to fulfill its obligations to the Group of Soviet Forces in Germany. As Hoffmann declared, "During this transition period, fulfillment of the constitutional obligations of the NVA will have to be very seriously limited."[72]

One of the biggest problems—and one that would haunt the Bundeswehr when it took over control of the former East German military— was guarding weapons and munitions. It was clear at this time that keeping these weapons and munitions safe would be a major undertaking. For example, with the dissolution of the Kampfgruppen, the NVA acquired about 1,000 armored vehicles, thousands of machine guns, about 50,000 antitank weapons with 500,000 shells, more than 360,000 machine pistols, and 135,000 pistols with over 300 million bullets.[73] How was the NVA to guard the tremendous amount of weaponry in the country (one of the most militarized in the world) especially given the fact that many units had less than 50 percent of their authorized strength? To quote Hoffmann:

> The central depots and the depots of the various military districts were filled beyond capacity: Large amounts of equipment had to be moved out of the depots and stored in the open—as a result of the shortening of military service and the failure to call up reservists the jobs could not be done with the available personnel.[74]

Career soldiers were now forced to take over guarding installations—a task previously delegated to conscripts. In fact, Gen. Joachim Goldbach estimated that after April 26 there would be a shortage of 2,000 men for guarding munitions and weapons, and Gen. Manfred Grätz stated that by September the military would have 20,000–25,000 fewer soldiers than at present.[75] According to Hoffmann, Grätz was faced with an impossible task: where to utilize the limited forces available to him—a dilemma made even more difficult by the lack of any guidance from the government over what kind of a military the country needed. The result was that "guarding [of munitions] had been made impossible."[76] In essence, not only was combat readiness a sham, there was now real concern over a second Beelitz. The NVA was on the verge of total collapse.

A former NVA officer who was directly involved in the manning problem drew a vivid picture of just how serious the situation was when he noted that by the end of January they had only ten soldiers for the fire department at one major base. Four of them left, leaving only six. It was necessary to have three on duty at all times just to operate the equipment. "In the final analysis this meant that the soldiers had to put in 360 hours per month—and that did not include a single hour of training." By April, another former East German officer reports that the total number of soldiers fighting fires was down to three—and this at a time when ammunition and weapons were stored in the open![77]

The lack of personnel also limited the destruction of weapons, which the GDR was obligated to carry out under the CSCE agreements. A new Office for Disarmament and Conversion was created to help with the process, but that still left open the question of who was going to do the work and ensure that no weapons fell into the wrong hands. Communications troops could no longer carry out their tasks. Even legal officers were refusing to become involved in disciplinary matters. In short, the situation had reached crisis proportions.

Meanwhile, within the NVA conditions continued to deteriorate. On February 22, for example, the chief of staff spoke of a rapid collapse of discipline and order. An East German military spokesman confirmed a week later that "the number of desertions, absent-without-leave cases and unapproved extensions of leave had risen significantly. . . ."[78] Probably the best expression of the confusion that faced the NVA was made by an officer who said, "First they took away the war from us, then the victory, and now even the enemy."[79]

This sense of frustration translated into decreasing support for the Modrow regime. From January to March, trust in the Modrow government declined from 53 to 42 per cent among soldiers, from 67 to 61 percent among NCOs, and from 91 to 90 percent among officers.[80] In March, soldiers and NCOs from an air force unit sent an open letter to the MOD threatening to go on strike if they were not released from military service by March 15.[81] From a military standpoint, this collapse of discipline and morale coupled with the decreasing number of soldiers on active duty made it impossible to carry out some of the simplest tasks.

To make matters worse, by the middle of February, in an opportunistic move to improve its sagging electoral chances, the PDS made an end of conscription a key component of its election campaign. It argued that such a step would raise the prestige of professional soldiers and be better for the country as a whole.[82] Regardless of the logic of the PDS position, from the NVA's standpoint, this was another nail in the military's coffin. It was bad enough to have discipline collapsing and desertions rampant, but now the military had to fight off attacks from one of its hitherto strongest supporters—which was bound to have an impact on the willingness of young men to serve in its ranks.

By the time of the election on March 18, the NVA had reached rock bottom. Soldiers from the elite Friedrich Engels Guard Regiment demonstrated—in uniform—in East Berlin against their poor living conditions and their outmoded Prussian military customs.[83] The fact that the country's most elite formations were on the verge of collapse was a clear sign of the deep deterioration within the military itself.

Military-to-Military Contacts

In spite of all the talk about increased contacts between the NVA and the Bundeswehr, little had happened by the end of 1989. In late December, Hoffmann announced that "the GDR is ready for discussions without preconditions and open to the ideas of the other side."[84]

In the second half of January, General Grätz met with Adm. Dieter Wellershoff in Vienna at a military doctrine seminar.[85] The East Germans saw this meeting as the start of more formal contacts. They proposed the creation of consultative groups made up of veterans of both defense ministries in order to reach agreement on how to avoid incidents in the border regions. The GDR was ready to appoint liaison officers for that purpose, and the NVA was also prepared for contacts in other areas. However, Wellershoff reportedly refused to respond to Grätz's suggestions to broaden contacts.[86]

Hoffmann claimed that he spoke about the matter with Rainer Eppelmann, who would later become the country's defense minister, noting that in spite of efforts on the part of the NVA, the Bundeswehr showed no interest in increased contacts. Indeed, Hoffmann's bitterness was evident from his memoirs where he complained, "In the West they were acting as if the NVA no longer existed. . . ."[87] In fact, as subsequent events would show, the East German concern was justified;

from West German Defense Minister Stoltenberg's standpoint, the NVA *had* ceased to exist.

In spite of Stoltenberg's hostility toward military contacts, some did occur. In January, reporters from the newspaper *Volksarmee* visited an armor unit near Bonn. Shortly thereafter, Willi Weiskirch, the military representative from the West German Bundestag, visited an NVA regiment.[88] More expanded military contacts, however, would have to wait until the upper ranks of the Bundeswehr changed policy. As Hoffmann put it with regard to a meeting at the highest level, "The leadership of the NVA had no hesitation. However, we were not ready to beg for a meeting."[89]

Military-to-military contacts improved somewhat in February. Toward the end of that month, representatives of the Main Staffs of the Bundeswehr and the NVA met in Koblenz. They agreed that Gen. Klaus Naumann would meet with an NVA general toward the end of March and that a meeting between the two defense ministers would take place in April.[90] At the same time, the general inspector of the Bundeswehr issued a directive concerning members of the NVA. In it he informed members of the Bundeswehr, "Our view of a person and our values obligate us . . . in a special way to tolerance, to patience and understanding. A feeling of victory and superiority have no place."[91] While German-to-German contacts in the military sphere had a long way to go, the atmosphere was beginning to improve.

Modrow's Last Hurrah

Given the failure of the West Germans to respond to his earlier overtures, Modrow felt he had to achieve something if he was to enforce any semblance of order and stability on the GDR. In a last-ditch effort to save the GDR, Modrow came out with a plan entitled "For Germany, a United Fatherland."[92] The plan foresaw the unification of Germany over a two-year period. Boundaries between the two countries would gradually cease to exist. Elections in both Germanies would lead to a single parliament, which in turn would lead to a single constitution and eventually a single government in Berlin.

The key idea of Modrow's plan was one of a gradual growing together, rather than a takeover of the East by the West. This was the major concern of many East Germans, including members of the NVA. Absorption of the GDR by the FRG would not be limited to political unification—it would also have widespread economic and social implications. Within the military, most officers feared that unification would lead to the end of the NVA, with its members being tossed to the wolves.

The plan also had a very clear foreign policy and security component. While he admitted that for practical purposes the Warsaw Pact no longer existed, Modrow argued that it was crucial that nothing upset the military balance in Europe. How could the Russians not be concerned about the possible extension of Germany toward the East, which is exactly what would happen if the FRG, which remained a member of NATO, took over control of the GDR? The only reasonable answer, Modrow purported, was neutrality for both states.[93]

For his part, Kohl rejected any thought of neutrality. "Neutrality would isolate Germany in Europe."[94] Even Hans-Jochen Vogel, the leader of West Germany's main opposition party, the SPD, opposed the idea of neutrality: "I don't think we want to follow a separate German path in Europe." However, the problem that was confronting both Modrow and Kohl was that the pace of unification was outpacing any attempt to handle it in a systematic fashion. As Teltschik put it, "The events of the last months show that reality can quickly overtake such ideas."[95]

Kohl and Modrow discussed the East German situation on February 3, 1990. Modrow told Kohl that the situation was declining daily—in fact, authority at the local level in many places was almost nonexistent. He warned Kohl that unless the GDR received DM15 billion immediately there would be a financial disaster in March. Two days later, together with Lothar de Maiziere, the leader of the GDR's CDU party, he declared that "a collapse can no longer be excluded."[96] The Polish Foreign Minister called East Germany "a country without a government."[97]

Shaken by reports of the seriousness of the situation within the GDR, Kohl told the CDU-CSU faction the next day that he planned to enter into discussions with the GDR on economic and monetary reform as soon as possible. In effect, the issue was simple: if the deutsche mark did not go the people, the people would continue to go to the deutsche mark. These discussions would begin just as soon as East Germany held its first free election, scheduled for March 18. Kohl was prepared to talk with an East German leader about all aspects of unification, but only under two conditions: first, that the idea of neutrality was not acceptable, and second, that the new leader had been elected in a free and open election.

Meanwhile, in an effort to stabilize the situation, Modrow had added eight more figures from the opposition to the coalition government. This meant that for the first time, the PDS[98] had less than half of the thirty-five cabinet seats. All of the new members were designated ministers without portfolio, and they represented a variety of parties and organizations—running the gamut from the New Forum to Democratic Awakening. Of future significance to the NVA was the appointment of Eppelmann, a Protestant pastor who had been a conscientious objector under Honecker, to the cabinet. Eppelmann, who openly admitted that he knew little about the military, was to play a key role in the remaining days of the NVA. As he would later say, "I will be responsible for the Army, a manly world about which I have known little up until now."[99] For the next few months, however, his responsibility would be indirect; he would oversee developments in the military but would not have any direct line responsibility for events within the NVA.

The fourth meeting of the Round Table—which focused on military issues—was held in February. In addition to hearing a report on the role of the NVA during the October and November 1989 demonstrations, the group also discussed the development of a new military doctrine.

The feeling that Bonn was ignoring events in East Germany was made worse by the announcement by Stoltenberg that "East German military personnel who pass through the Berlin Wall can serve in the West German Army."[100] In response—and with a strong feeling of frustration—Hoffmann complained, "A deserter remains a deserter, and I believe this is the case for Mr. Stoltenberg and not only for us."[101] For Hoffmann and his colleagues, it was just one more sign that instead of trying to help maintain stability within the NVA, the West Germans were working to destabilize it. According to one report, by March 15, some three hundred officers and NCOs from the NVA had applied to join the Bundeswehr.[102] However, despite Stoltenberg's comment, the Bundeswehr did not accept any former NVA personnel until after German reunification was a reality.

Moscow Moves Toward Reunification

In an effort to better understand Moscow's attitude toward German reunification, while at the same time calming Russian fears about a united Germany, Kohl met with General Secretary Gorbachev in Moscow on February 10, 1990. Gorbachev confirmed the earlier-announced Soviet position, stating, "Between the Soviet Union, the FRG, and the GDR there are no differences of opinion about unification and the right to strive for it." He continued, "The Germans themselves will decide the question of the unity of the German nation, and must themselves determine the form of the state, the speed of reunification and at what time and under what conditions this unity will be realized."[103] From the West German standpoint Gorbachev's comment marked a major step forward.

The only condition Gorbachev attached to his approval of German reunification was that a reunited Germany should not be a member of NATO. Modrow quickly picked up on this theme. In an interview he gave to *Volksarmee*, Modrow argued for a "neutralized" Germany. As far as the NVA was concerned, Modrow maintained, "For the immediate future, I see a need for its continued existence." He again made the argument that since both the Warsaw Pact and NATO continued to exist, the existence of the NVA was vital for European stability—a position endorsed by the Round Table.[104]

More sophisticated political observers such as Horst Teltschik realized that Gorbachev's meeting with Kohl marked a watershed when it came to reunification. As Teltschik put it, "This is the breakthrough!"[105] Once a meeting between the four victorious World War II powers and the two Germanies was held in Ottawa to work out "the external aspects of German unity, including questions of the security of neighboring states," most observers agreed that regardless of what the Soviets said in public, Moscow would not continue to insist on neutrality for a united Germany.[106]

Modrow probably did not realize that reunification would come as fast as it did. Furthermore, he was probably aware that his argument for the continued existence of the NVA was primarily a negotiating tool. This was not the case for the average NVA officer. To be sure, everyone suspected that the end of the GDR was on the horizon. However, trained as they were to take their guidance from political authorities, many officers and NCOs read the results of the Moscow summit as a confirmation that, whatever happened, the NVA would continue to be around in some form. Besides, Gorbachev had assured the GDR that he would not let it down. Furthermore, there were statements by other key Western figures confirming the importance of a neutral, united Germany. For example, West German Foreign Minister Dietrich Genscher and Social Democratic foreign policy strategist Egon Bahr both took this position at this time.[107]

Modrow Visits Bonn

Modrow's February 13 visit to Bonn to discuss reunification was a disaster. To begin with, it was now clear to everyone—including the East Germans—that the GDR would become part of the FRG and that Bonn was merely tolerating Modrow and his colleagues. To cite only one example, the East German CDU had practically become part of the FRG's CDU, an ominous sign for the upcoming elections.

When he got to Bonn, Modrow continued his push for a gradual coming together of the two German states. He was sharply rebuffed by the West Germans, however, who made it clear that they had won the inner-German Cold War. The election was only a month away and all signs pointed to a crushing loss for the reformed Communists. To quote Teltschik, "The Chancellor is no longer interested in reaching decisive agreements with a helpless Modrow."[108] As a result, Kohl put off formal discussions until after the March 18 elections.

Kohl did agree to the creation of a joint committee to consider an economic and currency union, but he continued to refuse to provide the GDR with the aid package Modrow was seeking. Furthermore, he demanded that the West German mark be introduced in the GDR. For practical purposes, this latter step would unify the two countries economically.

Not surprisingly, Modrow was furious at his treatment by Kohl. In response to questions concerning his visit to Bonn, he stated, "I will not get on my knees." However, there was nothing he could do—Kohl held all of the trump cards. Members of the NVA were as discouraged as their civilian counterparts. Admiral Hoffmann believed that the writing was now on the wall; it would now only be a matter of time before the GDR ceased to exist and the ideas of neutrality and demilitarization were dropped.[109] The problem for the average member of the NVA was that things were moving so fast, and that the chaos and confusion they were dealing with every day made it difficult to keep up with the latest nuances of East-West German relations.

The Future of the NVA

The NVA leadership continued to support the existence of the NVA. On February 18, Rainer Eppelmann, the country's future defense minister, who was at that time serving as a minister-at-large with special responsibility for security questions, visited the GDR's Defense Ministry. During his visit he argued that "the existence of the National People's Army on the territory of the present GDR is an essential necessity even after the People's Chamber elections on March 18."[110] The NVA would not exist forever, but Eppelmann made it clear that he believed it would become an integral part of the new, unified German armed forces.

To make matters worse, Hoffmann reported that Eppelmann's comments were very well received by the NVA officers present. According to Hoffmann, Eppelmann's comments "largely corresponded to the ideas and feelings of the professional soldiers present, aroused a sense of trust and overcame their skepticism toward the oppositional pastor and former conscientious objector."[111] Furthermore, both Eppelmann and Hoffmann came out in favor of creating a joint East-West German Military Commission after the election to work out details on how the two armies would be combined.[112] As a result of Eppelmann's remarks, as well as the call for a joint commission, it was not surprising that a number of career East German soldiers believed that they would have a future in a unified German military.

Meanwhile in Bonn a debate was under way. Genscher, always concerned about Moscow's potential veto of German reunification, continued to insist that NATO's protective shield should not be extended to cover the GDR once it became part of the FRG. Stoltenberg disagreed. He argued in favor of including the former GDR within NATO. How, he argued, could only part of Germany be protected by NATO? How could a united Germany not station Bundeswehr troops in eastern Germany? Kohl, upset at this open disagreement between two of his senior officials, intervened. The West German leadership announced that "no Bundeswehr troops whether or not assigned to NATO will be stationed in the GDR"—for the time being, a victory for Genscher.[113]

As far as the East German suggestion that a joint commission should be created to work out plans for a unified German army was concerned, Stoltenberg rejected it. "We are waiting for a democratic government which will be installed very soon after March 18 and with this government we will have talks about many issues and not with some communist defense minister now."[114]

The future was not long in coming. On March 18, the first free election in GDR history was held. In an election in which 93.38 percent of the populace voted, the CDU won an overwhelming victory. The East German citizenry gave a strong endorsement to a democratic society and a free market economy. It was a clear mandate for German unity. A unified German army was now only a matter of time.

Conclusion

One major contrast between the Modrow government and the Krenz interregnum was the top leadership. Unlike Krenz and Keßler, Modrow and Hoffmann attempted to provide the kind of leadership that the NVA needed. Nevertheless, one could argue that Hoffmann could have been more assertive or that Modrow was too removed from reality in believing that the PDS still had a future.

All leaders—political or military—are captives of their past to a certain degree, and this was true particularly of Modrow. His effort to find a "third way" was as doomed in the GDR as was Gorbachev's similar effort in the former USSR. As events have shown, there was no "third way," at least not when it involved these countries.

Hoffmann's handling of matters during this period should not go without criticism. For example, he could have taken a more forceful position when it came to issues like civilian work by the military, but such an attitude on his part could have been dangerous, especially at a time when the military seemed on the verge of collapse. He appears to have realized just how tenuous the situation was. Had he mishandled the Beelitz situation, for example, East Germany could well have fallen into civil war, and unification might never have occurred. Faced with these difficult circumstances, Hoffmann probably did the best one could expect. Certainly when compared with the dogmatism and inaction of Keßler, Hoffmann came across as a very dynamic and hard-working leader—refusing to lose hope in spite of being faced with a hopeless situation.

Nowhere was this difficulty in dealing with an instable and quickly changing world more evident than when it came to the question of military reform. Hoffmann, Süß, and a number of other NVA officers devoted a considerable amount of time and effort to trying to come up with a plan that made sense. The problem, however, was that they had no idea what the new GDR would look like—or, as time went on, whether it and the NVA would continue to exist. In fact, by the end of the Krenz period, it was clear that it made no sense to talk about military reform. The few reform steps that were taken, such as the end of use of the term *Genoße*, and the changes in regulations, were taken piecemeal; they were not the result of carefully thought-out plans, but of desperation as in the case of those introduced in the aftermath of the incident at Beelitz.

The one exception to this pattern was the attempt to depoliticize the NVA. One could argue that the continued use of political officers as part of the new educational establishment was a mistake, but every other communist military which went through this transition did the same thing—who else were they to call on to inculcate values, given their background and structure? Even so, the military was more or less successfully depoliticized—at least when compared with the kind of armed forces that existed under Honecker. Hoffmann made a major effort to get rid of those officers who were too closely tied psychologically to the old regime. Given what he was working with, it is fair to say that Hoffmann did a reasonable job in systematically depoliticizing the NVA.

It soon became obvious to Bonn that the sickness of the East German regime was even more serious than most had realized. As a result, Kohl decided to wait for the GDR to collapse on its own. In so doing, he probably made the situation in the GDR and the NVA more difficult, but one can hardly blame the West Germans for not wanting to do anything to prop up a government they had bitterly opposed for more than forty years.

For the NVA professionals, as the situation deteriorated—with more time being spent on civilian work, discipline collapsing, and the inability of the Modrow government to handle things becoming increasingly apparent—it should have been obvious to them that their situation was hopeless. And there is no doubt that many of them did feel that way. At the same time, however, their political naïveté—fostered by the *ancien régime*, which tried to isolate them from politics—as well as their focus on the catastrophic situations they were facing on a daily basis, tended to insulate them from the full realization of just how hopeless their situation was becoming. Somehow, many of them believed that they would have a future in a united German military.

Looking back at the period from mid-December 1989 to the elections on March 18, 1990, it is clear that neither Modrow nor Hoffmann really had a chance to introduce the kind of changes that were needed to keep either the GDR or the NVA viable. The situation was moving so quickly, and the political-military environment was so confused, that neither of them was able to control events. The NVA was faced with what Hoffmann called "*perestroika* at supersonic speed."[115] Indeed, it is no exaggeration to suggest that events controlled them, rather than the other way around. They seemed no sooner to get control of one situation than they would discover that something had occurred to upset their plans completely—a deadly situation for a military which based itself on planning and predictability.

15 March 1990. Soldiers demonstrate against their living conditions.
Credit: DPA

Minister Eppelmann and naval officers discuss the situation in the navy. Admiral
Hoffmann in the background, Vice Admiral Born at the far right.
Credit: Former Defense Minister Eppelmann

5

The First Democratically Elected Government: Eppelmann Crusades for Two German Armies

The Warsaw Pact is on the verge of collapse. The GDR has appointed a Minister of Disarmament and Defense! I'm quite serious! Does the Ministry of Disarmament intend to be a part of the Warsaw Pact? And if so, will its participation be a fiction?

Marshal Dmitri Yazov

I see not only the soldiers, the military and the generals. . . . I see in them also the fathers of families with their now destroyed careers, with their disappointments.

Rainer Eppelmann

Despite the victory of Lothar de Maiziere and the East German CDU, the real winner in the election of March 18 was Helmut Kohl. Kohl had put the full weight of the West German CDU behind de Maiziere and was credited by most analysts as the architect of the CDU's victory. De Maiziere's platform of reunification meant that he would be head of a caretaker government. In spite of Modrow's efforts, the old, "reformed" Communist system was never accepted as legitimate. Modrow himself recognized that his six-month experiment with democracy was a failure, noting that the "democratic" Volkskammer "did not enjoy great respect toward the end of its half year activity."[1]

The soft-spoken de Maiziere devoted most of his energy to bringing about a monetary, social, and economic union. He also decided to bring back the old five *Länder* in place of the fifteen regions that the East Germans had set up. This would put the GDR's geographic regions on a par with those in West Germany. He also pledged to remove the remaining parts of the Berlin Wall as well as the fortifications along the former East German-West German border.[2]

113

The process of reunification was already well advanced. With monetary union, Bonn would be responsible for the GDR's economy, especially for factors such as fiscal and monetary stability and fighting unemployment.

From a political standpoint, initiative—and leverage—were now in the hands of the West Germans. Whatever de Maiziere did, it was Kohl who would call the shots.

Most observers expected unification to take at least two years. In a news conference on March 20 Kohl stated that in spite of the CDU's landslide victory, he "did not expect an all-German election this year." Indeed, surveys conducted in West Germany showed that although the majority of West Germans supported reunification, 66 percent opposed rushing into union and 78 percent wanted to hold a referendum first. In East Germany, some 54 percent opposed a hasty union.[3]

Eppelmann Becomes Defense Minister

On April 9, de Maziere announced the creation of a "Grand Coalition." The new government included the Christian Democrats (eleven posts), the Social Democrats (seven), the Liberals (three), the German Social Union (two) and the Democratic Awakening (one). For the NVA, the last was the most important—Rainer Eppelmann.

Eppelmann was an unlikely candidate for the position of defense minister. Born in Berlin in 1943, he studied architecture, but later switched to theology and became pastor of East Berlin's Samaritan Church, which was a center of underground opposition. Eppelmann was imprisoned by the East German authorities for eight months because of his refusal to serve in the NVA. In addition, he was constantly in trouble with the Stasi because of his pacifist activities. In the early 1980s, for example, he led an appeal for "Peace without Weapons" and was briefly imprisoned for opposing the deployment of nuclear missiles in East Germany.

In October 1989, Eppelmann gave up his church duties to cofound the DA shortly before Honecker fell from power. He became its formal head in early March just prior to the elections when the then-chairman, Wolfgang Schnur, resigned after admitting that he had been a spy for the Stasi. In February of 1990, Eppelmann became minister without portfolio in the Modrow government.[4]

One of Eppelmann's first acts when he moved to the defense post was to change the name of the ministry from the Ministry of Defense (*Ministerium für Verteidigung*) to the Ministry of Defense and Disarmament (*Ministerium für Abrüstung und Verteidigung*). Indeed, according to one source, Eppelmann refused to take over the ministry until de Maiziere agreed to this name change.[5]

Eppelmann was accompanied to the ministry by three other civilians. The first, Werner Ablaß, had also been active in church affairs, in addition to holding other positions, such as insurance salesman. He would become Eppelmann's primary deputy in the defense ministry. The second, Frank Marczinek, had spent more than eight years in the NVA before leaving in January 1989, thus making him the only one of the four with any military experience. He had primary responsibility for technology, disarmament, and conversion as well as for preparing military personnel for civilian life. The third individual, Bertram Wieczorek, a medical doctor, had primary responsibility for the ministry's relations with the Volkskammer.[6]

On April 10, the four new defense officials appeared in Strausberg at the headquarters of the NVA to assume their new positions. Eppelmann's first action there was to talk with Theodor Hoffmann. The latter had seriously considered resigning his position, believing that time and politics had passed him by. As he said, "The last months had taken a lot out of me and I was . . . fed up with things."[7] Admiral Hoffmann's subordinates, however, felt he should stay in the military since he knew the internal situation better than anyone and, besides, he had already developed good contacts with the various politicians and political groups in the GDR.

When they met, Eppelmann proposed that Hoffmann take over a newly created position—chief of the National People's Army. This would be the most senior military post in the armed forces. Hoffmann thanked Eppelmann for his confidence but suggested that it might be better to appoint a younger, still "unused" officer to this post. Hoffmann pointed out that he had been a member of the SED and had been appointed defense minister by an SED regime. To make matters worse, Hoffmann explained to Eppelmann that his parents had worked for the Stasi.

Eppelmann nevertheless insisted on Hoffmann's appointment. He knew that Hoffmann "had the trust of many men in the NVA. Based on the information I received he was accepted by the majority of officers. He was a person who had shown political courage and had led the Ministry during a difficult time."[8] Hoffmann eventually agreed:

> I promised the putative Minister of Disarmament and Defense that I would carry out my service honestly and loyally and that I would use my entire knowledge and ability to ensure that the NVA would continue to be a factor and a guarantee in the peaceful restructuring of the GDR and to stabilize the unification of both parts of our people.[9]

The appointment of a pacifist as defense minister seemed strange to say the least. Günter Schabowski, for example, called it "absurd."[10] Hoffmann also noted that a number of NVA officers found the situation bizarre: "Several serving military officers could simply not understand how NVA generals and admirals could freely subordinate themselves to a former conscientious objector and convinced pacifist simply because the regime had made him minister and the Volkskammer had expressed trust in him."[11]

For his part, Hoffmann seems to have considered Eppelmann's appointment a positive step. Hoffmann had met him previously and believed he was an honest man who could and would work in the NVA's interest. Eppelmann also impressed Hoffmann as an individual who showed initiative and was the source of many original ideas. As he put it, "I was of the opinion, that Rainer Eppelmann as defense minister would not be such a bad solution for the army."[12]

The rank and file of the NVA, on the other hand, viewed Eppelmann's appointment with a great deal of suspicion and apprehension. One major noted that "many found it absurd and embarassing to have to follow the orders of a pastor and a construction soldier." As a result, there was considerable tension in the air when five hundred senior NVA officers met Eppelmann for the first time in Strausberg on May 2 at a commander's meeting.

Eppelmann began by thanking them for having helped avoid a bloodbath the preceding October—in contrast to the situation in China. He also noted that NATO and the Warsaw Pact would continue to exist for some time and that the security interests of all of the states involved must be respected. Then in what must have sounded like music to the ears of these officers, Eppelmann expressed concern for the fate of NVA personnel, opposed ending conscription, and said that as long as the GDR continued to exist as a state it would "maintain the NVA at the appropriate level and structured in a defensive way. . . ." Turning to the post-unification period, Eppelmann argued that even then "there could be a second German army on GDR territory which, not integrated in any military alliance, would exercise its own, territorial safeguarding functions." Eppelmann also opposed the expansion of NATO onto GDR territory and called for the creation of a European security alliance in which both German states—and their armies—could serve a bridging function between the two sides.[13]

For the NVA's officers, almost all of whom were deeply concerned about their future, Eppelmann's comments were reassuring. This was especially true of his insistence on the continued existence of the NVA. Hoffmann had made the same points previously, but now they were hearing them from a civilian—from a man who could have been expected to oppose everything they stood for. Indeed, in the words of Ablaß, the meeting served to "break the ice."[14] A number of military officers now decided to take another look at their new boss. Maybe he wouldn't be as bad as they had expected. Maybe he would even do something positive for them and their families. Indeed, one of the few bright spots was that the number of desertions went down. Eppelmann felt the change: "The soldiers appear no longer to ask so often why they are doing their duty, for what shall they be utilized? The soldiers and officers appear to understand that I will give them a chance."[15]

Eppelmann himself saw his primary task to be working toward disarmament while at the same time facilitating the merger of the two German states. After all, the Volkskammer had voted to become part of the Federal Republic in accordance with Article 23 of its Basic Law. Toward this end, he worked to downsize the NVA: "My goal is to disarm the NVA. A year ago we had 170,000 soldiers and officers. Now we already have 35,000 fewer. During the next year I want to halve this army. . . ." Turning to weapons, he noted that in comparison with 1989 they had already cut weapons by 20 percent—and he intended to cut them by another 30 percent.[16] At the same time, Eppelmann was concerned about the human dimension. He understood fully the need to improve the transition—from soldier to civilian. As he put it, "I can't simply send the officers and NCOs home. They haven't learned anything else."[17] At the same time, he, like many others, could not conceive of just how fast the unification process would move and how difficult it would be to impose any sense of order or rationality on it.

The Russians and the March Election

The Germans were not alone in expecting unification to be a long-term process. According to Modrow, Gorbachev thought the Communists would win the March elections. After the CDU victory, Gorbachev realized there would be significant changes in the GDR, but he never anticipated the collapse of the country.[18] In response to the election, Moscow pushed a policy whose aim was to minimize a unified Germany's ties with NATO.

On March 22, Yuri Kvitsinski, the Soviet ambassador to West Germany, met with Chancellor Kohl, and Horst Teltschik, Kohl's senior advisor and the man most responsible for the unification of Germany on the West German side. Kohl told Kvitsinski to tell Gorbachev that he expected German-Soviet relations to be even better after unification than they had been before. For this reason, he said he was not interested in moving fast. Instead he said he wanted to work with Moscow to ensure that the transition was a smooth one.

For his part, Kvitsinski concentrated on trying to kill the idea of Germany's membership in NATO. He maintained that membership for a united Germany in NATO would be "unmanageable" for the Russians. There was too much opposition within the upper ranks of the Soviet leadership, he argued. Kvitsinski tried to sell Kohl on the idea of a Germany that was anchored in both the West and the East, and he proposed the creation of a 100-kilometer demilitarized zone. Kohl turned him down.

As he was leaving, Kvitsinski said that NATO membership would continue to be the most difficult problem for Moscow. "We should come up with something to solve this problem."[19] Moscow would hold to this position for the next several months. When Soviet Foreign Minister Eduard Shevardnadze visited Washington in April, he again pushed the idea with Secretary of State James Baker that Germany should be part of both NATO and the Warsaw Pact.[20]

Despite this apparent hard line on NATO by the Soviets, it soon became obvious that there was more flexibility than many believed possible in Moscow's position. On March 28, Nikolai Portugalov, a senior member on the Soviet Central Committee, met with Teltschik. Throughout their discussion, Portugalov made statements that suggested that Moscow's position had changed. For example, he made it clear that the Kremlin was not insisting on neutrality.[21] Perhaps, Portugalov suggested, Germany could have a status similar to that enjoyed by France: a member of NATO, but not militarily integrated into the alliance. According to Teltschik, it was also clear that Portugalov was very concerned about the possibility that the GDR could self-destruct before unification could be effected. "What would happen if state order collapsed in the GDR?" he asked.[22] At this point, the Germans believed that concern over stability in the GDR and the impact a worsening situation could have on their own domestic experiment were leading the Russians to show greater flexibility on the question of NATO membership.

Meanwhile, the West Germans were beginning to focus on the question of Germany's military future. On April 2, Foreign Minister Dietrich Genscher; Defense Minister Gerhard Stoltenberg; Major General Klaus Naumann from the MOD; Rudolf Seiters, the chancellor's special emissary to East Berlin; and Teltschik met with Kohl. The chancellor made it very clear that he wanted a firm date for the withdrawal of Soviet troops from East Germany and he came out in favor both of the continued maintenance of conscription and of the stationing of Bundeswehr troops in all parts of a "unified Germany."

The Soviet military seems to have had the most difficulty of any of the major players in reconciling itself to the new situation in the GDR and the Warsaw Pact. When General Goldbach returned from a visit to Moscow on April 25, where he had participated in a meeting of the Military-Scientific Council of the Warsaw Pact, he told the East German leadership that he found Russian Defense Minister Dmitri Yazov to be "very rude and unmovable." Yazov seemed unable to understand that the old relationship no longer existed and that the East Germans were entitled to their own opinion. As Eppelmann remarked, Yazov "is probably too old to change his ways. He belongs to the veterans of the Great Fatherland War, which means that he was already an active officer in the Second World War." Nevertheless Eppelmann noted that, like other Soviet officers, "Yazov will have to learn that when he wants to get something done he will have to convince us. Orders alone no longer suffice."[23]

Meanwhile, on April 28, de Maiziere and his defense minister flew to Moscow for talks with Gorbachev on a united Germany's future role in Europe. In advance of the talks, Shevardnadze had reiterated the standard Soviet line: "Membership of a united Germany in the North Atlantic Treaty Organization is unacceptable to us." Instead he argued again for the membership of Germany in both the Warsaw Pact and NATO.[24]

Based on press reports, there were significant differences of opinion between the Russians and the conservative de Maiziere. Moscow continued to hold to its hardline public position. As Gorbachev declared, "A unified Germany as a NATO member is not acceptable to the Soviet Union. Another compromise solution must be found."[25] For his part, de Maiziere argued in favor of NATO membership, provided "the strategy and structure of NATO are changed. There may be a situation where there will be no concern of our neighbors about our membership in NATO." In essence, what de Maiziere was arguing for was a NATO that was less militarily oriented and instead one that took on more political and economic functions.[26] Interestingly, the Russians were already showing greater flexibility in dealing with the West Germans than they were with their own allies.

The Hungarians told the West Germans that the main point of opposition concerning German NATO membership was the Soviet military. In view of the Red Army's responsibility for the USSR's security and the fear that a united Germany would further strengthen NATO's already impressive military forces, such an attitude was not surprising. This was certainly the position adopted by senior Soviet military officers in public. On April 13, for example, Gen. Vladimir Lobov, the chief of staff of the Warsaw Pact, publicly stated, "I don't think Germany should belong to any military bloc."[27]

The East Germans tried to assure Yazov and his colleagues that the GDR would not accept NATO troops within its borders and that it would not accept any NATO weapons. The East Germans promised to work closely with the Group of Soviet Forces in Germany, but they also criticized Russian troops for the environmental damage they had caused in the GDR—a criticism Yazov did not appreciate.[28]

On May 7 the new Minister of Disarmament and Defense led the first official East German military delegation to Moscow since the election of the de Maiziere government. The purpose of the visit was the Pact's celebration of the forty-fifth anniversary of Germany's defeat. It was at this point that the East Germans began to note a new Russian approach to unification. Significantly, Gorbachev failed to argue against German membership in NATO:

> The Soviet people are for cooperation with this new Germany. The maintenance and construction of economic ties, the cooperation of our two great people on the basis of science and culture, a political dialog between them could profit civilization considerably and serve as a pillar for the Helsinki process. However, reliable guarantees are needed to ensure that unification of the two Germanies does not damage the interests of our security as well as that of other people and that strategic stability in Europe and the world is not destroyed.[29]

Shevardnadze supported the Gorbachev line, although Yazov remained opposed: A few days later in an interview in *Izvestiya* he reiterated that such an approach was "not acceptable to the Soviet people."[30]

The Situation within the NVA

Conditions within the NVA continued to deteriorate. On March 15, 1990, only a week prior to the election, soldiers from the elite Friedrich Engels Guard Regiment in East Berlin demonstrated—in uniform—against what they considered to be poor living conditions and "outmoded Prussian military customs." The soldiers held banners calling on the military leadership to make "repairs instead of parades" and to drop "Prussian military traditions." Even their commander expressed sympathy for the soldiers, agreeing that their quarters were badly in need of repair. This was East Germany's show unit—the one that guarded the Neue Wache, the monument in East Berlin to the victims of fascism and militarism. If discipline had fallen this far in such an elite unit, how bad must things have been in a normal outfit?[31]

On the same day as the Engels Regiment strike, the Committee on Misuse of Power, Corruption, and Personal Gain had completed its work. The chairman of this group revealed that a number of senior officers had violated military regulations and had created rules that made it possible for them to obtain special privileges. He summed up the group's reaction: "Not only is the lack of a sense of what is right and wrong bitter for us, but above all the knowledge that the misuse of office was aided by an accommodating apparatus."[32] In fact, these investigations reached the highest ranks of the NVA. On January 19, it was announced that Heinz Keßler, the former defense minister, was under criminal investigation for using military aircraft for private hunting trips and private funds to build a house. Keßler was subsequently arrested on January 25 for "abusing" his authority, but on May 17, it was announced that charges against Keßler had been dropped because of a lack of evidence.[33]

Even though most of those investigated would never be brought to trial in the GDR, the fact that they were singled out by name in the military press further undercut military morale and prestige. Indeed, to many it appeared that everyone in the upper ranks of the NVA was corrupt. Faced with these findings, Hoffmann signed an order on March 20 creating a working group to look into the charges and report back to him on its findings by April 30.[34]

Meanwhile, in an attempt to counter suggestions that the armed forces were some how connected to the activities of the Stasi, military intelligence activities within the army were ended by an order issued on March 16. The military also sent a letter to de Maiziere stating that it would be loyal to the new government. "The members of the National People's Army and the Border Troops of the GDR feel fully bound to their obligation for the security of our country and are ready to carry out faithfully the tasks assigned to them by the government and the Volkskammer."[35]

On March 20, the Round Table held its seventh and last meeting. Despite all of the confusion that had surrounded previous gatherings, the military, suprisingly, seemed to find the Round Table useful. Said Hoffmann, "As a form of co-determination, which grew spontaneously out of the peaceful revolution of the fall of 1989, the Round Table proved useful for the discussion of basic military-political questions."[36] From the military's standpoint, the Round Table provided a vehicle for critics—many of whom understood little or nothing about military issues—to vent their spleen and at the same time hear an explanation of why the military was acting in a particular manner. An example was Hoffmann's presentation to the Round Table in February, in which he had to explain to its members why military personnel were not permitted to go on strike.[37] While such an explanation would seem unnecessary to anyone who has served in the military, in many cases he was dealing with individuals who had been conscientious objectors.

On March 25, the Volkskammer adopted a new military law (*Wehrgesetz*) that marked a major break with the past. No longer was there talk of the duty to subordinate oneself to the interests of the "military collective" and the commander acting on behalf of social interests. Gone also was the unconditional obedience common to past regulations. The new law not only omitted any mention of the Communist party, it expressly forbade membership in any political party for the period an individual was on active duty. The law marked, in the words of a West German officer, "a new beginning."[38] Or as Gen. Jörg Schönbohm, the future commander of Kommando-Ost, said, "It was only after the democratic election of March 18, 1990, that one began to reform the NVA as a party army in earnest."[39]

The NVA of this period was a far cry from the military that had existed some six months earlier. With the introduction of a one-year conscription obligation, it had shrunk almost overnight from 180,000 to 100,000. Pay for soldiers had been raised from about 150 marks to 250 marks per month. Furthermore, in contrast to the past when they couldn't even watch Western TV, East German soldiers could now travel to the West and go home fairly often—in civilian clothes. The soldiers had even created councils that met on a regular basis with senior officers.

Nevertheless, the mood in the NVA was grim. As one East German soldier described it: "The future of the Army is in a fog. No one knows if it is going to be here next week or not." And for those who were serving in the military, there was the obvious question—what would they do if they were released from active duty? As an East German officer put it, "All I know is artillery. I have no profession. Maybe I can be a truck driver."[40]

The military leadership announced at the beginning of April that some three thousand soldiers, the majority of whom had twenty-five years of service, would be released by the end of 1990. By 1995 the Defense Ministry was talking about an army of only fifty thousand men. Indeed, its spokesman said that serious thought was being given to the complete dissolution of the army by 2005.[41]

Admiral Hoffmann discussed the situation in an interview on April 9. He began by noting that combat readiness had fallen considerably compared to its level some seven months earlier. Only 15 to 20 percent of NVA forces were now on combat alert (compared to 85 percent prior to the events of the preceding October). In addition, East German sources reported that some one thousand soldiers had deserted, and

Bonn acknowledged that it had received thousands of written inquiries from the East and that more than three hundred soldiers had turned up at West German barracks asking to join the Bundeswehr. Hoffmann called the situation within the NVA a "crisis of motivation," and argued that the dilemma was a result not only of a "legitimation crisis in the NVA in general," but also of the increasing social insecurity of the soldiers.[42] Interestingly, he still believed the integrative process between the two military forces would "be a long process."[43]

Eppelmann and the NVA

Eppelmann faced a difficult predicament when he took over the NVA. As a human being, he empathized with the officers. He knew that many of them, after serving well and honestly, now faced the prospect of being thrown out of a job by a Bundeswehr that wanted nothing to do with them. Yet they could not be ignored, if for no other reason than the potential threat they represented to the regime. Putting that many disgruntled NVA officers and NCOs on the street would be a security risk. Indeed, de Maiziere made exactly that point in a conversation with Horst Teltschik.[44] Eppelmann, however, took great exception to suggestions that the NVA as it was structured at that time represented a potential security risk. "Anyone who tried to use tanks could possibly slow down the wheel of history by a couple of months; however, he would never again have anything to say in this country." The real danger, Hoffmann wrote, was some sort of "stupidity"—an act that could quickly get out of hand.[45] Some way would have to be found to ensure that the NVA retained enough order and discipline to avoid such a scenario.

This raised the issue of having two separate German armies. While Eppelmann's continual insistence on the two-army variant would eventually alienate many if not most of those in the NVA, it was important as part of his approach to the military. Eppelmann recognized that he was not a military professional and at the same time he was well aware that the East Germans were breaking new ground. There was no model of what to do or how to do it. At this stage, the idea of two armies made as much sense as any other—unless one was talking about complete capitulation to the West Germans.

Of all the arguments this writer has encountered on this topic, the one that makes the most sense is that Eppelmann decided early on that if he did not give such assurances, the NVA ran the risk of collapsing, with all the unforeseen consequences that entailed. Furthermore, by holding out for the two-army variant, Eppelmann believed that his chances of convincing the West Germans to treat NVA officers and NCOs in a more humane fashion—that is by offering them the possibility of service in the Bundeswehr—would increase.

In order to better coordinate the FRG and the GDR's Russian policy, Teltschik flew to Berlin to talk to de Maziere. The latter gave him a non-paper from the Russians that pointed out in detail why the Russians opposed German membership in NATO. At the same time, Eppelmann met with Soviet Gen. Pyotr Luschev, the military head of the Warsaw Pact, and assured him that East Germany would continue to honor its commitments to the alliance. He reiterated his view that as long as the Pact and NATO continued to exist, there would be two armies and added that, as far as he was concerned, even if Germany were to become a member of NATO, NATO forces would not be stationed in what was then the GDR.[46]

Conditions in the NVA Worsen

There was good reason for concern on the part of the political leadership over the state of the NVA. In spite of the decrease in the number of desertions, the situation was critical and worsening.

To begin with, in an effort to increase its electoral popularity, the PDS intensified its campaign to do away with conscription by the end of 1990. This idea was extremely popular among a large portion of the population, which resented and disliked the NVA. Gregor Gysi, the chairman of the PDS, never tired of making this point. On April 22, he said that his party "favored ending conscription by the end of the year."[47] Indeed, de Maiziere told the West Germans that the idea was so popular that no other party in the GDR could oppose it and hope to survive politically.[48] Given their already difficult problems in obtaining personnel to man the NVA, acceptance of such an idea would have had the most serious negative implications for the military.[49] To his credit, Eppelmann took the PDS head on and argued vehemently in favor of conscription, calling the twelve-month required military service "a piece of Democracy."[50]

To make matters worse, on April 23 a letter by three NVA officers (originally written in February) was published in the East German newspaper *Junge Welt*. This letter, addressed to West German Defense Minister Gerhard Stoltenberg, called for the dissolution of the NVA and its absorption by the Bundeswehr.[51] The letter proposed a three-stage process whereby the NVA would be dissolved, its installations placed under control of the Bundeswehr, and West German soldiers stationed in the GDR.

Eppelmann reacted very negatively to the letter. After trying unsuc-
cessfully to keep the newspaper from distributing it, he came down
hard on all three officers. The official Defense Ministry statement read
in part:

> The . . . letter is aimed against the constitution of the GDR. Because of the
> damage to the standing as well as the honor and value of its officer corps,
> these three officers were punished by being released from active duty.[52]

The swiftness and sternness of the response suggested that the level of
concern over the stability and cohesion of the NVA was even greater
than it appeared on the surface.

The primary worry of the average NVA officer and NCO was their
future. This was clear in a survey conducted of officers at the Friedrich
Engels Military Academy in March. The results shows that 97 percent
were concerned about their future careers in the armed forces, 94 percent about job security, 93 percent about the way those who left the
service were treated on the outside, 89 percent about their families'
situation, 85 percent about their lack of qualifications for a civilian job,
and 76 percent that they would be subject to an early, involuntary dis-
missal from the military.[53] A letter to the editor of *Neues Deutschland*
by a soldier from the border troops probably spoke for many in the
NVA: "Why are we going through border troop training when it has
been determined that the borders will no longer exist after July 1,
1990?"[54]

This sense of insecurity was matched by an increasing feeling of
alienation toward the GDR's political system. This was evident in
changes in the attitudes of soldiers, NCOs, and officers from November 1989 through May 1990. Responding to the question of whether
they felt a sense of loyalty toward the GDR, military personnel answered as follows:[55]

	Soldiers	*NCOs*	*Officers*
November 1989	59%	72%	—
January 1990	51%	72%	90%
May 1990	38%	58%	87%

In another survey, only 9 percent of soldiers, 18 percent of NCOs, and
26 percent of officers were in favor of the continued existence of the
GDR.[56]

Eppelmann observed:

> For many their world view was collapsing. People, who for years had
> been socialized in a special form of thinking with regard to the strategy

of such an army, find it difficult to relate to new laws and new forms of thinking.[57]

Or as another source put it, "There is deep anxiety throughout the NVA because the future is a blank."[58] One sign of just how bad morale was in the NVA came from reports of "major increases in German-speaking applicants for the French Foreign Legion since the beginning of the year"; the West German media claim that the vast majority of these applicants were from the NVA.[59] For members of the NVA it was a new world—one which few of them understood.

Morale in the NVA continued to decline. Hoffmann reported that between December 1989 and May 1990 close to fifteen hundred men had deserted, including sixty-five officers, thirty-three warrant officers, and eighteen cadets. This was the equivalent of an entire motorized infantry regiment.[60] The situation was so bad that the NVA stopped all proceedings against deserters—there were simply too many, and besides the FRG would not cooperate since it did not recognize these individuals as deserters in the normal military sense of the word. In addition, hundreds of NCOs and officers had applied directly to join the Bundeswehr, which turned them down.[61]

The ability of officers to enforce normal military regulations—procedures that would be recognized throughout the world as normal—was questionable. In one unit, officers complained that "they cannot persuade their men to get up in the mornings if it is raining." In addition, while blind obedience was normal in the past, recruits—who were free to wear civilian clothes and to return home every evening—boasted that they could "argue with their officers."[62]

By the middle of May Eppelmann admitted publicly that the NVA "is basically no longer capable of waging war, especially not against the other German army." He estimated that the NVA would be cut to between 7,000 and 10,000 troops during the next three years.[63] Ablaß also commented about the sorry state of the armed forces after a visit to the navy. According to him, in spite of claims that the exercise that he had witnessed was a success, it was clear that there were major problems—including the late arrival of airplanes taking part in the exercise.[64] In fact, this was to be the last joint exercise in which the NVA would participate.

When it came time for the "Friendship 90" joint exercise some two months later, the Ministry of Disarmament and Defense announced that the East German army would not be participating.[65] This was partly due to the condition of the NVA, but also, as Hoffmann put it, "What would be the sense of such an exercise for the soldiers of the NVA in August 1990 only a few weeks before they would leave the

Warsaw Pact and become part of the Bundeswehr?" After all, earlier in the year soldiers had refused to take part in such an exercise. The Russians were very upset and tried to force the East Germans to proceed. However, the East Germans dug in their heels and their involvement was modified so that each of the participating countries carried out command-post exercises on their own.[66]

Recognizing the severity of the problems confronting the NVA, Hoffmann created a new structure that would turn the military into both a cadre and training army. Combat readiness would be reduced to a minimum. The focus would be primarily on training and carrying out militia tasks. The transition would begin in the fall of 1990 and be completed in 1993. As part of this drawdown, a number of military bases also would be closed.[67]

An order issued in June confirming that officer schools would be continued was countermanded by one in July declaring that they would be closed and that those attending them would be released from active duty.[68] The border troops were disbanded on June 29. The East German military justice system was abolished a little over two weeks later when the new constitution came into effect.[69]

Finally, in order to bring the NVA into greater compliance with regulations governing the Bundeswehr, the military leadership issued Order 41/90, which put an end to service by women in the NVA. The West German Basic Law permitted women to serve only in medical units or as part of bands. As a result, authorities in Strausberg felt they had no alternative but to release the 1,346 women serving in the NVA at that time. In addition, all men over the age of fifty-five were to be sent home by September 30.[70]

The country's military academies were closed down as of July 25 and those studying at foreign military academies in Poland, Czechoslovakia, and the USSR were recalled. Meanwhile, there was a major debate over what to do with the GDR's generals. Eppelmann had several times called for some of them to be included in the Bundeswehr. However, by the middle of September, Stoltenberg had made it clear that he had no intention of taking any GDR generals into the Bundeswehr. In the end, the only one taken into the Bundeswehr would be a physician. An additional four former generals would be taken on as temporary advisors.[71]

The Collapse of the Warsaw Pact

While all of these problems were taking place within the NVA, one of the main pillars on which Eppelmann was basing his argument for two

German armies during a transition period—the continued existence of the Warsaw Pact—was collapsing. When the Pact's leaders met in Moscow on June 7, it was clear that its demise was only a matter of time. As Hungarian Prime Minister Jozef Antall stated, "We consider the Warsaw Pact an outdated organization . . . which has lost its function in the Europe of today." He continued, "We believe its military organization is not needed in the future and think it would be desirable that [the Pact] should be abolished in its current form by the end of 1991."[72] Indeed, the communiqué issued at this meeting noted that the Pact was reviewing its role and called for radical democratic change—a code word for less Soviet control.[73]

Two days later, Eppelmann announced that the military structure would be abolished by the end of the year. He also noted that the June 13–15 meeting of the Warsaw Pact defense ministers would be their last.[74]

The GDR formally withdrew from the Warsaw Pact on September 25, with unification only a few days away, as Eppelmann presented General Luschev, the Pact's military commander, with East Berlin's formal note of resignation.[75] The GDR's thirty-five-year-membership in the Pact was a thing of the past. The military that was considered by most to be second only to the Soviet army in quality only a year earlier, and the only "army of the Warsaw Pact which had placed its troops under Soviet control during peace time," was no longer a part of the Warsaw Pact.[76] The Pact itself would hang on for another five months, but for the GDR, it was already history.

The Politics of Reunification

Kohl and de Maiziere met in a hastily arranged meeting on April 25 and agreed that the monetary, economic, and social union of the two countries would take place on July 1, 1990. The East German currency would be replaced by the deutsche mark as the West German Bundesbank took responsibility for the monetary policies of both countries. In what was clearly a political decision to keep more East Germans from moving to the FRG, Kohl agreed to a 1:1 exchange rate between the East and West German marks even though the normal exchange rate was 1:3. In addition, the East and West Germans decided that as of June 1 there would not be any further pass controls on the inner-German border.

In spite of the importance of these events for German reunification, even Kohl did not expect it to be a quick process. In talking with Shevardnadze, for example, he said that he did not think reunification would occur until December 31, 1992—almost two years in the future.[77] This put Kohl in agreement with Eppelmann, who also argued that unification would not take place until 1992. Indeed, in mid-June he said that he believed that September 1, 1992, would be a realistic date for unification. That date would be the fifty-third anniversary of the German invasion of Poland.[78] "I am a person who values symbolic acts, that is why I like September 1."[79] However, Eppelmann showed considerable flexibility with regard to the timetable for unification, arguing on another occasion that he was more concerned about the conditions that had to be fulfilled than he was with the date.[80]

On May 18, the two Germanies signed a treaty, which for all practical purposes made the GDR part of the FRG. It provided for the creation of a social market and the conversion of East German marks to deutsche marks beginning July 1. De Maiziere hit the nail on the head when he observed, "The monetary, economic and social union makes the unification process irreversible." The treaty stated that unification could occur at any time and noted that the GDR could join the FRG in accordance with Article 23 of the Basic Law.[81] To become effective, the treaty had to be ratified by both parliaments—an action taken June 21–22. It went into effect on July 1.

By July 2 it was obvious that unification would come faster than many anticipated. On that day, the Volkskammer agreed to elections: October 14 for local elections and December 2 for all-German elections. It was difficult to delay the process once the East German populace had openly expressed its desire for unification.

In spite of these developments, Eppelmann refused to give up his efforts to delay the process for as long as possible. In his memoirs he argued that both sides needed time to learn more about each other—to ensure that they went into unification as equal partners. His obvious concern was that the new Germany would be dominated by Bonn and that the East Germans quickly would become second-class citizens. At the same time, Eppelmann realized that he was up against tremendous odds. "I fear that the pressure will be so strong that no time will remain. We are already being seen as a brake and as enemies of unification. No one listens to our arguments. When they listen, many politicians and journalists are astonished at how much remains unresolved."[82]

The first meeting of the East and West German defense ministers took place on April 27 at the Cologne-Bonn airport. The communiqué issued by Eppelmann and Stoltenberg stated that their goal was a unified Germany, one that was a member of the Atlantic Alliance but without NATO structures on GDR territory. With an eye toward the East, they pledged to take the security interests of their neighbors and especially the USSR into consideration. The two ministers also agreed to cooperate on a broad basis and to develop closer contacts between the two armies. The areas listed for cooperation were disarmament, arms control, and the destruction of arms. In addition, they pledged to work together in helping the East Germans understand the concept of democracy in the military (*innere Führung*), as well as on air safety, air traffic control, and cross border air traffic. They did not reach any decision on the nature of a unified German armed forces, but they agreed to another meeting toward the end of May.[83]

Eppelmann described the meeting as "friendly, but without any great warmth."[84] Hoffmann was even less happy. He was especially piqued by Stoltenberg's refusal to agree to closer contacts between individual soldiers or units. According to Hoffmann, Stoltenberg even opposed the participation of the two armies in ceremonial affairs. "Regular contacts could not be developed between individual facilities. Daily trips in civilian clothes to troop units or cultural presentations and establishments were the most intensive form of contact."

Naturally, there were basic political differences between the two armies. Hoffmann reported that he spoke with General Schönbohm, who would become Kommando-Ost, and the latter expressed surprise that Eppelmann had spoken of the continued existence of two German armies after unification and noted that there continued to be senior military officers in the NVA who had been faithful members of the Communist party.[85]

Beyond the basic feeling of resentment—believing that Stoltenberg was doing everything possible to avoid granting legitimacy to the NVA by not putting the two militaries on equal standing—Hoffmann was right that there was considerable suspicion on the part of the West Germans. They had been raised not to trust anything connected with the word "communist." Most West Germans, and Stoltenberg in particular, did not want NVA officers to join the Bundeswehr even though there was political pressure within the FRG to let them in at least in a symbolic fashion. As of April, for example, Stoltenberg was still saying that only those who had served for less than three years in the NVA should have an opportunity to join the Bundeswehr.[86]

At a meeting between Eppelmann and Stoltenberg at the end of May the two ministers called for closer ties between operations staff of units, troops, and institutions. At the same time, however, Stoltenberg held firm to the restrictions he had placed on contacts between the two armies. The new set of military contacts would begin as of June 1. As far as the West German defense minister was concerned, the NVA was on its way out as an institution and he saw no reason to treat it as if it were a real army.[87]

Stoltenberg continued to speak out against the idea of two German armies. At the thirty-first commander's conference in Fellbach on June 13, he confirmed that after a short transition period an all-German military would be created. Stoltenberg argued that the future of the East German military had to be seen against the background of major reforms that were under way within the Bundeswehr. The only rational way to handle these changes would be as part of a united German military force.[88] It was becoming clear that Stoltenberg's primary concern was with the dismantling of the NVA and the incorporation of its material and personnel into the Bundeswehr.

NVA Officers in the Bundeswehr: The Debate in the West

The inclusion of NVA personnel in the Bundeswehr was a hotly debated issue. The idea was as objectionable to many in the West as it was common sense to others in the East. In the West, there were two schools of thought. There were those who believed that long service in a communist state almost automatically disqualified NVA officers from serving in the Bundeswehr. As one Bundeswehr officer put it, "If an officer from the NVA were to be taken over into the Bundeswehr, I as a prisoner for many years of the SED regime, could only draw the appropriate conclusions and hang my uniform on the door of the closest Bundeswehr barracks." There were calls in the West for what Hoffmann called a "purge, pure and simple." And while he could understand the desire to exclude political officers and members of the border troops and to keep NVA officers from sensitive positions, Hoffmann maintained that there was no reason to treat East Germans as "outsiders and throw them to the wolves as some in the FRG were demanding."[89]

On the other hand, some West Germans sympathized with the NVA's plight. A lieutenant colonel wrote a letter to the editor arguing that although he disliked the idea of being forced to follow orders given by an NVA general, it was important for the West Germans to offer "a hand" to their NVA colleagues.[90] Another West German officer took a similar line a week later arguing that there was no question that the NVA had served a political system "that I deeply disapprove of." However, he continued, "political and soldierly thinking leads me as a German officer, who happily greets unity, to the conviction that I must seek contact with soldiers and officers of the NVA. . . ."[91]

The debate continued throughout the summer. On July 10, retired Lt. Gen. Paul Summerhoff published a letter in the *Frankfurter Allgemeine Zeitung* attacking the idea of including members of the NVA in the

Bundeswehr. He claimed that the latter were trained to hate, they were members of the SED, and the army itself was an instrument of repression.[92] Others questioned the rationality of permitting NVA professionals to join the Bundeswehr at a time when the West German military was being downsized. What right did communists, who had served the SED, have to join an army composed of noncommunists?[93] A day later, Günther Gillessen, a well-known West German editorial writer, argued that, since the Bundeswehr and the NVA were two radically different armies, the latter should simply be dissolved.[94]

There were many other voices in this debate, but it was relatively clear that there was a deep split within West German society as well as within the Bundeswehr. Gen. Werner von Schewen, who at this time was commander of the Leadership Academy (*Führungsakademie*) in Hamburg, remarked that the debate over this subject was extremely controversial, not only among students but on the part of faculty and other officers as well. The argument became so heated, according to von Schewen, that he finally decided to convene all of the officers and officials in the academy in a large auditorium. For three hours there was a wide-ranging discussion of the issue—to the point "that some almost came to tears." The range of opinions reflected those in society at large: "Some could not imagine such a situation and stated that they would quit the service. . . ." Others spoke just as passionately in favor of the former NVA officers being accepted into the Bundeswehr.[95]

Gorbachev Gives the Go-Ahead

Of all the momentous events of 1990, none was more critical for German unification than Kohl's trip to the USSR in July. Since the invitation included a visit to Gorbachev's hometown of Stavropol, the West Germans believed that Gorbachev was prepared to make major concessions on the question of German unity.

As Kohl flew to Moscow on July 14, the official party knew that this was the most important postwar visit to the USSR by any German leader and that they had two hurdles to overcome. First, they would have to get the four powers to renounce their control over Germany, a holdover from Yalta. Second, they would have to convince the Russians—and in particular Gorbachev—to agree to unified Germany's membership in NATO.[96]

During Kohl's stay in Russia, Gorbachev agreed to German reunification and conceded, "Whether we like it or not, the time will come when a united Germany will be in NATO if that is its choice."[97] The only qualification that was placed on Germany's NATO membership was that the alliance not be extended beyond its current borders. In practice this meant that troops from a united Germany could be stationed in the former GDR as long as they were not integrated into NATO. Russian troops would be withdrawn within three or four years, and neither nuclear weapons nor non-German troops would thereafter be stationed in the former GDR. In addition, Kohl agreed to reduce the overall size of the Bundeswehr to 370,000.[98] The question of the NVA did not even come up, suggesting that Gorbachev cared little about the issue.

Although the West Germans were overjoyed—Kohl called it "a breakthrough, a fantastic result"[99]—the East Germans were crushed. To quote Eppelmann:

> The world looks completely different. Four days ago I still believed that the transition period—in which an independent East German Army would exist—could last until the withdrawal of Soviet troops from German territory. I had assumed that would last at least three or four years. This perception has now collapsed. I received the news completely astonished and . . . almost in disbelief.[100]

Meanwhile, Foreign Minister Markus Meckel accused Kohl of "arrogance." He maintained that Kohl had not consulted de Maiziere before he concluded the unification agreement with Gorbachev and criticized the West Germans for not including de Maiziere in the talks. "One must ask why Mr. de Maiziere was not there in Moscow and in the Caucasus," he said. He also insisted on the need to continue to maintain two German armies for the indefinite future.

The West Germans were clearly irritated with East German inability to understand what was happening. In West German eyes, East Berlin had tied its economy to Bonn because the country was bankrupt. Having given up their sovereignty, they now had no business being present at the talks between Kohl and Gorbachev. In response to Meckel, Teltschik said, "If developments pass him by, that is not our fault."[101]

The military realized that "with the summit meeting in the Caucasus, the dice had been rolled, the fate of the NVA had basically been decided. The Federal Government had de facto a free hand for the shaping of all security and military-political relationships within the future unified Germany."[102] General Goldbach probably spoke for most NVA professionals when he observed, "From today's knowledge it is bitter to have to say that the NVA was a product and an instrument of Soviet policy, that it together with its state was superfluous and allowed to collapse as Soviet power politics fell apart."[103] General Streletz was even more pointed in his criticism of Moscow: "We certainly did not consider that our best friend and comrade in arms, the Soviet Union or the Soviet Army, would hang us out to dry, that Gorbachev and Shevardnadze would not only betray us but sell us out."[104]

East Berlin's greatest fear had been realized. Moscow had made a deal at the expense of the GDR over the heads of the East German leadership. In return for massive economic assistance from Bonn, Gorbachev was prepared to sacrifice the GDR and with it the NVA. After all, the GDR was no longer the strongest economy in Moscow's sphere of influence and the NVA was far from the dynamic, high quality military it had once been.

Not surprisingly, the average NVA professional felt a deep sense of betrayal. He had stood loyally beside his Russian comrades when it involved actions against Czechoslovakia and when it came to creating an armed forces that was more loyal to the Kremlin than any other. Where were the Russians when the situation was reversed and the East Germans needed them?

When asked about their views of the Russians, the former NVA officers made a clear distinction between the Russians and their government. As one officer put it, "Gorbachev and the Russians are two different things." Almost without exception, all former NVA officers expressed a positive attitude toward "the Russian people." A number of them noted that they had studied in the former USSR, that they had friends there, and that "we still visit each other."

Attitudes toward Gorbachev were more complex. Some felt that Germans owed him: "Without Gorbachev there would not have been any German unity." Others, however, felt that his policy toward the GDR was "dishonest." Once he saw how the wind was blowing, he dropped the NVA "like a hot potato." As one officer described it, Moscow's policy toward the GDR was "a dark chapter for the older officers of the NVA." Another observed, "I see the behavior of some politicians and Soviet military officers, who betrayed their comrades in arms, . . . in order to satisfy their new bosses, negatively."

The final obstacle to German unity was removed on September 13 when the four World War II allies signed the "Treaty on the Concluding Settlement with Regard to Germany." It terminated the rights and responsibilities of the Four Powers in Berlin and Germany. Germany was now free of external political controls.[105]

Eppelmann Looks for Gimmicks

One of the things that created a deep sense of distrust and even hatred toward Eppelmann on the part of NVA officers was his tendency to make promises and invent gimmicks that he somehow thought would sanitize NVA officers in the eyes of the Bundeswehr or increase the chances that the NVA would continue to exist as an independent military for the immediate future. For example, in May Eppelmann raised the idea of creating a joint Polish-German brigade. If nothing else, he believed the establishment of such a unit would put NVA officers in a position where they would be playing a key role, thus forcing the West Germans take them more seriously. He raised the issue during a visit to Poland at that time. Publicly, the Poles agreed to "study" the idea, but both Hoffmann and Ablaß reported that privately Gen. Wojciech Jaruzelski, the president of the country, did not consider such a step "politically realistic."[106]

Then, on July 6 *Neues Deutschland* reported that Egon Bahr, the well-known West German SPD foreign policy specialist, had been appointed an advisor to the NVA in the area of "security policy."[107] Not surprisingly, given his close ties to Eppelmann, Bahr argued against a quick unification of the two armies. Instead, he maintained that although a single army was the goal, carrying out unification should be a long, carefully planned process.[108]

Eppelmann's next and most controversial idea was the introduction of a new oath to replace the old one in which soldiers swore allegiance to defend the old communist regime. To add symbolic importance to this gesture, he ordered that it take place on July 20, the anniversary of the attempt by Count Claus Schenk von Stauffenberg and others to assassinate Hitler. The new oath called upon soldiers to "always fulfill with discipline and honor . . . military duties according to the laws of the German Democratic Republic." In addition, soldiers swore "to devote all my energy to maintaining peace and protecting the GDR."[109] Eppelmann's decision to introduce this new oath raised hackles in the East as well as the West. NVA officers objected; one lieutenant colonel called it nothing more than "a compulsory social decision, especially for the professional soldiers." Anyone who did not participate in it would quickly be out of work, with all that meant for his family. In any case, what was the purpose? As this officer said, "I was forced . . . to take an oath to the German Democratic Republic"—which might not have been so bad if he had not already taken one when he was sworn as an officer some twenty years earlier.[110]

For their part, the West Germans ridiculed the whole idea. They could not understand why Eppelmann was putting the NVA through this process at a time when the army's days were numbered. Eppelmann responded by stating that the only way two armies could be combined was if they were both dedicated to democracy, and he believed that the new oath as well as his order that the main building in Strausberg be renamed in honor of von Stauffenberg did exactly that. Furthermore, the Bundeswehr could think what it wanted, but as long as the GDR had an army, "which has a defensive task, the soldiers and officers must identify with the oath."[111] Publicly, Eppelmann also seemed to believe—rather naively—that the fact that these men had taken an oath that separated them from the communist regime would "make the forces acceptable to NATO," and ensure that the majority of the 60,000 or so who were still active in the NVA would be taken over as part of the new unified German Army.[112] Most officers within the NVA agreed with their West German critics who considered the undertaking a "farce."[113]

Finally, aware that none of his other ideas had worked, Eppelmann hatched a suggestion, some ten weeks before unification, that the NVA should become a territorial army. If anything, this was a last-ditch effort to save something for the NVA. The problem was that the idea was dead on arrival, as everyone except Eppelmann seemed to understand.[114] Regardless of Eppelmann's motivation, he often created more problems than necessary in the way he handled matters.

Civil-Military Relations

In considering the relationship between the military and the government, it is important to keep in mind that East German officers were not used to dealing with civilians. Like their Soviet counterparts, for most of their military lives they had lived in a relatively closed society where contacts with civilians were much less frequent than was the case in the West. Furthermore, most of the civilians they were now interacting with showed early on that they understood very little about the armed forces and how they functioned. Most NVA officers, for example, took a very dim view of the Volkskammer, whose members they believed knew next to nothing about military operations. The same was true for the regime. To quote one Western historian, "Because of the many neophytes in the cabinet, the de Maiziere government often seemed to perform like a group of amateur actors."[115]

Added to the belief that the country's leadership was inept was a feeling that the de Maiziere government, and especially Eppelmann, was letting them down. To begin with, the military high command gained most of its information on what was happening to it from the press. Furthermore, Eppelmann or Ablaß would often make decisions without involving the country's military leadership.[116] For example, a commission was set up within the GDR government to look at the issue of how to bring the two German armies closer together. Hoffmann had a very hard time getting the political leadership's agreement to put a military man on it, and more often than not, when the commission met, the military representative was excluded.[117]

Another example of what the military saw as the civilian side's failure to consult with the country's military leaders was the decision to release all officers over the age of fifty-five.[118] The military only learned about the decision after action had been taken.

Hoffmann made it clear throughout his memoirs that he especially disliked the way Ablaß dealt with the military. Many military officers believed Ablaß was primarily interested in improving his own relationship with the West Germans—even if it came at the expense of the NVA. Hoffmann felt Ablaß was carrying on secret negotiations with the West Germans and was particularly perturbed by Ablaß's comment that if things did not go his way, the West Germans would not take any NVA officers. Indeed, Hoffmann and Ablaß appear to have had a number of battles over the latter's decision to leave the military out of the decision-making loop.[119]

To make matters worse, the civilian leadership managed to undercut everything the military leadership was trying to accomplish. For example, during a speech Marczinek gave to the Bundeswehr's Führungsakademie in Hamburg on June 22 on the evolution of civil-military relations in the GDR,[120] he spoke of the need to get rid of the "Stalinist" elements in the NVA. Hoffmann responded by writing a furious letter to Eppelmann and the military's trade union, the *Verband der Berufssoldaten*, demanding Marczinek's resignation. Marczinek eventually apologized to Hoffmann for his remarks, but the damage had been done. The civilian authorities that NVA officers were so loyally serving had stabbed them in the back.

Tempers were not improved by Eppelmann's tendency to promise more than he was able to deliver. One could argue that his call for two German armies was a combination of naivete and a belief that he had to make such statements to keep the disintegrating NVA together, but in the end his actions alienated further an already dispirited group of professionals. Hoffmann complained about the chaos that seemed to reign on the civilian side of the house: "I concluded that when it came to a decisive stage, this regime was not able to take a clear position with regard to its armed forces." Or as he said elsewhere, "This minister lied to us worse than the old leadership."[121]

Feelings of bitterness were not limited to Hoffmann; many other officers were outspoken in their condemnation. After all, Eppelmann was part of this new democratic regime that they had been led to believe treated people in an honest, open fashion. From their perspective, however, Eppelmann did just the opposite. He lied to them. As one put it, "For me he is no minister."[122]

Indeed, it seems to have been Eppelmann's deception of the rank and file that upset them the most. As one former major put it, "We all clearly noted that the NVA would be sliced up according to the "Salami principle" and liquidated. Why didn't Eppelmann say that to us right away? It would have saved us many illusions and disappointments." A former vice admiral concurred, "I know of no circumstances in which I can say, 'Honor to Pastor Eppelmann.' I had thought that a Christian would have been more honest," and a former lieutenant colonel added, "Today, he is not called Eppelmann for me, but 'dishonest Eppelmann.' That was not honest of him."[123]

Answers to the questionnaire prepared for this book show that although a number of former officers were unhappy under Eppelmann's leadership, few were ready to blame him personally. Most felt he was unqualified for the job ("Given his qualifications, I was amazed at his willingness to take on such a position," said one. "He was overtaxed," agreed another), and very naive when it came to military matters and how to deal with the FRG. Indeed, one officer commented, "Officers were naive to pay attention to him." Much depended on how well the individual knew Eppelmann. Those who had close contact with him were impressed by his sincerity and by his attempts to do something for NVA officers. Indeed, one former officer pointed out that Eppelmann played a major role in the decision by the Bundestag to give former NVA officers their full pensions beginning January 1, 1997. In any case, Eppelmann certainly fared better than his deputy Ablaß, whom one former officer noted was "much colder."

Eppelmann seems to have recognized the feeling of dissatisfaction on the part of many NVA professionals toward him. For example, in his September 28 speech to the generals who were to be retired the next day, he apologized for not having been able to accomplish many of the things he set out to do—including the "equal incorporation into a unified all-German armed forces."[124] Eppelmann was a man who cared deeply about the military officers entrusted to his care, which few expected when he was appointed. Unfortunately, not only were events out of his control, but like many of the new East German officials who had come from the dissident community, he was not capable of dealing with the many complex issues that he faced.

This feeling of bitterness directed at Eppelmann and his civilian colleagues was also aimed at the entire communist system. Eppelmann was disliked because he seemed to bungle things and he had misled the NVA. But far more serious was the system that had created the mess that these officers inherited. A former East German admiral, who called September 28, the date of his forced retirement, the "bitterest time of his life," expressed the sense of betrayal by the system he had served so long and faithfully:

> The increasing doubt, the recognizable corruption and ignorance, also the repeated incompetence of leading functionaries in the party and society, the increasingly narrow doctrinaire thinking, tied together with the repression, persecution and exclusion of dissidents . . . all that was demanded or declared a temporary occurrence, which was not typical for this society.[125]

It was hard not to share the resentment felt by these officers. Some of them were opportunists, some were ideologically convinced of the righteousness of their cause, and others simply enjoyed the military and its lifestyle. Some undoubtedly got what they deserved. The bottom line, however, was that a large number of them served honestly and honorably and now had begun to realize that they had been betrayed by the people and the system they had protected for so many years.

The Curtain Falls: The NVA's Last Hurrah

The last Commander's Day was held in Strausberg on September 12, 1990. Hoffmann gave a very emotional speech. He recognized that the end of the NVA and the GDR would be a source of happiness to some, but a cause for concern for most of those in his audience. He thanked everyone present for their services and noted that the previous November the NVA had stood the test by ensuring that the East German revolution was a peaceful one. "I believe that our recognition of the change, our guaranteeing of its peaceful character and our loyalty was the right decision. That is evident even today." He called upon Eppelmann to work to ensure that NVA professionals were treated fairly by the new German government. And then looking back over the past year he observed, "Our goal from the beginning was to bring the armed forces into the unification process intact, that means to work so that the armed forces were brought into unification disciplined, in order, and well trained even when it came to the personnel problems we faced." In closing, this admiral, who had devoted the majority of his thirty-eight years of military service to the navy, passed on to his listeners the well-known sailor's wish of "fair winds and following seas."[126]

A constant theme on the part of the former East German officers who responded to the questionnaire was that Hoffmann's freedom of maneuver was very limited, but that his presence was a positive factor. A former tank officer called him the "hero" of the period, and a former colonel and chief of staff noted that "he worked to ensure that order and discipline were maintained, that the NVA's property was not misused, and, given his limited possibilities, that members of the NVA were treated fairly." In effect, based on the comments of these former officers, Hoffmann should have felt a certain sense of satisfaction. Given his relatively unknown status when he took over the NVA and the very difficult situation that confronted him, the fact that his compatriots judged him in a very positive light was a major accomplishment.

On September 14, Eppelmann paid his last visit to the ground forces, and on September 27 the honor regiment in Berlin held its last parade. Then on September 30, all members of the political administration, together with officers from the intelligence, justice, and propaganda branches, and all soldiers older than fifty-five were released from active service.[127]

Conclusion

The last roll call of the NVA took place on October 2, 1990. At 1:15 the flags were hoisted, and at 1:30 Ablaß gave a short speech. He thanked the members of the NVA for their service and spoke of the future of Germany as a united country.[128] In discussing his feelings on this day, Eppelmann expressed concern for officers and soldiers of the NVA and how they would be handled by the Bundeswehr. In this regard it is noteworthy that he did not blame any of his failures on his own people; to the contrary he had nothing but praise for them and their accomplishments. Instead, Eppelmann placed primary blame for what had happened to NVA professionals on the Bundeswehr. He felt more could have been done, "but unfortunately I encountered very little empathy among my colleagues and the generals from Hardthoehe."[129]

Leaving aside the validity of Eppelmann's statement, it was clear that the future of the former members of the NVA was very much in the hands of the FRG's defense ministry and its generals. Many from the West would continue to look askance at the presence of any "Ossis" in the Bundeswehr and would make their views known in quiet, often subtle ways.[130] Fortunately, there were other Bundeswehr professionals who would work hard to ensure that the East Germans, with their very different military culture, were given an even break.

The new world would not be as good as many in the NVA had hoped for, nor would it be as bad as others had feared. For some it would be the beginning of a new life in a very different political and military environment; an experience that would challenge both sides, but one that would also tell us a lot about these officers and the problems they experienced as they made the transition to life within a democratic polity.

July 22, 1990. NVA soldiers take the new oath of allegiance introduced by Rainer Eppelmann.
Credit: DPA

July 22, 1990. (*Left to right*) NVA Chief of Staff Manfred Grätz, GDR Defense Minister Rainer Eppelmann , and NVA Chief Theodor Hoffmann salute during the introduction of the new oath of allegiance.
Credit: DPA

142

Vice Admiral Born, Minister Eppelmann and Admiral Hoffmann observe naval maneuvers.
Credit: Former Defense Minister Eppelmann

NVA Chief Hoffmann and GDR Defense Minister Eppelmann meet with a delegation of NVA soldiers.
Credit: Former Defense Minister Eppelman

Part III

Integrating the NVA into the Bundeswehr

6

Integrating NVA Personnel into a Democratic Military: The Machinery

> We come not as Victors to the Vanquished, but as Germans to Germans.
>
> General Jörg Schönbohm

> We lost a war without having fired a shot.
>
> A Former NVA Officer

On October 3, 1990, the day Germany was reunified, the Bundeswehr faced a task unprecedented in the annals of recent European military history: how to deal with members of a formerly hostile army that had not been defeated on the battlefield, as had been the case with the Wehrmacht, nor collapsed as a result of internal strife, as occurred in a number of countries during the twentieth century. Not only did the Bundeswehr have to figure out what to do with some 60,000 former members of the NVA—as well as their formidable stocks of equipment and munitions—it also was forced to find a way to integrate many of its former opponents into its own armed forces at a time when major reductions were mandated as a result of an agreement reached by Helmut Kohl and Mikhail Gorbachev in July 1990.

Designing the Machinery of Integration

Initially, West German Defense Minister Gerhard Stoltenberg had had two goals: to counter Russian attempts to force the Bundeswehr to downsize to a fraction of its former size, and to avoid incorporating former NVA professionals into the Bundeswehr.

Stoltenberg recognized that he would have to compromise on the size of the Bundeswehr, but he wanted to keep it as large as possible. On July 2 he suggested that the force level should be 395,000 (including a navy of 25,000). According to Horst Teltschik, Kohl agreed in principle with Stoltenberg's proposal, but did not commit himself to specific numbers. Foreign Minister Dietrich Genscher fought for a lower limit of 350,000 because he believed it would be easier to sell to the Russians. The problem with this proposal, as Kohl pointed out, was that if the FRG went into the negotiations with Genscher's number of 350,000, during the course of discussions Bonn would be forced to make concessions and the actual number would probably end up around 280,000.[1] In fact, the number finally agreed upon by Kohl and Gorbachev was 370,000.

As to Stoltenberg's second goal, he wanted as little as possible to do with those from the NVA who had served the SED. How could they be expected to suddenly be loyal to a democratic polity? Stoltenberg reportedly favored a proposal made by the Foreign Ministry that a structure be set up to handle all of those who had served the SED state—regardless of organization. This would have eliminated the need for the Bundeswehr to become involved in the fate of former NVA officers at all.[2] The Bundeswehr had not addressed the issue of what to do with NVA officers if unification were to come about—primarily because few of them seriously expected it to occur. As the editor of *Soldat und Technik*, a retired colonel, said, "The preparation time for this historic and once-in-a-lifetime event was less than short."[3]

In time, however, it became clear to the military leadership that at least some former members of the NVA would have to be taken into the Bundeswehr as a part of Kohl's overall attempt to show East Germans that they were welcome in this new, united Germany. The task then became one of organizing the practical details of the transition. Although it was clear that political officers, officers over fifty-five, and those who had worked with the Stasi would be excluded, this left a large pool of potential candidates.

On August 10, Stoltenberg and Eppelmann, the FRG and GDR defense ministers, agreed to the former's suggestion that a liaison group of civilian and military officers be sent to East Germany to facilitate the transition process. The group arrived on August 17 and began its work in the Ministry of Disarmament and Defense on August 28 under the leadership of Brig. Gen. Eckhard Richter. The primary task of this liaison group "was not about reforming the military as was assumed. It was more a question of to what degree the existing leadership organs, troops, and fleets should be reduced immediately, or reformed and included in the Bundeswehr." They saw their task as laying the basis for the dissolution of the NVA and its incorporation into the Bundeswehr.

Kommando-Ost Is Created

On August 14, Stoltenberg informed Lt. Gen. Jörg Schönbohm that he would be taking over as commander of Kommando-Ost, as the new German command structure in the former GDR was to be called. Schönbohm had been serving as chief of the Bundeswehr's Planning Staff and was scheduled to become commanding general of III Corps in Koblenz. From Stoltenberg's standpoint, however, the highly capable and politically sensitive Schönbohm was needed more in the former GDR, where there was a serious danger that the NVA could completely disintegrate, than at the command for which he had been scheduled.[4] The East Germans were informed of Schönbohm's appointment on September 20 in a meeting in Bonn between Werner Ablaß, Stoltenberg, and Schönbohm.[5]

It was at this point, after considerable discussion, that Stoltenberg laid out the basic rules that were to guide the transition process. Bonn's senior military officers agreed that because the NVA had been an instrument of the SED, it would cease to exist after the two countries were united. Beginning September 1, all NVA conscripts undergoing basic training would be trained by Bundeswehr personnel in accordance with its precepts. On October 3, former NVA members would become part of the Bundeswehr, subject to the FRG's constitution and expected to follow the provisions of the Bundeswehr's policy of *innere Führung*. On that date the Bundeswehr would take over command responsibility for all equipment that formerly belonged to the NVA.[6] Each NVA unit would be reconstituted with both Bundeswehr and NVA personnel.

Finally, starting October 15, all forces in the former GDR would come under Kommando-Ost. Kommando-Ost, consisting of two military districts (Leipzig and Neubrandenburg), would be placed directly under the command of the Ministry of Defense in the person of the general inspector of the Bundeswehr.[7] Several divisions would be created that would command six home defense brigades and four home defense regiments with their command and support elements. All of these troops would remain outside of NATO's command structure until all Soviet troops had left the former GDR.[8] Kommando-Ost would operate for a six-month transition period from October 1990 to April 1991 (though in fact it lasted until June 30, 1991, when it was replaced by the Korps and Territorial Kommando-Ost).

To implement this plan, the military decided that all key positions in the former GDR would be filled by Bundeswehr officers.[9] There was to be no doubt who was in charge. One senior West German officer who was directly involved in the transition process said, "We want complete responsibility, we are not here as advisors, but as leaders. That goes not only for commanders, but for staff officers as well."[10]

A special working relationship was created between the East German divisions and their West German counterparts to provide support for the NVA units as they went through the transition process. In addition, at a meeting on September 12, the Bundeswehr set up a procedure to select Bundeswehr personnel who would serve in the former GDR during this transitional period. Toward this end, Stoltenberg called for volunteers. Many of those selected were sent east on very short notice—one officer noted that he had only a week's warning.[11]

Bundeswehr personnel arrived in the GDR on September 17 to prepare for their upcoming task. A week later Bonn again made it clear to these men that their job was not to "integrate" the NVA into the Bundeswehr; rather, it was to dismantle the NVA. The task was urgent. When the NVA personnel were added to the Bundeswehr's on October 3, the size of the Bundeswehr would rise to about 590,000 soldiers. In order for the Germans to be able to meet the criteria outlined in the agreement Kohl concluded with Gorbachev, it would have to be reduced to 370,000 soldiers by December 31, 1994.[12]

Schönbohm laid out in his memoirs what he saw as his major tasks at that time:

> In short it consisted of taking over the NVA, to guarantee its security and control, to dissolve troop units platoon by platoon, to release the overwhelming majority of soldiers, to concentrate the mass of material, weapons and munitions, to build new units of the Bundeswehr and to work together with Soviet troops in order to facilitate their withdrawal.

In the meantime, Schönbohm's greatest problem was to prevent chaos. The NVA had almost collapsed, and the West Germans were worried that unless the East German military had a better "sense of clarity for their future . . . , Kommando-Ost would face very serious problems."[13] In addition, the Bundeswehr was concerned not only that some of the soldiers themselves might do something stupid, but that some of the radical left-wing groups in the former GDR might move to seize NVA weapons.

One West German participant outlined his priorities:

> First, we were to replace all commanders of major formations from the brigade level up with officers from West Germany. Next, we were to re-

place commanders of medium-sized units [regiments and battalions] that were to be retained as part of the Bundeswehr. Third, we were to provide West German officer advisers to those ex-NVA units which were being disbanded.[14]

Structurally, Kommando-Ost would have a combined staff of 240 officers and NCOs from the West and 360 from the former NVA. By the time he reported to Strausberg in October, Schönbohm's command contained some 93,000 former members of the NVA as well as 1,300 Bundeswehr soldiers active at all levels in the transition process.[15] Kommando-Ost's primary task was "to transform the militaries in unified Germany into a new structure." It was also responsible for safeguarding equipment and munitions from the NVA, the border troops, the Stasi, and the Kampfgruppen. Furthermore, Kommando-Ost was in charge of training the 15,000 conscripts who had been called to the colors on September 1, as well as the retraining of NCOs and company/platoon commanders (estimated at between 15,000 and 17,000) for the following year). Kommando-Ost was also charged with providing support for Soviet forces during their troop withdrawal.[16]

It is hard to overstate just how daunting was the task facing Kommando-Ost. Not only did it have to develop a new infrastructure to replace the one possessed by the NVA (one which had almost nothing in common with the West German system), but painful personnel reductions had to be carried out, facilities had to be rebuilt according to much higher West German standards, environmental damage at many NVA facilities (not to mention the problems at former Soviet bases) had to be overcome, and a massive amount of equipment and munitions had to be guarded as well as disposed of. At the same time, Schönbohm and his colleagues had to find a way to reach out to the former NVA professionals, most of whom not only felt they had been betrayed, but initially were very suspicious of the "Wessis."[17]

To facilitate the work of Kommando-Ost, Stoltenberg appointed Ablaß to be the head of a field office of the Bundeswehr's Regional Administration Office,[18] but only for the transition period. During that time the primary function of his three-hundred-member office was to assist the Bundeswehr leadership in understanding local conditions and needs. In addition, this office served as a liaison bureau for local officials in the former GDR.

Ablaß's assignment to this coveted position convinced many NVA officers that they had been right all along that he had been currying favor with West German military officials at their expense. A West German officer's comment that Ablaß had been appointed because he had proven himself to be "a discreet and competent conversation partner," served only to strengthen the belief by many NVA professionals that in dealing with representatives from Bonn, Albaß had put his own interests ahead of those of members of the NVA.[19]

Another problem was uniforms. What kind should the former NVA soldiers wear? Obviously, they could not expect to become part of the Bundeswehr dressed in their old NVA gear. Acutely sensitive to the psychological aspects of the unification process, Schönbohm persuaded Stoltenberg to use the NATO olive-green uniform. These uniforms were available in the necessary numbers and sizes and would be sufficient to outfit troops from both the West and the East. Indeed, Schönbohm underlined the importance of this decision when he said, "It was of decisive psychological importance that soldiers in a *single* German army should wear the same uniform."[20]

How to Handle Former NVA Personnel?

Successful militaries the world over have certain characteristics in common. One of the most important is a willingness to carry out orders once a political decision has been made. And, make no mistake, the decision to incorporate former members of the NVA into the Bundeswehr was not a military decision. From a military standpoint, it made no sense as the Bundeswehr was being reduced and many career officers and NCOs were being forced to leave. If anything, taking former NVA personnel into the Bundeswehr could hurt morale.

In spite of their personal feelings, however, once the federal government made a decision to include former NVA members in the Bundeswehr, the country's military leaders quickly fell into line. For example, despite his earlier opposition, Stoltenberg worked to facilitate the process. On October 3, he issued an order to Bundeswehr personnel that stated, "We want to give as many of them as fair a chance as possible, to test their suitability for the soldierly profession or as a civilian employee."[21] At the same time, in order to bolster morale among those who had been members of the Bundeswehr prior to October 3, Stoltenberg stated on November 12 that no career soldier in the Bundeswehr (as of 30 September) would be forced to retire.[22]

Bonn decided that all former NVA soldiers over fifty would be given early retirement. As a pension they would receive two-thirds of the salary they had been receiving as NVA officers. The exact amount depended on the individual's age. All such officers would have to leave the armed forces by December 31, 1990.

Altogether, approximately 50,000 members of the NVA would join the Bundeswehr (including 25,000 short-term regular and professional soldiers). In order to bring some order into the process of incorporating former NVA professionals into the Bundeswehr, Bonn divided them into a number of categories. The first were the conscripts. They immediately became full-fledged members of the Bundeswehr, receiving the same pay as their Western counterparts.

The second category was the short-term regular and professional soldiers. These individuals were further divided into a number of subcategories. The first subcategory included those who would serve for an additional undefined period (the *Weiterverwender*). They would remain in their current positions, receive a temporary rank, and be paid at a rate to be decided by the Bundeswehr until the latter determined it no longer needed their services. The second subcategory consisted of those who were in "reserve" (*Wartestand*)—individuals for whom there was no position currently available. They would receive 70 percent of their former pay on a temporary basis and would be released at the end of six months, if not before. The next group consisted of short-term regular soldiers (*Soldaten auf Zeit*) who would serve for two years on contract with a rank in accordance with Bundeswehr regulations.

The third and final category consisted of short-term regular soldiers and professional soldiers who would serve more than two years and have the opportunity to become professional soldiers. Such assignments would be made based on the needs of the service as well as on the capabilities of the individuals concerned. Decisions on officers would be made only after they had passed an examination by an independent committee concerning their suitability (a process very much like that which was used in the Bundeswehr to determine the suitability of former Wehrmacht officers for service in the West German military when it was first established).[23]

According to a Bundeswehr officer who was directly involved in the absorption process, in practice, Bonn divided former NVA personnel into three categories. First, there were those individuals the West Germans wanted to leave the military within three months (i.e., by December 31). They were promised a lump-sum gratuity of between 5,000 and 7,000 deutsche marks based on their rank and service. The second category included officers whose services the Bundeswehr needed until most of the units to be disbanded had been dissolved. Finally, there were those who would be offered the chance to stay for a longer period.[24]

Any individuals from the third group who wanted to serve for an additional two years and then become a professional soldier had from October 1 to December 15 to apply. Original plans called for accepting up to 20,000 professional and short-term regular soldiers, who would be offered a two-year contract. During that time they would go through a "testing period," one which would both give the soldier an idea of what life in the Bundeswehr was like as well as provide Bundeswehr officials with an idea of his suitability for long-term service. As one observer noted:

> On the one hand it gives the NVA soldier the possibility to consider thoroughly the finality of his decision [further service or a release from duty] and on the other hand, it gives superiors and the personnel leadership, who are running this test, time for evaluating a soldier who was socialized in another system and in another army.[25]

Once the evaluation was complete, individuals could be accepted for conversion to regular Bundeswehr officers at any time during this two-year period. After two years of service all differences between officers from the former NVA and those from the Bundeswehr would disappear.

The rank former NVA officers would be assigned in the Bundeswehr was a question that would be decided by the West Germans. As the relevant document noted, "The Federal Minister of Defense determines which rank they may temporarily hold. He will take into account their conduct, training, length of service, career path, and function within the NVA and will place them in an appropriate rank in the Bundeswehr." Furthermore, it was made clear that professional or short-term regular soldiers *would* be released for a number of reasons: if they requested it, when their term of service ended, if they had violated human rights or the law, or if they had worked for the Stasi. Such individuals *could* be released: if a professional soldier had served the minimal required time, if they lacked technical qualifications or personal aptitude, if they were not needed, or if their position was eliminated.[26]

Schönbohm and his colleagues faced a very difficult personnel situation. They needed former NVA soldiers—the number of Bundeswehr troops allocated to Kommando-Ost were not sufficient to man the units they were taking over. To quote one Bundeswehr officer who was sent to the East to reorganize an artillery division:

> My main problem was manpower, or rather the lack of it. In all, I had more than 120 officers, 100 NCOs, 400 soldiers, and 100 civilians. My mission—to reorganize and transition the ex-NVA artillery organization into a Bundeswehr division artillery—could not be accomplished by myself. In addition to the ex-NVA manpower already mentioned, I had a team of West German officers: three lieutenant colonels, all of whom had already been artillery battalion commanders; one major; three captains; and one lieutenant. I also had two teams, each consisting of a captain and two warrant officers, who were responsible for basic training.[27]

In November, Stoltenberg stated that he would need more than the 50,000-man limit imposed by the Bundestag's Budgetary Committee on October 24, just to guard the munitions and weapons depots in East Germany.[28]

In spite of the Bundeswehr's need for the services of these men, there was no way Hisso von Selle or any other Bundeswehr officer could promise them that if they stayed their future would be guaranteed. Only a very few would eventually be taken into the Bundeswehr on a permanent basis. Indeed, while an individual could apply to become a temporary soldier for two years, they first had to be accepted by the Bundeswehr. Further service beyond the two years would only be decided later by West German authorities. Schönbohm was in a quandary. As he said, "We needed the help of officers and NCOs from the NVA, but we couldn't deny that over the long haul we could only take a limited number of them into the Bundeswehr."[29]

During this transition period, a number of former NVA personnel had begun to ask themselves why they should hang around. Indeed, one could only wonder at the logic of those in Bonn who set up this arrangement. Soldiers who waited around for six months got nothing when they were released while those who left early received a hefty gratuity!

Former NVA Members Respond

Hoffmann was embittered by the whole process as October 3 approached. Bonn had spoken about equality, but this was far from the reality. "There was no longer even a hint of equal partnership, also no reference to the right of former NVA members or institutions to have a say. All decisions were in the hands of the minister of defense and his deputies."[30] While one could understand Hoffmann's bitterness—which was shared by many other NVA officers—the fact was that the East Germans and their political system had lost. Why should the Bundeswehr permit former NVA officers or the now-defunct Ministry of Disarmament and Defense to have a say on such a touchy subject? Given their former loyal service to the hated SED state, they were lucky that they were being given a chance at all to serve in the Bundeswehr.

Within the NVA, morale was continuing to sink. On September 13, for example, Eppelmann went out of his way to deny reports that 60–80 percent of professional soldiers had resigned. But at the same time, he admitted that if the current wave of resignations were to continue, those percentages could be reached by the end of the month.[31] The reasons were not hard to find. Despite reports that the West Germans would take a number of NVA officers into the Bundeswehr, the average officer and NCO knew only too well that this was problematical. Not only had they been betrayed by their own political leadership and the Russians, they now faced the prospect of trying to join a military that had given them every reason to believe they were unwanted.

Former NVA soldiers faced a crisis. The realization that they would be thrown out on the street with little or nothing to do at a time of high unemployment was a sobering prospect. A former NVA naval officer serving in the Bundeswehr toward the end of November captured the precariousness and dangerous nature of the situation when he observed, "Soldiers may not stand on the streets because they know where the weapons and munitions are currently stored. I have a stomachache releasing soldiers and officers here in Rostock with an unemployment rate of 30 percent. They have to be employed, regardless of where."[32]

For his part, Schönbohm was fully aware of the problem and was earnest in his efforts to resolve it. As he wrote, "Those soldiers who were forced to leave the armed forces, to the degree possible, should be given the opportunity to improve their transition to civilian life through career training programs.[33]

Bonn continued to make it clear to its personnel that it would not countenance any attempt on the part of its personnel to treat former NVA officers as second-class citizens. On September 24, the general inspector issued an order that stated:

> In accordance with the principles of the Unity Law from the day of unification we are all soldiers of the Bundeswehr. I expect the duty of comradeship to be taken seriously. Our different backgrounds [*werdegänge*] and differences of opinion cannot be permitted to endanger the unification process. There may not be any sweeping judgements or prejudices. Radical forms of speech and behavior by individuals cannot be justified. . . . We can only bring about reorganization and change together.[34]

Defense Minister Stoltenberg reiterated this point in a speech in early October when he promised that there would not be Bundeswehr soldiers of "first and second class." And he assured his listeners that the differences in pay scales would disappear after the transition period.[35] Schönbohm would repeat this message over and over throughout his tenure as commander of Kommando-Ost. He called for patience, "above all, understanding for the former soldiers of the NVA, who are under tremendous psychological pressure."[36] He never tired of pointing out that former NVA soldiers—many of whom had lived for forty years under a communist dictatorship—"have the right to make a mistake."[37]

Operationalizing this lofty sentiment would not be easy, however. It would require important concessions on the part of both sets of officers. It would also necessitate considerable understanding and patience as the East Germans became members of a democratic armed forces at a time when they still harbored deep suspicions toward their new colleagues. They would have to perform their duties in an exemplary fashion while learning to live in a new and confusing environment.

From the standpoint of the former NVA officers, no better person could have been chosen to carry out this difficult task than Jörg Schönbohm. Despite his earlier expressions of dislike, even disdain, for what the NVA represented, once he had been given the task of incorporating former members of the NVA into the Bundeswehr, he devoted all of his efforts to ensuring that they were given a fair chance. He worked hard to make certain that their living conditions (which were abysmal) improved, while at the same time standing up to those in Bonn who wanted little or nothing to do with former NVA personnel. Indeed, if it had not been for Schönbohm, the world these officers and NCOs entered on October 3 would have looked looked much bleaker and developed quite differently.

One of Schönbohm's first actions as the head of Kommando-Ost was to visit as much of the former GDR as possible. He was determined to change the public attitude that had been fostered by many years of life with the NVA and the Soviet armed forces. Both the East German and Soviet militaries were shut off from civilians. Military personnel kept to themselves and there was minimal contact between the two societies. Schönbohm was out to change all of this. He—and his fellow officers—visited every town and spoke to every civic leader they could find. He wanted to convince the East German populace that the Bundeswehr was different from the NVA they had known.

He had some successes. For example, on October 19 Schönbohm arranged for the oath taken by new recruits to take place in the center of the small town of Bad Salzungen. A few thousand people attended. Schönbohm invited an Evangelical pastor to be present on the platform while the ceremony took place, but the pastor declined his invitation, refusing to be part of a military "spectacular." Yet after the ceremony, the pastor told Schönbohm that the ceremony was conducted much differently than he had anticipated. Perhaps, he said, everyone should be more flexible in dealing with each other. According to Schönbohm, "For me, that was an encouraging experience."[38]

The Spoils: Equipment and Munitions

Few Westerners—even Warsaw Pact specialists—realized the extent of the vast stores of equipment and munitions the GDR possessed prior to unification. The liaison teams sent to the GDR soon discovered that the NVA had more firepower than the entire Bundeswehr, even though the latter was four times as large. This included almost 300,000 tons of munitions. The Bundeswehr inherited 2,272 tanks, 7,831 armored vehicles, and 2,460 artillery pieces. In addition, the air force had about four hundred planes and the navy around sixty ships. Finally, the Bundeswehr became the proud owner of an additional 1.2 million hand weapons and around 100,000 motor vehicles.[39]

What was even more impressive was the way in which this equipment was maintained. It received far better care than the military personnel who serviced it. For example, while there were problems with the heating system in barracks, the equipment was kept in well-heated halls. As one article described, "In the NVA, technology and weapons were taken care of in a first-class manner: however, people played no role."[40] Schönbohm's most immediate task was to find a way to guard this massive acquisition.

The problems it would face in trying to guard NVA equipment should not have come as a complete surprise to the Bundeswehr. NVA officers had warned several weeks earlier that in view of disciplinary problems they couldn't guarantee that weapons dumps were being guarded. Indeed, they spoke of increased thefts.[41] Bundeswehr officers assigned to the former GDR themselves reported that "often munitions were not only in bunkers, but since they were filled to capacity, munitions were stored in the open." In addition, electricity often was turned off to the high voltage wires surrounding the bunkers, requiring the assignment of greater numbers of soldiers to guard them. The guard rooms were also in horrible condition.[42]

It was soon discovered that securing these munitions would take far more men than anyone expected. One source reported that the Bundeswehr had estimated that 11,000 soldiers were needed just to guard munitions.[43] From a morale standpoint this made a bad situation worse. Conscripts in the former GDR were spending 40 percent of their time on guard duty, in contrast to the West where a conscript spent only 5 percent of his time in the same fashion. In fact, the situation was so bad, according to Schönbohm, that officers through the rank of captain were being assigned to watch duty, and even staff officers found their names on the watch lists.[44] The situation would worsen. General Werner von Schewen tells of news he received at Christmas that warned that all of the qualified officers who were guarding the munition and fuel dumps would leave the Bundeswehr by the end of the year![45] Needless to say, there was a mad scramble to find enough Bundeswehr officers in the West to fill the gap.

The problems facing the Bundeswehr were made more difficult because the munitions were unstable and made for weapons that were not in the FRG's inventory. Schönbohm wryly commented that "For the first time in my life as a soldier, I have too much ammunition."[46] Unfortunately, not only could he not use most of it, but given the limits placed on Germany by Conventional Force Agreement limitations, Bonn had to find a way to eliminate a lot of it.

The East Germans had recognized the problem early on and had tried to give some of their weapons and munitions back to the Soviets. Faced with their own problems of weapons disposal, however, the Russians had refused to accept them. The NVA then made an effort to cut back on the size of its inventory by donating some equipment to the Third World. On September 1, the Ministry of Disarmament and Defense reported that the GDR had given sixty-five heavy trucks, trailers, smaller trucks, and water tank trucks, as well as camp kitchens and mobile homes, to Ethiopia, Angola, and Mozambique.[47] However, in view of the amount of equipment on hand, such actions represented a drop in the bucket.

Bonn managed to get rid of some of the NVA's equipment by passing it on to the United States for use during the Gulf War in 1991. Most of this material consisted of trucks, water tanks, generators, engineering equipment, and chemical and biological warfare protective equipment. Altogether it was worth some $1.2 billion.[48]

The Bundeswehr also had to determine what if any kinds of weapons it wanted to keep. To help it decide, Bonn set up criteria: There had to be a need for the equipment, it must be in good technical and working condition, it must fit into the Bundeswehr's structural needs, resupply must not be a problem, it must meet Bundeswehr specifications, and using it must make some sense.[49]

One of the few weapons systems that the Bundeswehr decided to put into its inventory, if only on a temporary basis, was a squadron of twenty-four MiG-29s. The planes used more fuel than their Western equivalents, but the opportunity to obtain world-class aircraft, together with the pilots and technicians to fly them and keep them in the air, was too good to pass up.

Bonn decided to sell, give away, or destroy the thousands of tanks, helicopters, ships, and other equipment from the NVA. Transportation and armored personnel vehicles were sold to Sweden. Berlin gave armored personnel carriers to Pakistani peacekeepers in the former Yugoslavia and gave other combat vehicles to Kazakhstan, Kyrgyzstan, and Mongolia. Bonn also supplied a considerable amount of equipment to relief agencies. According to one report, "In reply to 13,000 requests, some 7,000 well-mounted vehicles of all kinds, 3,000 trailers, a considerable amount of firefighting and disaster equipment, and 19 million pieces of clothing" were given to relief agencies.[50] Meantime, civilian contractors were employed to destroy what was left—the bulk of the equipment. By 1995, the process of getting rid of East German military equipment was nearly complete.

The NVA Professionals' Background

Before discussing in detail the problems encountered by former NVA professionals in their bids to become regular Bundeswehr officers and NCOs, it is important to understand their mindset—by comparing their backgrounds with those of their new Bundeswehr colleagues. To begin with, it is worth emphasizing that the former NVA officers had been the sworn enemies of the Bundeswehr. As one former NVA air force officer put it, "Only a year and a half ago, I had Bundeswehr personnel in my radar sights. Now they're inviting us over."[51]

In this sense, former NVA officers and their Bundeswehr colleagues had a similar background: Both had been taught to view the others as potential enemies. There was an important difference, however, between the two. The former NVA professionals were being asked not only to join, but actively to support, a system they had sworn to oppose for their entire service lives. Many Bundeswehr officers were fully aware that this placed the NVA professionals in a difficult situation. As one West German NCO remarked, "How lucky I am to be standing on the right side."[52]

Most NVA officers claimed that although the party leadership did not "succeed in creating a genuine hatred [Feindbild] toward the soldiers of the Bundeswehr," they would have been prepared to do their duty if called upon. "I did not know from whence the enemy would come, but if he were to cross our border, then he would be my enemy. That concept was clear."[53] At the same time, the predominant emotion was one of jealousy—the Wessis had everything, while the NVA officer had lived in a world of need for many years.

It is important to keep in mind that NVA personnel were far more isolated from everyday life than were their Bundeswehr colleagues.

> One lived mostly in residential areas especially built for NVA members. Contacts with the civilian populace were limited, one discovers in many places a state within a state. The press and public relations limited themselves to nice official statements.[54]

Not only was hatred of the West—and the FRG in particular—pounded into their heads on an almost daily basis, they were barred from watching Western TV or listening to Western radio. They also were not permitted to have contacts with individuals from the West or even to possess Western currency. This does not mean that some did not "sneak" a listen to forbidden sources of information, or that they would run out of their apartment when a relative from the FRG came to visit. But a career military officer had much to lose. "The risk that one accepted in order to be better informed was not worth it to the officers."

Everything in an officer's life was directed toward the Soviet Union—his advanced education, his tactics, his strategy, and his force structure. In short, there was a minimal amount of information available that would permit him to develop ideas in opposition to those advocated by party leadership. In fact, one source claimed that NVA officers were politically worse-informed than the civilian population, and on many occasions "even less aware of what was going on in the outside world than those civilians who lived in the same apartment house." Even trying to learn English could lead to unpleasant questions. Why does the officer want to go that route? Is he planning to defect?[55]

The severe military obligations placed on an NVA officer further increased his isolation. Combat readiness was much higher in the NVA than it was in any Western military—including the Bundeswehr. To give the reader some idea of just how prepared the NVA was for combat, consider that the NVA had eleven motorized divisions, six active and five in reserve—all could be in the field and ready to go within two to three days.[56] As far as the navy was concerned, all ships had to be able to be under way within sixty minutes and half of them were on constant alert.[57]

According to a former East German officer, an active division, "had to be ready to have 85 percent of its personnel and materiel fully combat-ready and to be able to leave its base in forty-five minutes, regardless of whether it was a weekday or a weekend or over Christmas or over Easter."[58] By contrast, the largest contingent the Bundeswehr ever had on alert (in the 1960s) was 30 percent of its troops.[59] Indeed, one of the biggest contrasts between the East German and West German military systems was the different way each handled duty at Christmas. During the holidays, 85 percent of Bundeswehr soldiers were on leave at home, while 85 percent of NVA personnel were in their barracks.

On the average, this meant that NVA officers put in more than sixty hours a week—and in some cases more than seventy-two.[60] The normal workday lasted at least ten to eleven hours, often longer. The crippling hours worked by NVA officers meant that time with their families was very limited. For most, a Sunday afternoon free after 2 p.m. was the most that could be expected.[61] For the average soldier the situation was even worse:

> He had permission to leave the base once per week. A third of the air defense forces were in a constant state of combat readiness. The units of the air force had to be ready to leave their base with completely loaded weapons systems and support equipment within two hours.[62]

In short, the NVA was an "Army for war—a war machine. While in the Bundeswehr the individual occupied center stage, in the NVA everything was sacrificed for combat readiness."[63] There were at least two reasons behind this high level of combat readiness. First, from a political standpoint, it helped prove to the Russians that the NVA was an indispensable ally in the event of war, because no other East European military force could have reacted so fast with such a formidable military force during a crisis. Hans Peter von Kirchbach, who commanded a former NVA division after October 3, confirmed that the division he took over could be under way in less than sixty minutes. He also noted the presence of a Soviet alarm system right in the East German unit, which placed this unit under the direct control of the Kremlin in the event of a crisis.[64] The GDR's military prowess, combined with its economic strength (when measured against other East European states), was aimed at persuading the Russians not to make a deal with Bonn at the expense of East Berlin.

The second goal of the high level of combat readiness was to keep officers from having time to think about political questions, while at the same time convincing the rank and file of the danger presented by the imperialistic West. From a political standpoint this meant that "all of our thoughts and actions were measured by combat readiness and combat capability." In short, there was no time to worry about political issues except at higher levels or on a military staff. The same was true of ethical questions. "We had no time to think about things such as a soldier's truth or career ethics."[65] Duty came first. After all, the NVA would not be in such a high state of alert if it were not being threatened by NATO and the FRG. Unfortunately, from the party's position, "these arguments stood on weak feet and on occasion were really primitive."[66]

The NVA's very high level of combat readiness began to slip beginning in 1986 with the increasing use of NVA troops in the civilian economy. Nevertheless, the important point was that the vast majority of officers (certainly those at the level of an army captain or above) had spent most of their lives living under these extreme conditions. Indeed, some would find it difficult to adjust to the much more lax life of a soldier in the Bundeswehr.

The NVA was one of the most politicized militaries in the entire Warsaw Pact, but it would oversimplify matters to assume that the average NVA officer was only "a loyal instrument of the communist dictatorship."[67] While some joined for ideological reasons, many young men became members of the NVA because they were enamored of the technology, the chance for adventure, or the opportunity to improve their standard of living. The party was always present, but it was not the all-consuming organization that many in the West believed it to be. Listening to former NVA officers, one gets the impression that when they first joined, party membership (required of almost all officers and NCOs) was passive. As one moved through the ranks, the individual learned that there was no separation between military service and party membership. There was a tendency to assume that the party was right, probably because that was the only view of reality these very busy, overworked officers encountered.

At a basic level, the average NVA officer seems to have developed a belief in the rightness of socialism, a commitment to a system that he believed was actively working for peace in Europe. To quote one NVA officer, "To be a good soldier one had to be a good socialist." At the same time, the SED's ideology did not infiltrate every aspect of an NVA officer's life. To be sure, there was the occasional "hundred percenter," an "SED party functionary in uniform," but as one West German observer said, "I never encountered conviction in the sense of the 'real existing socialism,' rather the belief that socialism was better than capitalism and that the NVA had contributed to peace through its contribution to the balance of forces."[68] For practical purposes this meant that the NVA officer was trained to go along with the general goals as outlined by the party. He was a party soldier in the sense that he accepted the party's general guidelines, not because he was a fanatic communist. The longer he served, the more he accepted the party's presence as a fact of life; something that was as much a part of military life as cleaning a rifle.

Whatever his level of submission to communist ideology, every individual was subject to party discipline. One East German officer who participated in a number the events of 1989–90 at a very high level accurately observed that the reason that NVA officers did not react creatively when the situation began to change prior to unification was "found in the policy of the SED which, when it did not suppress independent thinking, still channelized it and offensively fought critical thinking."[69]

Anything that might create a sense of ideological pluralism, that might shift a soldier's psychological allegiance to anything outside of this narrow party-military environment, was strongly discouraged. The SED's efforts to isolate the NVA officer from external influences has already been discussed. These efforts extended to what the party considered "unhealthy" internal factors.

Religion serves as a good example. The party leadership made it clear that such ideas "stopped at the door of a military facility."[70] Less than 10 percent of NVA officers were baptized. In addition, the party apparatus carried out a very aggressive campaign against religious membership of any kind. No NVA officer could openly proclaim his allegiance to a religious community. If he did, he ran the risk of having his military career cut short. Indeed, the civilian population often viewed the military as a hotbed of antireligious feeling. This strong sense of mistrust created very serious problems for Schönbohm and Kommando-Ost. When the Bundeswehr first arrived in the East, many clergy and believers in the former GDR saw very little difference between the NVA and the Bundeswehr when it came to hostility toward religion.

Another factor that served to isolate NVA personnel from their surrounding environment was the all-pervasive sense of secrecy. Everything within the NVA was secret—civilians often knew very little of what was happening in the military.

Life within the military was strictly regulated by the "need to know" philosophy. Information was highly compartmentalized; if a soldier did not require information to do his job, it would be withheld from him. Naval officers knew nothing about ground force capabilities, and even officers who were part of the ground forces had very limited knowledge when it came to a unit's operational plans. NVA officers were not trained to ask questions. In fact, asking for information you might not be authorized to see could get you into serious trouble. Better to keep your mouth shut and mind your own business.

As a result, discussions—especially political discussions—were more limited than in some other communist militaries. They were so atomized that the idea of discussing politics with fellow officers almost never arose. This was part of the reason according to one study conducted in the GDR, in contrast to the armed forces of Poland and Hungary, military reform never really took hold in the NVA. "Forces from the SED willing to consider reform were neither conceptually nor organizationally able to negotiate, to formulate the further development in the GDR of a politically relevant reform wing."[71] It seemed as if the majority of NVA officers were locked in a state of political unconsciousness. They were used to others doing their thinking for them.

Leadership Style

Another major difference between the NVA and the Bundeswehr was the relationship between superiors and subordinates. In the NVA, superiors were not approachable. When it came to dealing with senior officers—or officers at all, for the enlisted—"discussions with officers were a one-sided affair. Personal opinion was not a matter for debate."[72]

Schönbohm ran into this sense of isolation in speaking to a number of former NVA officers. His open, easygoing, approachable style was a surprise to them. As he recounted the situation, "One of the officers said to me, 'I have been an officer for 18 years. The fact that I can talk so freely with a general is for me completely new.' "[73] This sense of isolation on the part of senior officers was a reflection of their different approach for dealing with subordinates.

Not only were NVA officers less approachable than their West German counterparts, they were also more numerous and carried out different functions. In the NVA, the ratio of officers to enlisted personnel was 1:8; in the Bundeswehr, the ratio was 1:40.[74] As von Kirchbach described it, "In a division staff of the NVA, which controlled about 10,000 men, there were more officers than in a corps staff of the Bundeswehr which was in charge of 70,000 men."[75]

The ratio of NCOs to enlisted personnel in the NVA was 1:1; in the Bundeswehr, it was 1:3. Thus the NVA was immensely top-heavy. One observer estimated that 50 percent of NVA officers were performing tasks NCOs did in the Bundeswehr.[76] In fact, the NVA had nothing approaching the NCO arrangement within the Bundeswehr. The Bundeswehr delegated authority, the NVA did not. As a result, junior personnel in the NVA did not assume leadership responsibility. As another observer noted, "With the exception of warrant officers and senior NCOs, who had served for a long time, both in their own eyes as well as in the eyes of the officers they were a special kind of 'senior soldiers'—they took on command and leadership positions only in exceptional circumstances."[77] By contrast, NCOs in the Bundeswehr were well known for their independence and self-confidence, traits that were severely lacking in the NVA. The Bundeswehr thus needed to create an NCO corps within the former NVA units.

The top-heavy nature of the NVA officer corps led to a much faster promotion rate than in the Bundeswehr. Therefore it was necessary for the Bundeswehr to equalize the officer rank structure between the two military forces.

Another area of considerable difference between the NVA and the Bundeswehr was discipline. In the NVA, the catchword was "blind obedience"; it was part of the oath taken by every NVA soldier. As

Gen. Ulrich de Maiziere, the former inspector general of the Bundeswehr, noted, "The oath left no room for a conscience"—a sharp contrast with the Bundeswehr, where "conscience stood above an order."[78]

In general, life in the NVA was considerably more brutal than that
in the Bundeswehr. Von Kirchbach told a story of a civilian who had
come into his office after he had taken command in Eggesin. The man
said he had been shoveling snow when two NVA officers approached.
Because he was wearing an NVA jacket, they mistook him for an NVA
soldier. The two officers beat him so badly that he was hospitalized
with serious injuries. Von Kirchbach investigated the matter, and confirmed the man's story. The NVA officers thought the man was a soldier intentionally missing from a returning formation.[79] A Bundeswehr
officer caught hitting a soldier in such a manner would have been dismissed from the service.

Life in the NVA also was characterized by a sense of dual morality,
an officially accepted one versus a private, individual morality. Apply-
ing the rules of private conscience to public life could be dangerous to
one's career. For example, everyone realized that the five-year plan was
a joke. Statistics were notoriously inaccurate and no one seriously believed them. Nevertheless, the individual officer had no choice but to
parrot the official party line. If the party lecture, which soldiers had to
attend, said that the GDR was ahead of the FRG in a particular area,
the fact that such data were inaccurate was irrelevant. After all, the
idea of a free press was completely unknown. "In this climate, opportunistic personalities were created, which made it very difficult to build
genuine comradely relationships."[80] If an individual did not play the
game correctly, he had to deal with the possibility that his "incorrect"
ideas would be reported to the so-called "Abteilung 2000," populated
by Stasi officers. Over the long run, it was the officers who were best
at deception who were often most successful in their careers.

Another result of this aloof leadership style in the NVA was the ha-
rassment of junior conscripts by more senior ones. Called *dedovshchina*
in the Russian military, this process was a way of helping officers maintain discipline. More senior conscripts kept their juniors in line with
threats, promises, and intimidation. This permitted officers to remain
above the fray. After all, the junior conscripts could always take com-
fort in the fact that they would eventually be senior conscripts and
perpetuate the cycle. One former East German officer described the
dynamics: "In units filled with conscripts of varying service years,
there was always discrimination and repression of the more junior
ones. Neither discussions nor punishment helped. We were never able
to deal correctly with this problem."[81] Indeed, the whole idea of law as
it was understood in the West was completely foreign to the NVA. Law

was for maintaining order and ensuring that the party/government's wishes were carried out. "There were no legal principles which gave the member of the military any . . . political, social, cultural or juridical rights vis-à-vis the state."[82]

From a military standpoint, the NVA's leadership style also was harmful because it stifled initiative. Since leaders did not trust the rank and file, everything was determined from above. As a former NVA officer complained, "The real absurdity came about because the same command authorities who drew up the littlest detail constantly demanded that all tasks be carried out creatively and with initiative."[83] The NVA leadership—like their Soviet colleagues—never understood that micromanagement destroys initiative. Criticism was tolerated, but only to the degree that the facts and opinions were in agreement with the prevailing point of view.[84]

Creature Comforts

Another significant difference between the NVA and the Bundeswehr was living conditions. Given the brutal hours worked by NVA personnel, one might have expected officers to go to great lengths to ensure that their people were treated properly. This certainly has been the approach taken in most Western militaries. In fact, however, the living conditions afforded enlisted NVA personnel were horrible. These were conscripts (as opposed to professional soldiers) about whom no one seemed to care.

According to one report, a typical barracks had only eight showers for more than two thousand men![85] The bathrooms and the toilets were antiques—at the level of 1936 technology.[86] Schönbohm noted, "We had to close all of the 141 kitchens"—they were all far below Western standards.[87]

Von Kirchbach's description of the NVA's barracks was especially graphic. "The rooms, washrooms, toilettes are almost all completely in disrepair. They stink horribly. In spite of sometimes recognizable efforts to improve the situation with the means on hand, in general, total structural and technical neglect is visible."[88] Other observers came to the same conclusions. "The living standards for soldiers were even worse. They had to be content with extremely old furniture, filthy washrooms and toilets and showers. There was a central shower building in the barracks, but it was closed for hygienic reasons and because the building was unsafe."[89]

Conclusion

Whether for good or bad, former members of the NVA were now part of the Bundeswehr. For some, the relationship would be a short one. They would be leaving for lives in the civilian world at their earliest opportunity. The DM 7,000 those who left collected looked good to a lot of men who saw the money as a way to start a new life.

Others, however, would opt to stay on in the Bundeswehr; to try to continue their military careers. It would not be an easy undertaking. Not only would they have to convince the West Germans of their military expertise, but they would also be required to prove that in spite of their very different backgrounds they could and would adapt to the world of the Bundeswehr. Making this transformation would be not only difficult, it would at times be humiliating. They were competent military officers who had proven that they could function in one of the world's most demanding military environments. Now they had to admit that much of what they had learned was wrong and be prepared to learn to operate in a very different fashion. What was once right was now wrong—and vice versa.

This also would be a very trying period for the West Germans. At a time when the Bundeswehr itself was being downsized, they had to work with soldiers who had been their sworn enemies only months before. Furthermore, in spite of their years of learning to hate everything the NVA as a party army had stood for, these individuals also had to be prepared to defend their new colleagues against continued attacks from those in the Bundesrepublik who found the presence of former NVA personnel in the Bundeswehr to be an abomination. In fact, there would be occasions when Schönbohm would be locked in what seemed to an outsider to be mortal combat with the defense ministry in Bonn over how these individuals were treated.

Patience would be at a premium on the part of Bundeswehr officers serving in the East. These were the men on the front lines, the ones who would spend countless hours trying to reshape the rudiments of the NVA into Bundeswehr soldiers. They did this knowing full well that many of their new colleagues would be forced to leave the unified German military regardless of how well they performed.

October 3, 1990. Defense Minister Gerhard Stoltenberg (*Rear*), Former GDR Defense Minister Eppelmann (*Front*), and Bundeswehr General Jörg Schönbohm as the NVA became part of the Bundeswehr.
Credit: DPA

October 19, 1990. The first swearing-in ceremony of new recruits in Bad Salzungen in the former GDR.
Credit: DPA

September 9, 1990. Officers from the NVA attend a course in Fürstenfeldbruck.
Credit: DPA

September 9, 1990. East German officers attend a class put on by the Bundeswehr.
Credit: DPA

7

The NVA Professional: Making the Transition

Relearning takes time. No one can expect that former NVA soldiers will have already understood and digested everything in a couple of weeks.

General Ulrich de Maiziere

We will only have a Bundeswehr when . . . where a soldier comes from no longer plays a role.

Brigadier General Hans Peter von Kirchbach

The task facing the Bundeswehr was enormous. How could thousands of former NVA officers and NCOs be integrated into an army that was based on totally different principles than the one in which they had spent the majority of their military careers? The problem was not so much hostility to the new process (most who felt that way had left the NVA prior to unification) as it was a sense of confusion and insecurity.

The NVA Professional and the Transition

Before describing the actual steps taken by the Bundeswehr to integrate these individuals, let us take another look at the kind of military officer and NCO who entered the Bundeswehr on October 3, 1990.

Shocked and Confused

Former NVA professionals were uncertain about their future and afraid they would soon find themselves thrown out of the military into the chaotic world of unemployment, where the individual's military qualifications, which were much more specialized than those of officers in the West—would be of little value in finding a job. As General von Kirchbach, a senior West German officer who dealt with these individuals on a daily basis, said, "Everything was dominated by the question, 'What will happen to me?' 'Do I have a chance in a unified German armed forces?' "[1]

The problem was not only concern for the officers' physical well-being. It went deeper than that. Their identity was at stake. The collapse of the SED regime not only had destroyed any ideals that the NVA professionals had left, it also had created a deep sense of depression. "The collapse of the SED regime left the soldiers of the NVA not only in a crisis of identity and acceptance, but it frequently also led them into an existence crisis."[2] Many of them believed they had honestly and faithfully served the GDR and the party that led it. "The knowledge that in all these years of our soldierly existence we trusted a leadership that proved itself to be corrupt and incapable of leading and guiding this state was very painful for us."[3]

Not only was he insecure about his future, the NVA professional he was not even certain who he was. Was he nothing more than an opportunist? How could he turn his back so easily on the years he had put in the NVA? Was it all for nothing? Had it been a waste of time? Where would he find his identity in the future?

Closely coupled with this feeling of uncertainty was one of humiliation. Describing the most difficult problem he faced in joining the Bundeswehr, one former officer stated it was "changing my uniform and then being seen in public." Obviously, he did not consider this change to be a positive experience.

Furthermore, having held one of the most prestigious positions in the former GDR, some officers were now faced with the prospect of becoming manual laborers. This was a serious problem for individuals who came from a system in which "a large part of the GDR populace absolutely views the NVA with a certain degree of pride—it symbolizes German [Prussian] precision and discipline, which is expressed above all at the official parades and changes of the watch."[4]

Then there were the monetary benefits. In the old days, a company chief received a salary of 1,375 to 1,425 East German marks a month, while a colonel received about 2,600. This compared to a teacher who earned 1,300 a month or a nurse in an intensive care unit who earned just 760 per month.[5] Yet the average NVA professional did not see himself as privileged when it came to his salary. As one put it, "Any skilled worker who put in as many hours as we did would have earned the same or more in salary."[6] Nevertheless, he was envied by civilians because many of them believed that he was far better compensated than was the case.

In addition to pay, civilians believed that NVA personnel had excellent access to housing in a society where it was at a premium.[7] In fact, the military housing was more modest than most civilians realized, and often involved a long waiting period before a unit became available. Nevertheless, if he were forced to leave the Bundeswehr, a soldier would have to fight for the increasingly expensive housing on the same basis as everyone else. The former NVA officer would have to start all over again from the bottom, and there was no guarantee of success. After all, the Bundeswehr had made it clear that only a few East Germans would be taken over—thus even if an officer did follow the new approach to military affairs advocated by the Bundeswehr, there was a good possibility that he would be brushed aside. From a practical standpoint, this made many of them afraid to do anything that might lead them afoul of their new bosses. As one source recalled, "I saw how a Western sergeant cussed out a lieutenant from the NVA . . . who said nothing because he was afraid that he would be tossed out."[8]

Functioning in a Democratic Polity

Former NVA officers did not understand the rules of the new game. The idea of a democratic army, not to mention philosophical concepts such as *innere Führung* made little sense to them. The concept of "soldier's rights" sounded like the ultimate in silliness. From the NVA professional's standpoint, the military's task had always been to carry out its missions, and individual rights could be brushed aside if they got in the way. What if a few soldiers were roughed up? If that helped get the job done, then it was justified. What if soldiers did not live as well as officers in the West believed was appropriate? After all, this was the army and life was not supposed to be a bed of roses. Soldiers should learn to live with deprivation; if they ever went into combat, life would be a constant state of deprivation.

The purpose of discipline was to force a soldier to obey orders. And the officers had the authority to enforce discipline. "A company commander in the NVA could give out up to three days of arrest, and a platoon leader up to seven days restriction."[9] Why not use it?

In the NVA, an officer's ability to enforce order was less restricted by regulations or law than was the case with his counterpart in the Bundeswehr. In the Bundeswehr, penalties could only be enforced when an individual clearly violated a regulation or a law. This was not the case in the NVA, where an officer's ability to discipline a soldier was broader.[10]

In addition to discipline, NVA officers also were used to relying on premiums to inspire soldiers to better performances. In any given year, the NVA devoted about 20 million marks to rewarding outstanding performances by individuals of all ranks.[11] Each regimental commander had between 100,000 and 200,000 marks available to distribute to his troops, with complete discretion over how the money was spent. Those who performed as he wished would receive a premium, those who didn't (or whom he simply did not like) would be left out.[12] To give the reader some idea of how widespread this practice was, one officer reported that in the course of his twenty-six years of military service, he had received 53 awards; a second obtained 93 over thirty-one years, and a third received 114 during a career of thirty-four years.[13]

Clearly, a great deal of education would be necessary to integrate these individuals successfully into the Bundeswehr. Not only did they need to be trained to understand a whole new approach for dealing with subordinates, considerable effort was required to help them overcome their aversion to questioning the opinions of superiors.

Part of this hesitation to question authority came from the world of secrecy inhabited by NVA officers. One could never be sure how sensitive information was or how others in authority might respond to it. Better not to speak than to get in trouble.

To understand their thought process, it is important to remember that NVA professionals were coming from a "subject," not a "participant," political culture. They had been trained to follow orders; not to participate in decision-making. Regardless of how crazy or ridiculous an order was, their task was to carry it out, not to question it. The idea that a subordinate could or should raise his voice to suggest an alternate approach was utterly foreign to them. As a consequence, former NVA officers tended to sit back and wait to be told what to do.

The NVA officers' ability to adapt to the new world was made even more difficult by the heavy dose of politicization they had experienced over the course of their careers. In addition to carrying with them many ideas unique to a socialist political system, they were not used to the idea of political participation as Bundeswehr soldiers understood it. For NVA officers, politics meant obeying the orders of the ruling party, not thinking for themselves. This is not to suggest that they were ideological puppets or that they believed everything they were told. Rather, politics was a passive area for them. There was no need to think through difficult political questions; the party would provide them with the needed information. Adapting to an army like the

Bundeswehr, which was built on the idea of political participation, would be very difficult.

As strange as it might sound to Western ears, an East German officer, like his Soviet colleague, was less politicized—if one takes that term to mean involvement in politics—than his Western counterpart. Politicization was a control device, a mechanism that ensured that the NVA officer did not think about politics. It was aimed at ensuring that he left politics to the politicians, while the party-political apparatus ensured that he carried out orders.

Resentment toward the FRG

Regardless of the sweet-sounding comments by Stoltenberg and Schönbohm about reaching out to former NVA officers, there was still a strong feeling of resentment on the part of the Easterners. It was bad enough that had they lost; now they were being forced to accept their conquerers as mentors. Their first encounters were especially difficult. Remembered von Kirchbach, "Only a few officers could look the Wessis in the eye. Their first contact with the enemy of many years was not easy."[14]

To make matters worse, many of the former NVA professionals saw themselves as "second-class" soldiers—which many Western observers agreed was a valid perception. A number of factors contributed to this feeling. NVA officers often felt that they were only being kept around until Bundeswehr officers from the West had mastered East German technology or until order had been introduced into the former GDR. As one NVA officer bitterly said, "The Bundeswehr makes it very easy for us: You are not needed anymore—begone! We have accepted many privations. Should that be for nothing?"[15]

Added to this perception of expendability was the fact that—with the exception of conscripts—they were paid considerably less than their West German counterparts. "Our sergeant receives half of that which his colleague makes in the West—even though they do the same work, one officer declared. "Those from the NVA have the same number of service years, perhaps have done more difficult work than in the Bundeswehr—and that counts for nothing."[16] Or as another East German officer complained, "I perform the same work [quantitatively and qualitatively] as a Western officer and receive only 60 percent of his salary."[17] Even in 1998, former NVA officers are only paid 85 percent of what their West German colleagues earn. And this discrepancy goes beyond pay to include perks such as per diem. Another source commented, "Who is supposed to understand when a Bundeswehr colonel coming from the NVA is sent to Bonn with his driver from the

Federal Republic and gets only five marks a day? His driver gets 33 DM and a colonel from the West gets 46 DM a day."[18]

Although he was sympathetic to many of their concerns, salary was one area where Schönbohm firmly supported Bonn's policy. He believed "the soldiers of the former NVA must be handled the same as all other members of governmental service, if only because the Bundeswehr cannot be separated from the rest of the population in the five new Länder and may not be different in that—as earlier was the case with the NVA—he enjoys special privileges."[19] NVA officers might resent the way they were treated with regard to pay, but Schönbohm was focusing on the long term. He would fight to see that they were treated equally, but he would not work to win them special privileges.

Another cause of resentment was the Bundeswehr's decision to reduce the ranks of officers accepted from the NVA—on some occasions by two grades. The problem resulted from the prevously discussed top-heavy nature of the NVA officer corps. NVA officers were simply too young for their rank, compared with their Bundeswehr counterparts. As a consequence, "almost all colonels, lieutenant colonels and majors were downgraded by one rank because they were far too young. . . ."[20] A two-grade demotion was especially hard to accept. "A battalion commander in the grade of major was taken over as a technical officer as a senior lieutenant. A lieutenant colonel and regimental commander must decide whether he wants to serve longer as a captain."[21] In some cases, staff officers found themselves performing duties as drivers or guards.[22] West Germans did not see this drop in rank as anything other than an attempt to rationalize the rank structure between the two armies. Not surprisingly, this view was not shared by many NVA officers.

A final problem the NVA professionals faced was linguistic. East Germans, for example, often used words like "republic, object, kadar, technology," all of which sounded strange to West Germans.[23] Part of the problem was that "many of the military concepts were—as was only discovered later—word-for-word translations of the Russian, which to West-Germans made no sense."[24] Not only did the two sides use different concepts, they often used the same words (for example, "security, supply, freedom, etc."[25]) but gave them very different meanings. In short, every time an East German soldier opened his mouth he underlined both his origin and his second-class status. In the eyes of some West Germans, he was nothing more than a Russian puppet, and his language proved it!

The result was that many NVA officers found it difficult to deal on a one-to-one basis with West Germans. The West Germans faced an uphill battle if they genuinely wanted to convince their former NVA colleagues that they considered them equals.

Lack of Initiative

A cornerstone of almost all Western, democratically oriented militaries is initiative. It is assumed that in many circumstances it will be critical for the individual in charge to take personal responsibility and come up with creative solutions to problems. With its overwhelming desire to control all aspects of military life, however, the East German military leadership railed against the lack of initiative on the part of its personnel but did little to encourage it. If anything, initiative was actively discouraged. Life in the NVA was highly structured. Nothing was left to chance.

Those who showed initiative ran the risk of getting into serious trouble. All parts of their lives were predetermined. As von Kirchbach described it, "The daily function of a company chief was determined in detail by the battalion. Even a battalion commander had less freedom than a company chief in the Bundeswehr."[26] The idea of delegating authority—the heart of Western militaries—was underdeveloped in the NVA.

Once the former NVA soldiers entered the Bundeswehr, they were confronted with a whole new world. To quote one source, "I did not have as much decision-making power in the NVA. When it came to details, I always had to ask my platoon leader. Now as a sergeant major, I have to handle everything on my own."[27] Ex-NVA officers and NCOs thus tended to lie back, to resist Bundeswehr efforts to get them to assume the initiative.

The NVA Officer on October 3

If a single word could describe the NVA officer as he entered the Bundeswehr, it would be atomized. In addition to building a highly competent, technically sophisticated officer corps, the SED had also succeeded in creating isolated officers. Each soldier lived in a world of his own—connected by collegiality with his colleagues, but also separated from them by factors such as secrecy, the Stasi, rigid rank structure, and strict and all-pervasive politicization procedures.

His years in the highly structured NVA had produced an officer who was devoted to performing his job (even if it took long hours) and who was trained to follow orders—whether in the political or military sphere. His contacts with the civilian world were minimal, he used language he had learned in a Russian-influenced military environment, and he was insecure and unsure of himself in this new world. He was not certain what was expected of him—nor if he would be rewarded by the Bundeswehr if he performed satisfactorily.

Introduction to the Bundeswehr

The Bundeswehr inherited some 90,000 former NVA soldiers. Of that number, 51,000 were former career soldiers or temporary career volunteers; the remaining 39,000 were conscripts. By the latter part of 1990, this group was down to a total of 24,000 officers and 18,000 warrant officers and NCOs.[28]

Each soldier had to decide by October 12 whether or not to apply for further service in the Bundeswehr. Those who did not wish to join the Bundeswehr had until December 31, 1991, to leave. They could use this time to improve their qualifications for a job in the civilian world. A number of them chose to leave. Indeed, between September 1990 and January 1991, some 22,000 officers were released from active duty, some voluntarily and some because there was no place for them in the Bundeswehr. By the end of January, according to Schönbohm there were just "9,400 (officers) left."[29]

In terms of numbers, some 73 percent of the officers and 95 percent of the NCOs who applied at one military unit were taken over for a two-year test period.[30] Fifteen hundred more were taken into the Bundeswehr as two-year temporary career volunteers than was originally planned. It has been suggested that this push for larger numbers on Schönbohm's part was primarily a "social act."[31]

Although human concerns probably played a role, there were two more important, practical reasons for Schönbohm's action. The first sprang from Schönbohm's feeling that he had to do something to counter the deep sense of suspicion the former NVA officers felt toward the Bundeswehr by convincing them that he was willing to meet them more than halfway in their quest for job security. In fact, one author jokingly referred to this increased number as the "Schönbohm donation," a result of his constant badgering of Bonn to provide more of these men with an opportunity to continue their careers for at least the next two years.[32]

From a political standpoint, this was an important accomplishment because it showed Kommando-Ost's impressive ability to carry on a bureaucratic battle with personnel specialists in Bonn who were always trying to reduce the number of NVA officers taken into the Bundeswehr.[33] It also signaled to the NVA professionals that he was prepared to go to bat for them.

The second reason why Kommando-Ost fought for these increased numbers was just as important. How could Bundeswehr officers make a valid determination on whether an individual should be permitted to join the Bundeswehr when they knew so little about him? His service record was of limited value, and his performance in a three-week course or in short conversations told them little. They couldn't even evaluate his ability to perform his job based on what they had seen. By allowing more former NVA professionals to join the Bundeswehr for a two-year period, Schönbohm felt they would be in a better position to select those who would be best suited to continue their careers in a united German army.[34]

In addition, a number of extended-service personnel would be employed under a special status. Of this group, which included about 1,400 experts and medical officers, 4,500 could be selected as either professional soldiers or temporary career volunteers with contracts for four to twelve years. "The task is to pick the most suitable through a qualified evaluation."[35]

It is important to recognize that Schönbohm went far beyond just trying to keep greater numbers of former NVA personnel on active duty in dealing with these individuals. To cite only one example, when he visited thirty-five ex-NVA pilots—all of whom had become superfluous as a result of unification and had to find new employment—he discovered that the biggest problem was that they could not speak English. Without English, they could hardly hope to become civilian pilots. It would cost DM 1,000 each for an English training course, and Schönbohm "promised to find the money, but I had no idea where I would get it."[36] The bureaucrats argued that there were already enough English speakers and hence no need to spend money on these pilots. Having made a promise, however, Schönbohm persevered in the face of bureaucratic and public opposition. Only after a five-week odyssey through the German bureaucracy was he able to find someone who was prepared to come up with the money.

Unfortunately, as in every large bureaucracy, those who often made critical decisions were unfamiliar with the situation on the ground. Bureaucrats in Bonn knew little or nothing about the former GDR, and when they did visit Kommando-Ost, most restricted their visits to its headquarters in Strausberg rather than going out to the field where the most serious problems were. As a consequence, Schönbohm fought a constant battle to ensure that his troops were given the flexibility and resources that they needed. Schönbohm recounted a conversation he had with his chief of staff: "We were in agreement that we must prevail in dealing with the sub and staff directorates of the Federal Ministry of Defense, even if in that way we did not make additional friends."[37]

The problem was not only bureaucratic. Public resentment against the presence of these former communists in the Bundeswehr continued for some time. Schönbohm said that when he visited Mainz in April, students asked, "Is it really necessary to attempt to build the Bundeswehr with former communists? Why can't you release all of them?"[38]

Schönbohm recognized early on that he had to back up his many comments about giving the former NVA professionals a fair chance with actions. He did this on numerous occasions. In the end he succeeded in winning greater "maneuvering room" from Bonn, which was important not only for his ability to function as Kommando-Ost but also for his attempt to convince the former NVA soldiers that he was worthy of their trust and that they had a future in a unified Germany, even if in the all-German army.

Training New Soldiers

One of the Bundeswehr's first actions was to provide NVA members with special training. This led to some interesting situations. For example, up to September recruits were trained according to the old NVA standards. Then there was a brief pause. On October 3 they put on the new uniforms of the Bundeswehr and continued their basic training as members of the new unified German army.[39]

Meanwhile, three-week courses were developed to "acquaint them with the peculiarities of *innere Führung* and to familiarize them with a soldier's rights and obligations."[40] Technical courses would follow at a later date. Priority was given to acquainting these men with the new politico-military environment in which they would be operating. One source reports that by mid-1992 some ten thousand former NVA professional soldiers had taken part in such courses.[41]

The situation facing NVA professionals in units that were being disbanded was especially hard, or as Schönbohm put it, "psychologically very difficult."[42] The environment was much different in those units which were being retained and restructured. Instead of devoting their time to tearing down what they had spent so many years building, they were assigned tasks that had a more positive meaning.

Those soldiers who were accepted as temporary career volunteers for two years were required to complete a special training program. This program consisted of a self-study course on the principles of *innere Führung*, a four-week training program in a West German unit, a two-week class on *innere Führung*, and assignment to a work place.[43] The time they spent in the West working in a Bundeswehr unit was intended to permit them "to experience how the Bundeswehr lives, moreover with all the weaknesses and advantages."[44] During their work assignment, they would be evaluated by their commanding officers on their suitability for longer service in the Bundeswehr.

Given their background, the NVA soldiers reacted about as one might have anticipated. On the one hand, Bundeswehr officers who encountered them early on noted that they were still marked by "the Soviet command tactics, doubtless more soldierly and disciplined in external appearances than the Bundeswehr. They think and argue militarily, conspicuously unpolitical." On the other hand, it was clear to the West Germans that the former NVA officers feared that their new colleagues would treat them as "losers."[45] There was also a strong sense of cynicism; a belief that, regardless of what the Bundeswehr officers said, they would not be treated fairly.

The Psychological Transition

One of the greatest difficulties facing former NVA professionals was making the psychological transition to the new world represented by the Bundeswehr. First, as Schönbohm himself noted, they had to recognize that they had a right to make a mistake. "When a solder says to me, 'Herr general, I realize that I have made mistakes in my life and for that reason I am leaving the army and will not remain a soldier,' then this shows the extent of the spiritual problems before which . . . these officers stand."[46] After all, the concept of *innere Führung*—which is so central to life in the Bundeswehr—called upon officers to be "examples," not "models," of behavior in carrying out duties. The latter would imply that superiors were perfect. Instead, the task of Bundeswehr officers was to show soldiers how to act. "Models" were more closely tied to the NVA's tradition, where officers were not expected to make mistakes.[47]

The only way to deal with the past was to admit that one had made a mistake and then look to the future. Focusing on the "good old days" prior to October 3 did no good and only led soldiers to avoid dealing with their current problems. As one former NVA officer said, "He who has decided to serve in the Bundeswehr can only do this by looking to the future. One may not look backwards, but to the contrary one must tap into new social relationships."[48] Another former NVA officer characterized the hardest adjustment he had to make: "To work out my own past and to find inner peace."

Fortunately, West German officers quickly recognized that NVA professionals had both the capacity and the willingness to learn. Unfortunately, change would be slow. Those who tried to circumvent the process by making "ersatz" conversions in their political loyalties and behavior were highly suspect. "From further conversations I was able to detect . . . that some former NVA officers had changed too quickly in order to be believable."[49]

Everyone knew that the transition would be painful, and one former NVA officer claimed that the process would take at least one or two years. Most helpful to this officer was what he learned about the failures of socialism, his understanding of the FRG's "system," the role played by the Bundeswehr in West German politics and his contacts with the members of the Bundeswehr.[50] Indeed, two years after the unification of the German armed forces, one analyst was still arguing that "former NVA professional soldiers need more time in order to be able to judge soberly their service in the NVA. In this regard, 'internal change' takes time."[51]

Yet, change was expected. During one of his first meetings with senior NVA officers, a colonel rose and told Schönbohm what many former NVA officers believed; namely, that they too had served the cause of peace and stability in Europe. Schönbohm responded by acknowledging that although he respected the positive role they had played in ensuring a peaceful transition from communism to democracy, the fact remained that the regime they had served had shown no respect for the rights of individuals. If such officers hoped to serve in the Bundeswehr in the future, "you must unconditionally free yourself from the past of the socialist armed forces."[52]

The psychological transition was not made any easier by the way the Bundeswehr handled its "trial period." A number of positions were double-filled—and in some cases triple-filled. The obvious conclusion was that not all of these individuals would be accepted into the Bundeswehr on a permanent basis. One or two of them would have to go. In a certain sense, it was like the Stalinist technique of assigning an understudy to someone about to be purged. As soon as the new person had learned the job, the incumbent would be removed.

NVA personnel had to overcome their reluctance to speak up as well as their sense of inferiority. They were not used to communicating beyond their own narrow areas of responsibility. "I noticed some soldiers lowering their eyes so our eyes did not meet," recalled one Western officer. He described the wooden appearance of many of his NVA counterparts, claiming they acted like "a puppet on a string."[53] Similarly, when Schönbohm spoke with some recruits on October 9, he noted that they were very reticent. "They did not answer my questions in large circles; only when they were in small groups did they become open."[54] The same situation repeated itself several days later at another base in the northeastern part of the former GDR. "The conversation with conscripts at lunch is arduous. They are restrained and inhibited."[55]

Officers exhibited similar constraints. Schönbohm, referring to a discussion he had with former NVA officers in Eggesin, said, "For former members of the NVA, it was a completely unusual situation that such a high-ranking superior came to them, made a presentation, and afterward wanted to discuss things with them." Learning how to deal openly with superiors was painful for NVA personnel at all levels. Indeed, it was difficult not only for lower-ranking personnel to learn that they could openly discuss issues with senior officers, but also for senior officers to learn that they had to treat their subordinates in the same fashion. A former NVA officer told Schönbohm, "We see how completely different the relationships are in the Bundeswehr than in the NVA, but we will need time to get used to them."[56]

For its part, the Bundeswehr assigned a critical role to West German officers, who were expected to set examples. "A lot more has to be expected from officers from the West in that he lives *innere Führung*. He must become familiar with the past of his new comrades." The officer from the West was expected to work closely with his new colleagues, make it clear to them that mistakes were a part of life, pass on responsibility to them, avoid raising false hopes, have endless patience, and avoid being overbearing.[57]

In time, NVA professionals managed to overcome many of their psychological inhibitions. Where conversations had at first been like monologues, gradually former East German officers and NCOs began to open up. They were still in a state of shock, but they were more willing to speak their minds than they had been on October 3.

The process would continue to be a gradual one, however. Indeed, writing almost two years later, a Western observer noted, "To be sure, former NVA professional soldiers are fundamentally more open and at this point more self-confident than they were in 1990, but they are always more careful and reserved in conversation."[58] The same was true of their ability to relate to the pluralistic nature of the Western system. In the past they had one channel of information, now they had many. While all militaries are hierarchical and depend on information coming from the top down, the Bundeswehr was much more tolerant of a variety of viewpoints on various issues than the NVA had been. As a consequence, "former career NVA soldiers are not able to process correctly the wide variety of information common to a pluralistic society and instead expect a clear orientation from above."[59]

Many still found it difficult to understand the concept of *innere Führung* and were unfamiliar with the new military disciplinary regulations. Schönbohm reported a conversation he had at the end of November 1990 with a former NVA senior NCO and an officer. Both had completed the basic course on *innere Führung*. He asked the NCO to explain it. The NCO was able to quote from the constitution and the military law, but clearly did not understand what it really meant. The captain did not do much better.[60]

As a result, when it came to dealing with subordinates, former NVA personnel showed "an underdeveloped ability in communication as well as a lack of sensibility for the special responsibility toward the individual recruit." Conversations with soldiers often sounded like orders.[61] In addition, former NVA officers also spoke in a formal fashion and had little grasp of West German legal concepts. They had little authority in the sense that Western militaries understood the concept. Former NVA officers also had to internalize the ideas of Germany's Basic Law, that is, the idea that in all spheres, "rights and freedom" were the key points. Individuals had specific rights—a hard concept for someone coming from a political system that had upheld few if any individual rights.[62]

Schönbohm evaluated the situation facing former NVA officers on July 1, 1991, when Kommando-Ost was disbanded. In addition to highlighting the important role that members of the Bundeswehr had played, he also emphasized his belief that the NVA officers would eventually adapt to life in this more democratic military: "Today I say without a doubt that soldiers of the former NVA understand the principles and recognize the fundamental differences and are ready to serve our united Germany. Since October 3 they have made a beginning and they will prove it in the future."[63]

The plan was to reduce the number of ex-NVA officers to 4,000 by the end of 1994,[64] but some 11,700 officers applied to extend their time beyond their two-year status to become regular members of the Bundeswehr. The acceptance of officers into this program ran from December 1990 until the summer of 1991. By June the number of former NVA officers was at 9,500.[65] Once the processing of those who applied to serve as temporary career volunteers had been completed, only 6,000 officers who had been accepted into the program would remain. Then would come the process of selecting those who would enter the ranks of the Bundeswehr as regular officers.

While each individual was serving his two-year term as a temporary career volunteer, an extensive evaluation of his performance was completed by his commanding officer. The reports were turned in by February 1992. These reports, together with the individual's service record, were given to a special committee, which evaluated the suitability of each of these men for further service. The committees selected 3,575 officers (fewer than the 4,000 that had been expected) to become regular officers or NCOs in the Bundeswehr. Some of these individuals were later found unacceptable for a variety of reasons: work with the Stasi, withdrawal of their application, other security problems, and so forth. As a result, some 3,027 officers (most of whom were under forty) were finally accepted for "continuing employment as regulars or temporary-career volunteers with extended terms of enlistment."[66]

Creating an NCO Corps

The Bundeswehr faced a very serious problem when it came to creating an NCO corps. As one senior East German officer put it, "There was too little value placed on the leadership quality of NCOs."[67] Schönbohm remarked that "of the total amount, we could fill 80 percent of our billets with senior NCOs from the former NVA." They would be taken over as short-term regular soldiers. The problem was that "when compared with needs, we have only 30 percent of the junior NCOs we need." The reason was simple: the NVA did not have an NCO corps in the Western sense of the term.

NCOs in the NVA were not used to command responsibility. An NCO in the NVA was a technician, a driver, an expert, but "not a squad leader in our sense."[68] Von Kirchbach provided a concrete example of what this meant in daily life: "It was quite common for a sergeant of the guard holding an NCO rank neither to feel responsible for the discipline of a soldier on guard nor to realize that it was his responsibility to straighten out inadequate performance of duty or at least report that fact. . . ."[69] The same was true of the welfare of soldiers; in the officer's mind this was the responsibility of an officer—a far cry from the Western concept that gave an NCO direct responsibility for the well-being of those placed in his charge.

In order to deal with this situation, Schönbohm took a number of steps. An NCO school was created in Delitzsch and began its work in April 1991. Its purpose was to train enlisted personnel to become Western-style NCOs. At the same time, exchanges between the West and East involving NCOs were stepped up. This was especially true of senior NCOs from the West. The idea was that by bringing them to the East and putting them in positions of authority alongside former NVA personnel, the latter would begin to learn how to assume personal responsibility—a foreign concept in the past. A report submitted to Schönbohm included this critique: "NCOs from the Bundeswehr-Ost are not in a position to carry out independently the tasks of the NCO of the day."[70] They didn't know how to get their subordinates to carry out orders nor to treat enlisted personnel in accordance with the precepts of *innere Führung*.

By October 1991, there were 9,100 NCOs active in the Korps and Territorial Command East. Of those, 7,859 were from the NVA (of which 1,358 were the *Weiterverwender* type) and 6,501 were temporary career soldiers on a two-year contract.[71] 12,300 soldiers applied for acceptance into the professional ranks of the Bundeswehr. Of that number, 11,200 were accepted—500 of whom were former junior officers whose work more closely accorded that done by senior NCOs in the Bundeswehr.[72] From these, 7,639 NCOs were eventually accepted as regular or temporary-career volunteers with extended terms of enlistment.[73]

In spite of these actions, problems remained. For example, General von Schewen noted that while 90 percent of senior NCO positions and 40 percent of regular NCO positions were filled, the situation was far from satisfactory. Despite efforts made to retrain these individuals through work in units in the West and training sessions, the premium the Bundeswehr placed on leadership meant that a significant number of them "will have to leave the military because of insufficient suitability." As a consequence, it seemed likely that a greater number of NCOs would have to be sent from the West to the East than had previously been planned.[74]

The process of integrating soldiers from the East and the West continued. However, new recruits from the East were also starting to enter the Bundeswehr. Beginning in January, the first 5,200 were called up and sent to the West. By April they had returned to their units in the East and, according to Schönbohm, were willing soldiers. "As a result of their pre-military training they had shown themselves to be better prepared than their comrades from the West."[75] In April an additional 3,309 of the 6,059 conscripts called up in the East were sent to the West. In a further effort to integrate the two sides, in the middle of 1992 Western recruits were sent to the East.[76] At the same time, officer candidates from the East were taken into the Bundeswehr. One report noted that some 400 of them had been approved by the Officers Testing Bureau and that by July 1, 1991, 250 of them had begun officers training school.[77] By 1996 roughly 6,000 officers and NCOs from the former West Germany were in the East, while some 7,100 officers and NCOs from the East were serving in the West.[78]

NVA Members in Retrospect

By 1996, some 9,784 former NVA members were still on active duty. Another 1,650 former NVA soldiers were employed as civilians by the

Bundeswehr.[79] Reviewing those who had been accepted for long-term service in the Bundeswehr, analysts found four different kinds of personalities. First, there were the military specialists. These individuals had few problems with their past because ideology played almost no role in their NVA membership. These were the easiest types of individuals to integrate into a unified German military.

In the second category were those who tried to downplay their past. They argued that they were not being used properly and were often full of self-pity. These individuals continued to have problems in adapting to their new environment.

The third group were those willing to admit their complicity with the "old regime" yet prepared to begin anew. Although such officers still had a long way to go, they were clearly on the road to adapting to the new Bundeswehr.

Finally, the fourth group included individuals who had come to grips with the current situation even though they still showed signs of attachment to the old regime.[80]

Improving Relations with the Public

As a part of his effort to change the attitudes of all East Germans toward the armed forces, Schönbohm instituted a policy of "openness." Not only would Bundeswehr officers visit bürgermeisters and other civic leaders all over the region, he would also give civilians access to military bases—almost unheard of under the NVA. His purpose was to convince East Germans that "the Bundeswehr is much different from the NVA." Or as he argued in even stronger language, "We must make clear to the population that we are a radically different army than the NVA even though a majority of our officers and NCOs previously belonged to the NVA."[81]

His task was not an easy one. Toward the end of November, he made a trip to Schwerin. He noted that a woman came out of a house, took one look at his uniform and stuck her tongue out. Believing he was a former NVA officer, she said, "All you did was change your uniform."[82]

In fact, representatives of the Bundeswehr were everywhere in the new states of Germany. Contacts were established with civilian authorities at all levels, including schools and other organizations. Indeed, the military worked especially closely with the employment offices and regional industries in an effort to find jobs for the many soldiers who were leaving the armed forces.

Getting the approval of the Protestant churches represented one of the most difficult tasks the Bundeswehr faced in dealing with civilian authorities. It is important to remember that the churches, and in particular the Protestant church, led the fight against the old SED regime, especially a number of its military programs. It was also the Protestant church that supplied many of the GDR's dissident leaders— Eppelmann himself being a prime example. Like most East Germans, the clergy found it very difficult to separate the animosity they felt toward the NVA from their feelings toward the new West German military. From the perspective of many of these individuals, an army was an army.

A key issue—insofar as Schönbohm and Kommando-Ost were concerned—was chaplains. Many West German soldiers were believers and the Bundeswehr had assumed that local clergy would provide religious services, as was the case in the West. Schönbohm raised the issue with Protestant Bishop Demke on December 3. Demke expressed serious concern because of the deep suspicion felt by many in the church toward the state and the military in particular. Chaplains would be paid by the state thereby tying them to it. Schönbohm's attempt to explain that these pastors would have theological independence and freedom to say what they wanted fell on deaf ears.[83]

The response by the Roman Catholic Church was more positive. In one instance, when Bundeswehr headquarters could not find a Protestant pastor to hold religious services—in spite of the fact that the majority of the personnel in Bundeswehr-Ost were Protestant—a Catholic priest agreed to hold them. By December agreement had been reached with the Roman Catholic Church to provide spiritual assistance for Bundeswehr personnel.[84] It would be some time before a similar agreement was reached with the Protestant Church.

Available evidence suggests that over the years the policy begun by Schönbohm was successful. By 1996, 78 percent of East Germans regarded the Bundeswehr as an integral part of society; only 14 percent saw it as something foreign. When asked for their opinion of the Bundeswehr, 75 percent of East Germans had either a very high (7 percent) or rather high (68 percent) view of it. Sixteen percent had a rather bad opinion of the military, while only 2 percent saw it as very bad.[85]

Looking to the Future

On January 1, 1995, all German forces in the former GDR were assigned to NATO. The Russians had left the country, and Germany as a whole now became part of the Atlantic Alliance. Included in this contingent was the IV German Army Korps located in Potsdam, together with two divisions, six brigades, one air-defense fighter wing, one sur-face-to-surface missile wing, two tactical air-control battalions, and a fast patrol boat squadron.[86] The official ceremony marking the incorpo-ration of these forces into NATO took place on February 3.

For many young East Germans, a career in the Bundeswehr repre-sents not only a secure job, but a means of social mobility as well. For them, an officer's career offers a way of entering an "elite" occupa-tional category.[87] This contrasts markedly with the situation in the West, where an officer's career "has lost its attractiveness."

By 1993, press reports indicated that almost a third of all volunteers in the Bundeswehr were coming from the former GDR. The reasons varied among recruits, but the opportunity to learn an occupation fig-ured high, as did the security that service in the Bundeswehr offered at a time of rampant unemployment in that part of the country.[88]

By 1996 former NVA personnel were present throughout the Bundeswehr. A report from Bosnia, for example, profiled a former NVA officer, Cpt. Lutz Arnold, commander of a company in a trans-port battalion, as he prepared to lead his troops to Croatia to partici-pate in peacekeeping efforts. What was most interesting about this re-port was the indication that the process begun by Schönbohm and the Bundeswehr in the East had shown positive results. For example, Ar-nold's troops liked him because he involved himself on their behalf—a characteristic that one would expect from a Western-trained officer but missing from the stereotypical picture of an NVA officer prior to 1990.[89]

This is not to suggest that the process has been problem-free. To cite only one example, Wolfgang Hoppe was a former NVA officer serving in the Bundeswehr who had won an Olympic gold medal in the bob-sled event. In September 1993, he was released from the Bundeswehr when it was discovered that when he filled out his application to be-come a temporary career volunteer, he failed to mention a two-year period when he worked for the Stasi. Regardless of his renown, the courts decided that because he lied on his application, the Bundes-wehr's decision to release him was valid.[90]

Conclusion

Looking back at the period from October 3, 1990, to the present, it is clear that much has changed in what had been the German Democratic Republic. Nevertheless, the East continues to be beset by major prob-lems—especially unemployment. The costs of reunification were much higher than anyone anticipated. Resentment among Germans in the West over the extreme tax burden they are bearing in the rebuilding of

East Germany is high; indeed, the pressure on Kohl's government to reduce taxes grew daily.

Meanwhile, many in the East remain resentful. The land of gold and plenty that they had expected when the d-mark moved east has not turned out to be the world of affluence that many in the east expected. Reconstructing East Germany and integrating its people into a unified Germany is still some time off. This must include not only the issue of bringing the East up to the material standards enjoyed by those in the West—in a certain sense that will be the easier part. Far more difficult, as the experience with the NVA showed, will be the psychological transformation that must take place—the move from a subject political culture to a participant one.

The military is always a part of its country's political system. However, as a structure, it is more cohesive, better disciplined, and better organized than most other groups in society. It is in a position to "attack" problems, to focus resources on solving whatever difficulties it faces. The Bundeswehr exhibited precisely these capabilities in dealing with the NVA. The Bundeswehr has done more than any other part of German society to bring about unification, both psychological and physical. The situation is far from perfect, but as Winston Churchill said about democracy, it certainly beats any other approach tried to date—especially in Germany. Indeed, I would endorse the observation by a West German analyst who said that the Bundeswehr has reason to be proud of having brought about unification more quickly and smoothly than any other part of German society.[91] The Bundeswehr still has a way to go—for example—as far as I am aware, no former NVA officer has yet reached flag rank—but the time will come.

The progress the Bundeswehr has made toward helping create a unified Germany should not be taken to suggest that other parts of the German polity should necessarily imitate all of its actions in dealing with former East German citizens. Some apply and some do not. However, it does suggest that a close look at the Bundeswehr's experience would be profitable.

This is particularly true on the issue of leadership. One may disagree with some of the actions that Schönbohm did or did not take. However, I suspect that few objective observers—and even fewer of the many former NVA professionals who now proudly wear the uniform of the Bundeswehr—would disagree with the argument that his willingness to fight for equal treatment for former members of the NVA was critical. In fact, when this question was asked on the questionnaire I used to supplement this study, the majority of respondents said he treated them fairly, although one noted that his ability to act was limited by "hard-liners in the CDU."

The vast majority of Bundeswehr officers and NCOs who were assigned to the East played a similar leadership role. Almost without exception, former NVA professionals reported that their encounters with these military men were positive experiences that helped them considerably in their adaptation process. A former NVA major observed, "When I noticed that the soldiers of the Bundeswehr were merely human beings like you and I, I also noticed how much I had been in error for years." Another major agreed, "What I experienced was completely different from what I expected. . . . Since that point in time I thought: 'Here you can compete, you won't come into conflict.'" A colonel probably said it best when he asked, "What would have happened if history had traveled in a reverse course? I doubt that we would have shown so much understanding."[92]

Without this leadership, the integrative process would still have gone forward. However, it is doubtful that it would have been so successful. Thus, in retrospect, it appears that Stoltenberg was right in deciding that Schönbohm's presence in this critical job was more important than the corps command he was slated to take. One can only hope that as former NVA officers assume increasingly senior positions in the Bundeswehr, they will recognize both their debt to Schönbohm and his colleagues who traveled to Kommando-Ost in late 1990 and their own obligation to continue the integrative process. Indeed, if Schönbohm's role showed nothing else, it was that individuals can and do make a difference.

8

Lessons from the NVA

The NVA was an army of the people. . . . For that reason, in a critical situation it stood on the side of the people.

A former NVA Colonel

My biggest difficulty in adapting to the Bundeswehr was the completely different character of the two armies.

A former NVA Colonel

It is now time to return to the two major issues raised in this book. First, why did the NVA not become directly involved in late 1989? Why, when the very existence of the state was challenged did the East German military remain in its barracks and facilitate the transition to democracy? Second, what does this tell us about a professional soldier in a party-state? What are the defining characteristics of such an individual, and what kind of an individual do such states produce?

Staying Out of Politics

Based on the results of this study, as well as the questionnaire that was completed by former NVA professionals, there were a number of reasons why the country's military did not resort to the use of force.

Orders are Orders

If one factor defined the existence of a party-state like the GDR, it was control. The party attempted to control everything in the political, economic, social, and military realms. While its control was never total, it made a constant effort to move in that direction. The SED was in charge, and everything was structured to ensure that its control within the party-state was as complete as possible. For this reason, East Germans, and especially NVA personnel, were used to carrying out orders. This brings us to the first reason why the NVA did not resort to the use of force.

As one former NVA officer succinctly said in response to the question of why force was not used in 1989, "No such order was given."[1] Militaries all over the world are built on a hierarchical structure and the NVA was no exception. It was not trained to act in a spontaneous fashion. Without an order, no military is likely to use force—at least not in a coordinated and large-scale fashion. Faced with such a situation, officers and other military personnel tend to be very cautious. As a former NVA major in the border troops noted, the situation was so confusing that the watch words became "Be careful; make certain that nothing happens."

That leaves the question of what would have happened if the order had been given? What would the NVA have done?

The Role of the Leadership

Given its hierarchical structure, the role of the political and military leadership in such a situation was critical. In this instance, the leadership's position was best summed up by a former lieutenant colonel who said simply, "The NVA leadership was not prepared to solve problems with the force of arms."

Without leaders who are ready to give such orders, the likelihood that the military will become directly involved in internal politics decreases dramatically. There is always the danger that the military will collapse and anarchy will result, but the chances that the armed forces will act in a coordinated, purposeful fashion in such circumstances are almost nil.

It is important to note that the leadership itself worked hard to avoid a situation where the military might have to be used against the populace. General Streletz's work in drafting the key order that was signed by Honecker forbidding the use of force in October was only one example. Admiral Hoffmann's trip to Beelitz in January 1990 was another, as were the efforts to avoid greater displays of military force at the point when the Berlin Wall was opened. With the exception of Heinz Keßler, the GDR's military leadership seemed to have understood just how dangerous the situation was. The roles played by Generals Goldbach, Grätz, and Süß in discouraging the use of force in November were also critical, as was the work by Hoffmann throughout his tenure in office. He and his colleagues showed considerable leadership skills in bringing the military through its year of turmoil until it became part of the Bundeswehr.

Another response to the question of why the leadership failed to order the use of military force is that it was worried that the soldiers would not carry out such orders. Those who thought this way were probably right for a number of reasons.

Disciplinary Problems

Disciplinary problems had plagued the NVA for some time. These problems seem to have begun with the party leadership's decision to make ever-greater use of military personnel in civilian work. Taking soldiers out of the controlled, highly disciplined, and isolated military environment not only removed them from military control and discipline, but also subjected them to the anti-regime influences prevalent in the civilian world. As a former chief of staff put it, "As a result of the use of whole units and formations for months and years in the civilian economy, by 1989 combat readiness had sunk considerably, military morale was down, and dissatisfaction on the part of members of the military had risen."

It is perhaps ironic that after all the party leadership did to isolate the professional military from the civilian world and thereby increase its political reliability, the whole effort was undermined by contradictory actions on the part of the leadership itself. Sending large numbers of troops to work in factories or farms undermined discipline and it undercut the military's ability to carry out training exercises—an important factor in the development of military cohesion. Without a strong sense of cohesion, there is little likelihood that the military could have been used in a calculated fashion against its own populace. At a minimum, it would have created uncertainty, something that would had given pause to even the most dedicated communist.

One former warrant officer said that after the first use of troops to back up the police in Dresden in October 1989, a number of soldiers and NCOs stated that they would no longer take part in such activities. "Even discussions with them did not lead to a change in opinion. They were returned to service at their bases." Or as an air force officer put it more generally, "I cannot imagine the use of force against the population." The point is that anyone who was even remotely aware of the psychological state of NVA soldiers in late 1989 would have known that ordering them to use force would have been a major gamble. What if they had shot their officers instead?

If more was needed to drive home further the magnitude of the problems that existed within the NVA, the increase in desertions did the job. Not only could the leadership not depend on the country's soldiers to carry out the orders given to them, it could not even be

certain that they would show up in the event their services were
needed.

The Soviet Factor

Another factor that would have been of concern to anyone contem-
plating the internal use of the armed forces was the role the Soviet
Army would have played. As more than one respondent noted, the
assistance of the Soviet Army would have been critical, and it was clear
to the SED and the military leadership that Moscow did not want to
get involved in an internal East German power struggle. This was especially true given the low level of discipline and the confusion that
reigned within the NVA at this time. Without the certainty of support
from the Soviet military, the use of force would have been an even
riskier undertaking.

Gorbachev's policies of *glasnost* and *perestroika* had had a major impact on the GDR. It was impossible to isolate the NVA from the cries of
"Gorbi, Gorbi" on the lips of hundreds of thousands of East Germans.

Most East Germans, including those in the armed forces, knew and
understood that major, liberalizing changes were under way in the
USSR and wanted the same thing to happen in the GDR. Why support
the regime in East Berlin when it was out of step with the USSR? The
strong pressures the regime had placed on the population—and especially the NVA—for close ties with the former USSR were beginning to
haunt them.

The Political Structure

Contrary to what often has been thought in the West, regular military
officers in communist armies have long recognized the value of the
party's political structure in maintaining cohesion in the armed forces
of a party-state.[2] This was also true of the NVA. The political structure
was valuable—as long as military cohesion remained at a relatively
high level. When cracks started to appear, however, it worked against
military cohesion.

Prior to 1989, one of the tasks of the political apparatus was to indoc-
trinate troops with a particular *Weltanschauung*. By the latter part of
1989, however, control over the political structure had been lost. No
one knew what the party line was on any issue of importance. As a
consequence, these same discussion groups had become debating organizations. Whereas in the past the political officer had lectured
troops on the party's view of specific events, by October and Novem-

ber soldiers were discussing among themselves what should be done and, in many cases, trying to tell the party what to do.

Training

Another factor that raised questions about the use of military force for internal purposes was the lack of training for such an eventuality. There is a big difference between maneuvering tanks on a battlefield and controlling unruly crowds in an urban environment, as countries that have tried to use the military for that purpose (e.g., the United Kingdom in Northern Ireland) have discovered. Troops intended for such purposes need specialized training if they are not going to worsen the situation. Consequently, had they been deployed against the civilian population during the events of October 1989, the NVA's value would have been limited and probably would have led to overreaction by soldiers who did not understand the situation and who were not trained to deal with it.

Political Drift

Confusion over where the country was going, together with an increasing sense of disillusionment on the part of the average military officer, also played an important role. By August 1989, the country was clearly adrift. One element that is important to any military is clear and decisive orders. Honecker's and later Egon Krenz's, failure to take charge and move things in a positive direction left the armed forces in a quandary.

A colonel cited the party's failure to deal with the refugee issue (the desire of East Germans to move west), noting that the Politburo's helplessness in handling matters "undermined its authority in the military." Then there were the disclosures about corruption—including in the military. This led to disillusionment not only with the political leadership, but with the military leadership as well. People who felt little or no allegiance to the country's political leaders were not likely to support them in a confrontation with the populace.

As several former NVA officers pointed out, this was exactly what happened in the GDR. "Soldiers recognized the contradiction between the State functionaries and the citizens of the GDR, and decided in favor of the people." A navy captain sounded a similar note when he observed that the "majority of soldiers shared the same opinion as the demonstrators on the street." A colonel concluded, "The regime was not worthy of being defended." Why defend a regime that was working against the interests of the majority of the populace?

The Ideological Factor

Although there were certainly those in the NVA who would have been prepared to use force to keep the old regime in power, one consistent response to the questionnaire was the comment that the NVA was not intended for use against internal enemies. East German soldiers had had two lessons drilled into their heads over the years. First, as one former colonel put it, they were trained "to resist external threats—not internal ones." Second, they were told they were an "Army of the People." Using force against the East German populace would have violated both of these premises.

It is easy for outsiders to dismiss the importance of such things in the eyes of military professionals. Nevertheless, the prevalence of such comments suggest that they were important to a large percentage of NVA officers. One respondent, a colonel, noted that sociological analyses conducted yearly from 1983 to 1987 showed that the majority of the officers and NCOs believed that "the NVA's only task was to defend the country from external threats." A military psychologist said that in the aftermath of the events of the summer and fall of 1989, "the officer corps understood itself increasingly no longer as a party or regime army, but as a people's army. Defense against external threats, no force internally." From a practical standpoint, what this means is that a party-state like the GDR needs to be very careful about the ideological lessons it teaches its soldiers. They may take some aspects of this training seriously and under some circumstances such lessons can influence the army's actions during a crisis.

All of the questionnaire respondents agreed that had the military been used, there would have been problems getting soldiers to carry out their orders, and furthermore that such an action would have probably led to a civil war—or a "bloodbath" according to one officer. There would even have been problems with the officers. As one officer said, "There was no readiness on the part of the majority of generals and commanders to take over responsibility for leading such actions."

Another factor that may have played a role in convincing the military leadership to support the people was the recognition on the part of many in the military that the populace was right—major reforms *were* necessary. The country could not be permitted to continue in its current state. This recognition of the need for change was as prevalent in the military as it was in the rest of society. Interestingly, a colonel noted, "In the beginning, the majority of members of the army believed that the anti-Honecker changes would be maintained and would work in the GDR." Why work to stop the process of reform—even if it meant the end of the party's control—if one believed that the kinds of reforms that were being demanded were necessary and long overdue?

It is therefore possible that the majority of NVA officers resisted the involvement of the army in internal politics not only because they feared such an action could backfire and lead to a civil war, but because they believed what the party had taught them—that they were an army of the people and that their purpose was to defend the country only from external enemies. Similarly, the majority of them appeared to believe that basic reforms were overdue and that by making meaningful changes, the system could be saved. It would be wrong to dismiss out of hand the claims by former NVA officers that they believed the use of force would have been wrong morally, that it would not have solved the country's problems, and that diluting party authority was criticial to reforming the country.

The Use of Military Force Internally

Taken together, the foregoing suggest a number of generalizations relative to a party-state's ability to deploy its armed forces against its own populace. A party leadership's ability to use its armed forces internally is dependent on several factors.

First, it must maintain strong control over the military. That is the chain of command must remain intact. The party must also find a way to isolate the military from unwelcome political and ideological influences. Heavy work schedules, prohibitions against watching or listening to "subversive" television or radio programs, and ideological indoctrination lectures are all techniques employed by such states. Similarly, to the maximum degree possible, it must avoid permitting its soldiers to take part in civilian work—a factor that will also decrease its isolation from the populace. The latter is particularly dangerous during a period of political instability. To the degree that control declines, the party's ability to employ the military against its own populace will also drop.

Second, it is critical for the leadership to demonstrate that it is in charge. In this regard, the party leaders must send clear and unambiguous messages to the armed forces. If the party-state sends confusing or contradictory signals, or even worse, if it sends no message at all—especially during a crisis—the military will soon be adrift, unsure of what it should do. Needless to say, the greater the degree to which it finds itself in such a position, the less useful the military will be to the party leadership.

Third, political stability is important. A regime like the GDR could probably have survived even if control over the military weakened—provided the country remained stable. Increasing instability, however, simply fed the sense of confusion and disillusionment on the part of the regular military; especially given the deterioration in military cohesion that was taking place. When soldiers looked around and noticed that there were demonstrations by average people, they began to ask themselves why. If the regime had been able to control information, then the regime's ability to use the military against the populace would have been significantly higher.

Fourth is the external factor. Given the GDR's close ties to the Kremlin, Moscow's intentions were also important. Polish Gen. Wojciech Jaruzelski was able to tell his populace that he declared martial law in order to keep the Russians out. For many Poles, such an explanation was credible—after all, the threat of a Russian invasion was real. The point is that with a serious external threat the regime is in a stronger position to argue that action by the armed forces will help save the country from a greater danger. As it was, the Russians not only did not back up the SED, they were a negative influence through their policies of *glasnost* and *perestroika*. Given the close ties between the former USSR and the GDR, organizations like the NVA could not help but be influenced by the policies advocated by its "big brother."

Fifth, party-state regimes must keep in mind that ideology is a two-edged sword. As long as the party leadership can maintain stability and a high degree of control over the armed forces, ideology will serve the party's interest. Once control begins to lessen, however, ideological structures and writings can work against the party.

Party-Army Soldiers and a Democratic Military

Based on the East German experience, we can pinpoint a number of factors that characterize officers in a party-army state. Understanding these factors is important if one hopes to help such individuals adjust to life in a democratic polity. An awareness of these characteristics is also important if we hope to be able to conceptualize civil-military relations in totalitarian, and to some degree authoritarian, regimes.

A Sense of Isolation

Because control is so important to a regime trying to control all aspects of soldiers' lives, there is a strong tendency for the regime to isolate them both from civilians and from other members of the military as well.

The East German political leadership went to great lengths to control the daily life of NVA personnel. Officers and soldiers worked long hours. They were almost always isolated in their barracks or on their bases. And they were kept away from the civilian population (except on those festive occasions when contact with civilians was encouraged).

The long hours and isolation on a base, when combined with the prohibition on contacts with the West—both personal and via the media—helped facilitate the party-state's efforts to inculcate its own preferred view of reality. In this way, soldiers were able to avoid cognitive dissonance—they seldom encountered facts or events that contradicted the world view conveyed to them by the party. Officers knew little of the outside world, and the heavy demands on their time meant that they would have had little time to think about it even if they had been given more reliable information.

The all-prevailing secrecy contributed to this sense of isolation. The NVA officer or NCO focused first and foremost on the job at hand. His knowledge of what his colleague might do in the event of combat operations was limited. Military information was highly compartmentalized. Needless to say, his knowledge of major battle plans was even more limited.

Strict Obedience

Although the strict sense of obedience in the NVA may have been due to the country's military history and the tendency to emulate the Russian or Prussian experience, there is no question that such a setup was useful to a totalitarian regime. The GDR was a "top-down" type of regime. If it could have, it would have treated all societal groups as described in the military slogan: "We give the orders, you obey."

This sense of obedience was reinforced in the NVA by the strict military structure—the sense that hierarchy is everything. General Schönbohm's comment about the shock that NVA officers felt when they discovered that he was willing to discuss issues with them on a one-to-one basis and to treat them with respect is an example of just how rigid such hierarchical relationships were in the NVA. This is not to suggest that all NVA officers were inhumane in their treatment of subordinates, but as a large number of respondents pointed out, "Military order in the NVA was very strict." The soldier's task was to obey.

Needless to say, this strict emphasis on discipline also influenced officer-subordinate relationships. While all militaries see a strict line of separation between officers and enlisted personnel, the situation in the NVA was far more rigid than in most Western militaries, and this was especially true when compared to the Bundeswehr. The aloofness that many NVA officers projected toward their subordinates, the willingness on the part of some to resort to draconian measures of discipline, the system's penchant for control—all discouraged the delegation of authority. Just as generals tended not to delegate authority to staffs and staffs tried to control all aspects of the units under them, officers were hesitant to delegate authority to their subordinates. As a result, the country lacked a viable NCO corps in the sense that is understood in the West. Officers routinely did the jobs assigned to enlisted personnel in the West. Warrant officers existed, but they were technicians, not the kind of leaders that Western militaries expect of such individuals.

Politicization

This brings us to the process of politicization, one that has been widely misunderstood in the West. Politicization as it is usually understood—inculcating the party's point of view in the minds of members of the NVA—helped further the goal of isolating members of the NVA.

Politicization also meant isolating members of the NVA from the political decision-making process. After all, the party knew best, and the overwhelming majority of professional military officers were party members. In a political sense, this meant that the military's task was to obey orders—to wait until the party had made a decision and then to carry it out.

This does not mean that individuals such as Keßler or Hoffmann were not involved in political maneuvering. Rather, it means that the majority of officers viewed themselves as a political subjects, not political participants. This stands in contrast to the U.S. experience, where the willingness to follow orders is backed up by a readiness to publicly question governmental actions—for example, on the issue of gays or women in the military. Had the SED issued a directive on such issues, NVA officers would have carried it out without question (although some might have grumbled privately).

No Autonomous Institutions

In the GDR, the party leadership made every effort to infiltrate all institutions. Based on the number of people who are known to have cooperated with the Stasi, they seem to have been successful. One respondent claimed that about 30 percent of the NVA officers also worked for the secret police.

It mattered little where one turned. The law was a servant of the SED, with lawyers and judges in both the civilian and military worlds bowing to the state. In essence, their task was to ensure that the wishes of the party were carried out.

For practical purposes, NVA professionals were often atomized. Frequently, they did not know whom they could rely upon. One's best friend, officemate, or shipmate could be a spy for the Stasi. As a consequence, most NVA officers realized early on that the only way to survive was to keep one's views to oneself. Those who stood out or showed signs of independence at the wrong time could easily find their careers at an end—as happened to those who opposed the GDR's participation (however limited) in the 1968 invasion of Czechoslovakia. In a nutshell, NVA professionals were not trained to ask questions, beyond technical issues.

Of all the institutions in the GDR, the one that appears to have remained most autonomous was the Protestant church. Its leaders and members fought a constant battle for more freedom and independence of thought. The regime battled back trying every trick in the book to undermine it. Antireligious propaganda was carried on openly in the NVA, and no officer or NCO could hope to be religious and remain in the military.

Incorporating Party-Army Soldiers into Democratic Militaries

The German experience has taught us much about the process of democratizing formerly communist militaries. Indeed, based on the Bundeswehr's experience, we can pinpoint some of the major problems that likely will be encountered when introducing a former communist officer into a democratic military.

Rules of the Game

One of the first tasks facing anyone dealing with members of a formerly communist military is the need to teach them the rules of the democratic game. As the West German experience shows, just sending officers and NCOs to a course on *innere Führung* or democracy does not mean that they will really understand how a democratic regime functions. Some came back able to cite the West German constitution by heart, but that did not guarantee that they understood how a Western polity functions. It was only by trial and error that one could expect to learn how to function in the chaotic world of a Western democracy. There were no simple rules as was the case in the more "ordered" world of the GDR.

Initiative

One problem that West German analysts cited over and over was the unwillingness of former NVA personnel to act on their own. Too many of these individuals simply waited to be told what to do; they felt their primary task was to carry out orders. This was not surprising given their highly structured world in which control was the regime's most important goal. West German officers assigned to Kommando-Ost spent countless hours trying to convince East German officers to be proactive, but the learning process was difficult when one was used to an environment where the quickest way to end a career was to act independently.

Similarly, former NVA officers and NCOs had problems dealing with delegation of authority. Not only were individuals in the lower ranks in the Bundeswehr given far more responsibility than in the NVA, superiors were expected to trust subordinates in a way that never existed in the NVA. For most of these professionals this meant learning anew how to deal with subordinates. No longer was an order sufficient; an officer was now expected to use persuasion to convince subordinates of the need for certain actions. The Bundeswehr remained a military organization, but for many of these former NVA professionals, adjusting to the different—less formal—way in which individuals of different ranks interacted was not easy.

Democratic Politics

Former NVA officers also had trouble adjusting to the world of democratic politics. Most Bundeswehr officers spent little time engaged in politics, but they were never afraid to make their political views and memberships known. For an NVA professional, this involved entering a new world, one in which politics meant more than just taking orders. Here the individual was expected to formulate his own ideas and have an opinion of his own. No longer could he leave politics to the party. Having lived in a world of secrecy and secret police informers, many NVA professionals had developed a tendency to hide their political views. Trying to convince them to express their own opinions was a difficult part of the transition from a politically passive to a politically active military officer.

In the same sense, he also had to learn that he and his family could now belong to whatever organization they found attractive. Religion was a private matter; in no case would membership in a religious congregation be used against an officer.

Dealing with Civilians

Although not a major problem, professionals from a party-military will also have to learn how to deal more effectively with civilians. Instead of living in an isolated military world, Bundeswehr personnel have constant contacts with civilians. They have never had the luxury of ignoring them as NVA professionals did. Now former NVA officers not only faced the prospect of having civilians live next door and interacting with them on a daily basis, they also had to be prepared for a much greater level of civilian interference in military affairs than they had been used to.

The Past

One of the most painful tasks facing former NVA professionals has been coming to grips with their past. Were the years they spent in the NVA wasted? Were they traitors for now serving in the Bundeswehr? Was their SED party membership a mistake? What about the dual morality that they had lived with on a daily basis—for example, knowing that the figures they cited to their troops about living standards were blatantly false, yet continuing to parrot them day after day? What about the corruption that had existed all around them?

For the East Germans, and probably for other militaries that go through this process, a certain sense of resentment is to be expected. It would be hard to find an NVA professional who did not believe that he had helped maintain peace in Europe during the years of the Cold War. To some, the incorporation of the NVA into the Bundeswehr was a conquest of the victors over the vanquished. By and large, such individuals—at least those who had strong views on this point—appear to have opted not to join the Bundeswehr. Yet it remained as a factor of some importance; one that the members of Kommando-Ost had to deal with frequently.

Concluding Thoughts

The task of incorporating or reeducating professionals from a formerly totalitarian regime was not easy. Based on what I have seen, the West Germans have done a credible job. Their willingness to use an open hand rather than a mailed fist was cited by almost all of the officers who filled out my questionnaire as an important factor in their assimiliation into the Bundeswehr. In addition, all of them agreed that it was important for the West Germans to be proactive in helping with the adaptation process. If the West Germans had not developed special courses and trained its officers and NCOs to deal with the process, the transition would have failed. All of the factors noted above must be dealt with in a systematic fashion.

In the end, however, patience and time are the two key elements.

Several of the officers who answered my questionnaire noted that it took three or four years to come to grips with their past.

The NVA now belongs to the past. One can still find parts of its uniforms being hawked on the streets of Berlin, but for practical purposes it no longer exists. Many of those who served in its ranks are now members of the Bundeswehr, but in time they will pass from the scene. In spite of the NVA's disappearance from the historical stage, however, the events of 1989–90, as well as the experience of those who joined the Bundeswehr, tell us a lot about civil-military relations in a party-army state.

In order for the party to be able to rely on the military in an internal crisis, certain conditions must exist. Should these factors be undermined, the nature of civil-military relations will change. In particular, the party's ability to use the military in a crisis will decrease significantly.

It is important for those in the West to keep in mind that just because an individual puts on a uniform in a party-army state it does not follow that he is prepared to use his weapons against his own people. Too often, Western observers have taken that assumption as a given.

It is also important to understand that those who serve in the ranks of a party-army can adapt to life in a democratic polity given time, a willingness to change, and acceptance by those in the new polity. Not all West Germans were happy at the federal government's decision to take even a limited number of former NVA professionals into the Bundeswehr. However, if the government's goal was to bring about psychological as well as social, economic, military, and political reunification, then the actions of individuals like General Schönbohm and his colleagues showed that it can be achieved—with considerable effort and goodwill.

Few of those who wore the uniform of the NVA were saints. At the same time, it is important to recognize that not all were sinners either. History could have taken a very different course if those in the ranks of the NVA had been less responsible. Strong leadership—the kind exercised by men such as Hoffmann, Streletz, and Goldbach—made an important difference. A civil war in the former GDR would have had a catastrophic impact on the course of history. At a minimum, it would have drawn the Russians in and probably would have meant Gorbachev's replacement by one of those who wanted to turn the clock back. It could—as one East German officer argued—have even led to "a third world war." Whatever the outcome, we would almost certainly not have seen the peaceful, united Germany that is now playing such an important role in Europe and the world. And for that we can be thankful—at least in part—to those who served in the NVA during the turmoil of 1989–90.

Appendix I

Key East German Military Leaders

Baumgarten, Klaus Dieter. Born in 1931, Baumgarten joined the Volkspolizei in 1949. He held a variety of positions within the Ministry of Interior related to the border troops and from 1959 to 1963 studied at a Russian military academy. From 1965 to 1970 Baumgarten was first deputy to the chief of the border troops, and in 1970 he left for Moscow to study for two years at the General Staff Academy in Moscow. From 1979 to 1990 he served as a deputy minister and as chief of the border troops.

Brünner, Horst. Born in 1929, Brünner joined the Volkspolizei in 1948. He held a number of different positions as a political officer and from 1962 to 1965 was head of the department at the Main Political Administration. From 1965 to 1968, Brünner was chief of the Main Political Administration of the border troops, then head of the Political Administration of Military District V. In 1985 he became a deputy minister of defense and head of the Main Political Administration, a position he held until 1989.

Fleisner, Werner. Born in 1922, Fleisner joined the Volkspolizei soon after it was created. After the NVA was founded, Fleisner studied at the Friedrich Engels Military Academy and soon was appointed chief of transportation in the NVA. In 1964 he became the deputy minister of defense in charge of armaments.

Goldbach, Joachim. Born in 1929, Goldbach also joined the Volkspolizei shortly after it was created. He served in the KVP and then joined the NVA as an armor officer. Goldbach attended the Malinovskii Armor Academy as well as the Soviet General Staff Academy. In 1972 he became a military district commander, a position he held until 1979 when he became chief of the rear services. In 1986 he took over as chief of armament and weapons and remained in this position until 1990.

Grätz, Manfred. Born in 1935, Grätz joined the KVP in 1952. A tank officer who graduated from the Soviet General Staff Academy, he became commander of the 8th Motorized Division, deputy head of Military Region V, and from 1982 to 1986, chief of Military Region III. In 1986 he was appointed chief of the rear services. In 1989 Grätz became chief of the main staff, a title he held until the NVA was disbanded.

Hoffmann, Heinz. Born in 1910, Heinz Hoffmann joined the Communist party in 1926. He emigrated to the USSR in 1935 and during the Spanish Civil War fought on the side of the loyalists. During World War II he was in the USSR. Hoffmann became head of the Main Administration for Training and in 1952 was appointed head of the KVP. Hoffmann completed the Soviet General Staff Academy and in 1960 was appointed minister of national defense, a post he held until 1985.

Hoffmann, Theodor. Born in 1935, Theodor Hoffmann enlisted in the Seepolizei in 1952. He became an officer and later attended the Soviet Naval Academy. In 1974 Hoffmann became the navy's deputy chief of staff for operational matters. In 1985 he was appointed the Navy's deputy chief and in 1987 took over as navy chief. He was appointed GDR defense minister in 1989 and in 1990 was made chief of the NVA.

Keßler, Heinz. Born in 1920, Keßler was drafted into the Nazi Wehrmacht but defected to the Soviets. He spent the war as a member of the Soviet-sponsored National Committee for a Free Germany. Keßler was chief of the East German air force from 1956 to 1967 and chief of the main staff of the NVA from 1967 to 1978. He served as head of the Main Political Administration from 1978 to 1985, when he became defense minister, a post he held until 1989.

Reinhold, Wolfgang. Born in 1923, Reinhold joined the Volkspolizei in 1952. After creation of the NVA, he attended a Soviet military academy and held a number of command positions in the East German air force. In 1972 he became head of the air force, a position he held until 1989.

Stechbarth, Horst. Born in 1925, Stechbarth worked as a farmer and in 1949 joined the Volkspolizei. He held a number of command positions in the NVA and later attended the Soviet General Staff Academy.

Stechbarth became head of the ground forces, a position he held until 1989.

Stoph, Willi. Born in Berlin in 1914, Stoph joined the Communist party in 1931. From 1952 to 1955, he was minister of the interior. In 1956 Stoph was appointed the GDR's first minister of national defense. He remained in this post until 1960.

Streletz, Fritz. Born in 1926, Streletz served for a year in the Wehrmacht. He joined the Volkspolizei in 1948 and in 1952 transferred to the KVP. After the founding of the NVA, Streletz attended the General Staff Academy. From 1964 to 1978, he was the deputy chief of the main staff, and from 1979 to 1989 he served as chief of the main staff.

Süß, Hans. Born in 1935, Süß joined the KVP in 1955. An air force officer, he graduated from the Soviet Military Academy in Kharkov and later attended the Soviet General Staff Academy. Süß became chief of staff of an air defense division and then from 1978 to 1988 served as the commander of the air force officers school. From 1988 to 1990, he was the chief inspector of the Ministry of National Defense and was the last chief of the Military Academy in Dresden.

Appendix II

Questionnnaire Answered by Former NVA Officers*

This questionnaire is for a book being written by an American specialist on former communist militaries. The book will be entitled, *Requiem for an Army: the Case of the East German Military*. Its purpose is to explain to Western readers the key role played by the NVA in the peaceful transition in the former GDR during the 1989–1990 time period, as well as to help Western readers better understand the difficulties faced by former NVA professionals as they adapted to the Bundeswehr. Your candid and complete answers will play a critical role in telling this story.

(Please write clearly or type answers. This questionnaire will be read by a non-native German speaker.)

Rank in NVA—1989–1990 _____

Position in NVA—1989–1990 _____

Age—1989–1990 _____

1. What factors do you believe account for the failure of the NVA to resort to the use of force in defense of the regime in late 1989?

---

*This questionnaire was translated into German for distribution.

2. Do you believe NVA forces would have used violence if they had been ordered to in October or December 1989? If not, why not?

3. What factor do you see as the most critical in breaking the bond between the government and the military—the point after which the majority of officers were no longer willing to call it "their own"?

4. What is your evaluation of the role played by Keßler? Was he too closely tied to the old regime to understand what was happening? Do you think he made a positive contribution during the events of October-November?

5. What was the impact of the opening of the Berlin Wall on the NVA?

6. How critical were the events in Beelitz when it came to the cohesion of the NVA?

7. How do you evaluate the role played by Admiral Hoffmann? Some say that he was critical in ensuring a peaceful transition. Do you agree?

8. How do you evaluate the role played by Minister Rainer Eppelmann? Do you think he treated the NVA fairly? Was he naive in dealing with the West Germans or did he have evil intent?

9. Do you feel a sense of bitterness vis-à-vis the Russians? After all, it was Gorbachev's decision in July that pulled the rug out from under Eppelmann's plans to keep two German armies alive and functioning during the transition period.

(For those who joined the Bundeswehr in October 1990)

1. Some claim that General Jörg Schönbohm as chief of Kommando-Ost played a key role in ensuring that former members of the NVA were treated fairly. Do you agree? Do you believe he made a difference?

2. What was the biggest difficulty you encountered in adapting to life in the Bundeswehr? Why?

3. To what degree did the Bundeswehr personnel sent to the East play a positive role in your adaptation to the new unified German army?

4. What was the biggest problem Bundeswehr personnel seemed to have in dealing with former NVA professionals?

5. What seemed to you to have been the most important factor in determining whether or not you would be permitted to continue your career in the Bundeswehr?

6. To what degree do you now believe that you still carry traces of your time in the NVA? What aspects of it are most influential in your life today?

7. If you had to go through the process of incorporation into the Bundeswehr again, what changes would you suggest in the approach taken by Bonn?

8. How do you feel about the series of trials that have been held involving former senior East German officers? Do you think they contribute to reconciliation? How do your colleagues from the West react to these trials?

Notes

Preface

1. Dale R. Herspring, *East German Civil-Military Relations: The Impact of Technology, 1949–1972* (New York: Praeger, 1973).

Introduction

1. Klaus-Jürgen Baarß, tape 25 in Jürgen Eike, "Interviews zum Film 'Die verschwundene Armee,'" Hereafter cited as Eike.

2. The term "NVA professionals" will be used throughout this book to refer to regular officers and NCOs. To be sure there were others who served in the NVA either as conscripts or for three or four year periods as "Soldaten auf Zeit," but in most cases such individuals had minimal influence—except in cases when such soldiers refused to follow orders.

3. There has been a tendency in the West to confuse politicization with political involvement. Politicization, as it is used here, refers to the party's attempts to ensure tight control over the military, as well as its efforts to inculcate the appropriate values in its personnel through an elaborate political apparatus. In this sense, the NVA was probably the most politicized military in the former Warsaw Pact. Political involvement, on the other hand, refers to actions by senior military officers in the political sphere. As this study will show, NVA officers played only a minor role in this area.

4. Dale R. Herspring, "The Military Factor in the GDR's Soviet Policy," *Slavic Review* 46, No. 4 (Winter, 1988).

5. "By the East, Quick March," *The Economist*, 22 August 1992, p. 37.

6. A recent bibliography of material on the GDR and its collapse reflects the lack of interest in the military—it includes only one reference to the armed forces. See Mike Dennis, "A Selected Bibliography of Articles and Books on the Collapse of the GDR and the Process of German Unification, 1991–1994," *East Central Europe* 19, No. 2 (1992): 199–238.

7. Horst Teltschik, *329 Tage: Innenansichten der Einigung* (Berlin: Siedler, 1991), pp. 109, 198.

8. See, for example, Karl-Heinz Arnold, *Die ersten hundert Tage des Hans Modrow* (Berlin: Dietz Verlag, 1990); Michael R. Beschloss and Strobe Talbott, *At the Highest Levels* (Boston: Little, Brown, 1993); Thomas Blanke and Rainer Erd, eds., *DDR: Ein Staat vergeht* (Frankfurt am Main: Fischer Verlag, 1990); Jeffery Gedmin, *The Hidden Hand: Gorbachev and the Collapse of East Germany* (Washington: AEI Press, 1992); Gert-Joachim Gläßner, *Der schwierige Weg zur Demokratie* (Opladen: Westdeutscher Verlag, 1992); Manfred Goertemaker, *Unifying Germany, 1989–1990* (New York: St. Martin's Press, 1994); Konrad H. Jarausch, *The Rush to German Unity* (New York: Oxford University Press, 1994); David Kiethly, *The Collapse of East German Communism* (Westport, Conn.: Praeger, 1992); H. Donald Hancock and Helga A. Welsh, *German Unification: Process and Outcomes* (Boulder, Colo.: Westview Press, 1994); Frank Schumann, ed., *100 Tage die die DDR erschütterten* (Berlin: Elefanten Press, 1990); Uwe Thaysen, *Der Runde Tisch Oder: Wo blieb das Volk?* (Opladen: Westdeutscher Verlag, 1990); Markus Wolf, *In eigenem Auftrag* (Munich: Schneekluth, 1991); and Hartmut Zwahr, *Ende einer Selbstzerstörung* (Goettingen: Vandenhoeck & Ruprecht, 1993).

9. Rainer Eppelmann, *Wendewege* (Bonn: Bouvier Verlag, 1992); Werner E. Ablaß, *Zapfenstreich: Von der NVA zur Bundeswehr* (Düsseldorf: Kommunal-Verlag, 1992): See Theodor Hoffmann, *Das letzte Kommando* (Berlin, Verlag E. S. Mittler & Son, 1993; and Heinz Keßler, *Zur Sache und zur Person* (Berlin: Edition Ost, 1996).

10. See Gregor Gysi, *Einspruch!* (Berlin: Alexander Verlag, 1992); Erich Honecker, *Zu dramatischen Ereignissen* (Hamburg: W. Runge Verlag, 1992); Egon Krenz, *Wenn Mauern Fallen* (Vienna: Paul Neff Verlag, 1990); Christa Luft, *Zwischen Wende und Ende* (Berlin: Taschenbuch Verlag, 1991); Hans Modrow, *Aufbruch und Ende* (Hamburg: Konkret Literatur Verlag, 1991); Günter Schabowski, *Das Politbüro* (Hamburg: Rowohlt Taschenbuch Verlag, 1990); Günter Schabowski, *Der Absturz* (Hamburg: Rowohlt Taschenbuch Verlag, 1991).

11. Helmut Kohl, *Ich wollte Deutschlands Einheit* (Berlin: Ulstein Buchverlag, 1996); Jörg Schönbohm, *Zwei Armeen und ein Vaterland* (Berlin: Siedler, 1992); Wolfgang Schäuble, *Der Vertrag* (Stuttgart: Deutsche Verlags-Anstalt, 1991); and Teltschik, *329 Tage*.

12. An example is the book edited by Volker Koop and Dietmar Schlößler, *Erbe NVA: Eindrücke aus ihrer Geschichte und den Tagen der Wende* (Waldbröl: Akademie der Bundeswehr für Information und Kommunikation, 1991). This book is based on discussions with a wide variety of former NVA professionals and provides an invaluable insight into life in the NVA from a variety of perspectives.

13. This term is almost impossible to translate into English. Suffice it to say that it refers to military leadership within a democratic political system. In such a system, democratic values such as respect for the individual soldier or sailor are of utmost concern. For a discussion of its role in reeducating NVA professionals, see "Innere Führung: eine gute Mitgift für die Bundeswehr Ost," *Truppenpraxis*, No. 2 (1991), 185–187.

14. While there has been a tendency on the part of some writers to assume

that the military is an autonomous institution, closer inspection reveals that it is heavily affected by what happens in the political sphere. This study thus proceeds from the assumption that politics is as influential in its impact on the military as it is on agriculture, education, or social services.

Chapter 1

1. Max Opitz in October 1959 from a lecture intended for the party school of the Institute of Marxism-Leninism of the Central Committee of the SED, as cited in Thomas M. Förster, *Die NVA: Kernstück der Landesverteidigung der DDR* (Cologne: Markus Verlag, 1979), p. 24.

2. Joachim Goldbach, tape 5, in Eike.

3. Autorenkollektiv, *Armee für Frieden und Sozialismus* (Berlin: Militärverlag der Deutschen Demokratischen Republik, 1985), pp. 48–49.

4. Frank Buchholz, *Armee für Frieden und Sozialismus: Die Geschichte der bewaffneten Organe der DDR* (Munich, Universität der Bundeswehr, 1991), p. 16.

5. Toni Nelles, "Der Aufbau und die Entwicklung der NVA: Schöpferische Anwendung des Leninischen Militärprograms durch die SED (I)," *Militärgeschichte*, 1970, No. 1: p. 23.

6. Buchholz, *Armee für Frieden und Sozialismus*, p. 21.

7. Ibid., pp. 27ff.

8. Ibid., p. 22.

9. Dale R. Herspring, *Russian Civil-Military Relations* (Bloomington: Indiana University Press, 1996), pp. 55–71.

10. Rüdiger Wenzke, tape 23, in Eike.

11. Buchholz, *Armee für Frieden und Sozialismus*, p. 75.

12. Klaus-Jürgen Baarß, *Lehrgang X* (Berlin: Mittler & Sohn, 1995).

13. Theodor Hoffmann, *Kommando Ostsee: Vom Matrosen zum Admiral*, (Berlin: Mittler & Sohn, 1995), pp. 51–68.

14. D. Heinze, tape 10A in Eike.

15. Kurt Gottwald, tape 19 in Eike.

16. Fritz Streletz, tape 10 in Eike.

17. Goldbach, tape 5 in Eike; and Horst Stechbarth, tape 35 in Eike.

18. Heinze, tape 10A in Eike.

19. Stechbarth, tape 35 in Eike.

20. See Herspring, "The Military Factor in the GDR's Soviet Policy."

21. Buchholz, *Armee für Frieden und Sozialismus*, pp. 79, 81.

22. As cited in Ibid, ff. p. 29.

23. According to several former East German officers, the Russians had a major hand in pushing the East Germans to adopt these more traditional German uniforms. It is also worth noting that contrary to what many in the West have assumed, the very distinctive East German helmets were not designed for the NVA, but were a new model Wehrmacht helmet left over from World War II. See Goldbach, tape 5 in Eike; and B. Bechler, tape 24 in Eike.

24. Buchholz, *Armee für Frieden und Sozialismus*, p. 23.

25. Erich Hasemann, *Soldat der DDR: Erinnerungen aus über dreißigjähriger Dienstzeit in den bewaffneten Organen der DDR* (Berlin: Verlag Am Park, 1997), p. 41.

26. Buchholz, *Armee für Frieden und Sozialismus*, p. 27.

27. This process is discussed by former NVA Major General Bechler, in tape 24 in Eike.

28. Buchholz, *Armee für Frieden und Sozialismus*, p. 446.

29. Joachim Goldbach, Die Nationale Volksarmee: Eine Deutsche Armee im Kalten Krieg," in Detlef Bald, ed., *Die Nationale Volksarmee* (Baden-Baden: Nomos Verlagsgesellschaft, 1992), p. 131.

30. Wenzke, tape 23 in Eike.

31. Buchholz, *Armee für Frieden und Sozialismus*, p. 45.

32. According to an East German source, ten PS (*Pferde Stärke*) meant that for every one hundred soldiers, there existed one tank, four trucks, and two jeeps. "Kurz und Knapp," *Volksarmee*, No. 9 (1969), p. 7.

33. "Zu den Grundfragen der Militärpolitik der Sozialistischen Einheitspartei Deutschlands," *Militärwesen*, June 1964, p. 779.

34. R. Schleicher, "Die NVA ist eine moderne und schlachtkräftige Armee," *Volksarmee*, No. 14 (1971), p. 3. For a more detailed discussion of the role of technology in the NVA during its early years, see Herspring, *East German Civil-Military Relations*.

35. Gottwald, tape 20 in Eike.

36. See Rüdiger Wenzke, "Zur Beteiligung der NVA an der militärischen Operation von Warschauer-Pakt-Streitkräften gegen die CSSR 1968," *Deutschland Archiv* 34, No. 5 (1990): 1179–1186, and Rüdiger Wenzke, *Die NVA und der Prager Frühling 1968* (Berlin: Ch. Links Verlag, 1995).

37. For Streletz's biographic information, see Buchholz, *Armee für Frieden und Sozialismus*, p. 642.

38. The term *Fähnrich* has nothing to do with the American or British term "warrant officer." Rather, the vast majority of such individuals were to become technical specialists, not leaders.

39. Buchholz, *Armee für Frieden und Sozialismus*, p. 56.

40. Hans-Werner Diem, "Die NVA in der Ersten Strategischen Staffel der Vereinten Streitkräfte des Warschauer Vertrages," in Manfred Backerra, ed., *NVA: Ein Rückblick für die Zukunft* (Cologne, Markus Verlag, 1992), p. 320.

41. Buchholz, *Armee für Frieden und Sozialismus*, p. 172.

42. For a more detailed discussion of this network, see Herspring, *East German Civil-Military Relations*.

43. Werner Rothe, *Jahre im Frieden: Eine DDR-Biographie* (Berlin: GNN Verlag, 1997), p. 81.

44. Wilfried Hanisch, "In der Tradition von Müntzer, Scharnhorst, Engels und Thaelmann?" in Backerra, ed., *NVA: Ein Rückblick für die Zukunft*, p. 257.

45. Buchholz, *Armee für Frieden und Sozialismus*, p. 46.

46. Streletz, tape 10 in Eike.

47. Kurt Held, Heinz Friederich, and Dagmar Pietsch, "Politische Bildung und Erziehung in der Nationalen Volksarmee," in Backerra, ed., *NVA: Ein Rückblick für die Zukunft*, p. 208.

48. Streletz, tape 10 in Eike.

49. Förster, *Die NVA*, p. 117.

Chapter 2

1. Goeffery van Orden, "The Bundeswehr in Transition," *Survival*, July/August 1991, p. 361.

2. Keßler's speech is contained in "Lehren, Forschen, Studieren für die militärische Macht," *Volksarmee*, No. 5 (1989), p. 2. For the announcement of Honecker's reductions, see "DDR zeigt mit konkreten Taten Willen zur Abrüstung," *Neues Deutschland* (hereafter *ND*), 23 January 1989. What is especially interesting is the fact that in addition to playing up the importance of these unilateral reductions, Keßler made it sound as if nothing significant had changed in the world—it was still a dangerous place requiring a high level of vigilance and combat readiness on the part of the NVA. See also, "Die Karten liegen auf dem Tisch," *ND*, 30 January 1989.

3. "Woche der Waffenbrüderschaft in Karl-Marx-Stadt eröffnet," *ND*, 18/19 February 1989.

4. As cited in Walter Laquer, *The Dream That Failed* (New York: Oxford University Press, 1994), p. 169.

5. As quoted in Frithjof H. Knabe, *Unter der Flagge des Gegners* (Opladen: Westdeutscher Verlag, 1994), p. 88.

6. See Thomas Gensike, "Mentalitätswandlungen in der Jugend der DDR," *Deutschland Archiv*, No. 12 (1992), p. 1266 as cited in Laquer, *The Dream that Failed*, p. 173.

7. Hans-Joachim Reeb, "Wandel durch Annäherung," *Truppenpraxis*, No. 2 (1991), p. 181.

8. Hans-Werner Weber, "Gläubigkeit, Opportunismus und späte Zweifel," in Backerra, ed., *NVA: Ein Rückblick für die Zukunft*, p. 58. Former security chief Markus Wolf took a similar position. See Wolf, *In eigenem Auftrag*, p. 29.

9. Wolf, *In eigenem Auftrag*, p. 38.

10. Schabowski, *Der Absturz*, p. 221.

11. Goertemaker, *Unifying Germany*, p. 58.

12. Keithly, *Collapse of East German Communism*, p. 108.

13. See Goertemaker, *Unifying Germany*, p. 60.

14. See Keithly, *Collapse of East German Communism*, pp. 111–114.

15. Keßler, *Zur Sache und zur Person*, p. 238.

16. Hoffmann, *Das letzte Kommando*, p. 17.

17. Schönbohm, *Zwei Armeen und ein Vaterland*, p. 38.

18. Hoffmann, *Das letzte Kommando*, p. 71.

19. See Herspring, *Russian Civil-Military Relations*, pp. 132–150.

20. Hoffmann, *Das letzte Kommando*, pp. 14–15.

21. Ibid., p. 17.

22. Eppelmann, *Wendewege*, p. 83.

23. See Hermann Hagena, "Die radikale Wende der Nationalen Volksar-

mee," *Europäische Wehrkunde* (hereafter *EW*), No. 4 (1990), p. 206; and "Hohe Offiziere der NVA und der Bundeswehr beendeten ihre Gespräche in Hamburg," *ND*, 30 March 1989. According to one senior NVA officer, this exchange of visits was opposed by the Bundeswehr. See Gerhard Kunze, "Feind und Kamerad—Zweimal 'Kehrt-marsch!' " in Backerra, ed., *NVA: Ein Rückblick für die Zukunft*, p. 89.

24. See "Wehrpflichtige begannen ihren Ehrendienst," *ND*, 4 May 1989.

25. Keithly, *Collapse of East German Communism*, p. 99.

26. According to Keßler, this was a key point in the evolution of matters in the GDR, since "from this day on, the very sick General Secretary of our Party, Erich Honecker, was never again well and with full concentration able to lead the work of the party and the difficult affairs of state." Keßler, *Zur Sache und zur Person*, p. 247.

27. Krenz, *Wenn Mauern Fallen*, p. 27.

28. Ibid., pp. 28–29. Schabowski argues that the main reason why Krenz was sent on vacation was that Honecker did not trust him to be decisive enough at the critical moment. See Schabowski, *Das Politbüro*, pp. 63–64.

29. "Gespräch mit Minister der BRD," *ND*, 19 August 1989. For a Western view of this meeting, see "Die Regierung der DDR bleibt bei ihrer harten Haltung," *Frankfurter Allgemeine Zeitung* (hereafter *FAZ*), 19 August 1989.

30. See "Bonn: Die DDR muß sich dem Rhythmus der Reformen anpassen," *FAZ*, 22 August 1989; and "Der Bundeskanzler bekräftigt Bereitschaft zu Treffen mit Honecker," *FAZ*, 23 August 1989.

31. "Die SED verteidigt die Notwendigkeit ihrer Führungsrolle in der DDR," *FAZ*, 28 August 1989.

32. "Der Medienrummel und die Realitäten," *ND*, 13 September 1989.

33. Jarausch, *The Rush to German Unity*, p. 31.

34. Keithly, *Collapse of East German Communism*, p. 141.

35. As cited in Beschloss and Talbott, *At the Highest Levels*, p. 132.

36. Schabowski, *Das Politbüro*, p. 52.

37. Schabowski, *Der Absturz*, p. 225.

38. For a copy of the statement, see "Der 13 Tag," in Schumann, *100 Tage die die DDR erschütterten*, p. 25.

39. See the distribution list on Mielke's memo of September 25, 1989, in Armin Mitter and Stefan Wolle, eds., *Ich liebe euch doch alle!* (Berlin: Basis Druck, 1990), 172.

40. Keithly, *Collapse of East German Communism*, p. 149.

41. Schabowski, *Der Absturz*, p. 231.

42. Krenz, *Wenn Mauern Fallen*, p. 32.

43. Keithly, *Collapse of East German Communism*, p. 153.

44. "Sich selbst aus unserer Gesellschaft ausgegrenzt," *ND*, 2 October 1989.

45. See Mitter and Wolle, eds., *Ich liebe euch doch alle!* pp. 180–186.

46. Hoffmann, *Das letzte Kommando*, p. 20.

47. Streletz, tape 10 in Eike.

48. Hoffmann, *Das letzte Kommando*, pp. 19–20. Emphasis added.

49. "Zuverläessige Verteidigungsbereitschaft—unser aller Anliegen," *Volksarmee*, No. 38 (1989).

50. "Das Leben ist das beste Studium," *Volksarmee*, No. 39 (1989).

51. "Soldaten des Volkes erfüllen täglich ihren Klassenauftrag in Ehren," *Volksarmee*, No. 39 (1989).

52. Hoffmann, *Das letzte Kommando*, p. 19. Streletz made the same point about the NVA having no "plans, no documents in the Ministry for National Defense or the National Defense Council concerning the internal use of the NVA." Streletz, tape 10 in Eike. The information on the orders issued is taken from Reeb, "Wandel durch Annäherung," p. 180.

53. Jarausch, *The Rush to German Unity*, p. 22.

54. Krenz, *Wenn Mauern Fallen*, p. 170.

55. Modrow, *Aufbruch und Ende*, p. 14.

56. According to one participant, those sent from the military academy were not of the highest quality. "To a large degree it was a question of staff officers and members of the teaching staff because the students were not there — they were in Berlin for the parade." W. Scheler, tape 8 in Eike.

57. Much of the material in this paragraph is based on interviews Reeb conducted with former NVA personnel who participated in the events in Dresden. Reeb, "Wandel durch Annäherung," p. 182.

58. Keßler, *Zur Sache und zur Person*, p. 264; and Hoffmann, *Das letzte Kommando*, p. 11. Thus the rumor that circulated around the GDR and especially in the media that the military had been given a *Schießbefehl* (order to shoot) was an exaggeration. The soldiers were told that the only circumstance under which they could use their weapons was if their life was threatened. The argument that a *Schießbefehl* was given is contained in Eckhard Bahr, *Sieben Tage im Oktober* (Leipzig: Forum Verlag, 1990), p. 58.

59. Ablaß, *Zapfenstreich*, p. 20. See also "Einsatzhundertschaften der NVA im Herbst 1989," *ND*, 8 February 1989.

60. Reeb, "Wandel durch Annäherung," p. 182.

61. Ablaß, *Zapfenstreich*, pp. 20–21; and Reeb, "Wandel durch Annäherung," pp. 179–180.

62. "Tagesbefehle zum 7. October," *ND*, 6 October 1989.

63. Scheler, tape 8 in Eike.

64. Schabowski, *Der Absturz*, pp. 239–240.

65. Günter Mittag, *Um Jeden Preis* (Berlin: Aufbau-Verlag, 1991), p. 18.

66. Schabowski, *Das Politbüro*, p. 74; and Krenz, *Wenn Mauern Fallen*, pp. 92–93.

67. Goertemaker, *Unifying Germany*, p. 74.

68. Schabowski, *Der Absturz*, p. 242.

69. Beschloss and Talbott, *At the Highest Levels*, p. 133.

70. Schabowski, *Das Politbüro*, pp. 78–79; and Schabowski, *Der Absturz*, p. 246.

71. Schabowski, *Das Politbüro*, pp. 79–80.

72. Jarausch, *The Rush to German Unity*, p. 57.

73. See "Erklärung des Politbüros des Zentralkommitees der Sozialistischen Einheitspartei Deutschlands," *ND*, 12 October 1989.

74. Modrow, *Aufbruch und Ende*, p. 18, and Schabowski, *Der Absturz*, p. 256.

75. Streletz, tape 10 in Eike.
76. As cited in Hans-Herman Hertle, *Chronik des Mauerfalls* (Berlin: Ch. Links Verlag, 1997), p. 85.
77. Krenz, *Wenn Mauer Fallen*, pp. 138–140.
78. Schabowski, *Das Politbüro*, p. 75.
79. Hoffmann, *Das letzte Kommando*, p. 23.
80. Knabe, *Unter der Flagge des Gegners*, p. 111.
81. "Gorbatschow in Ost-Berlin: Gefahren warten nur auf jene, die nicht auf das Leben reagieren," *FAZ*, 7 October 1989.
82. Beschloss and Talbott, *At the Highest Levels*, p. 133. See also Philip Zelnikow and Condoleezza Rice, *Germany Unified and Europe Transformed* (Cambridge, Harvard University Press, 1997), p. 84.
83. Gedmin, *The Hidden Hand*, p. 102.
84. Hoffmann, *Das letzte Kommando*, p. 22.

Chapter 3

1. Mittag, *Um Jeden Preis*, p. 179.
2. This discussion is based on Jarausch, *The Rush to German Unity*, pp. 59–60. For a copy of the speech, see "Rede des Genossen Egon Krenz," *ND*, 19 October 1989.
3. This was a clear play on his name which means "swallow."
4. "Opposition, Ordinary East Germans, Skeptical of Krenz," *Reuters*, 19 October 1989.
5. "GDR Leader Affirms Importance of SED-CPSU Alliance," *BBC*, 31 October 1989.
6. See "Gorbatschow hofft auf 'feinfühlige' Politik der SED nach dem Wechsel in Ost-Berlin," *FAZ*, 20 October 1989.
7. "Egon Krenz trifft sich mit Michail Gorbatschow," *ND*, 23 October 1989.
8. Based on Hoffmann's account, Yazov was not especially forthcoming on issues such as the GDR's attempt to give back its surface-to-surface missiles. Yazov argued that the Soviets had enough problems of their own with the destruction of such missiles and did not want to make things worse by adding additional missiles. Hoffmann, *Das letzte Kommando*, pp. 86–87. Later comments by Yazov would make it clear that he found it very difficult to understand, much less relate to, the changes that were taking place in the GDR.
9. This term *Wende* was to become a major phrase in describing change in East German politics in much the same way as *odnowa* in Poland or *perestroika* in the USSR. See "Kohl führt ein erstes Gespräch mit Krenz; Seiters reist demnächst nach Ost-Berlin," *FAZ*, October 27, 1989.
10. Schabowski, *Der Absturz*, p. 272; and Hoffmann, *Das letzte Kommando*, p. 25.
11. "Nachdenken, diskutieren, gemeinsam handeln," *Volksarmee*, No. 44 (1989); and "Für Streitkräfte ist klar: Zu jeder Stunde wird Klassenauftrag erfüllt," *ND*, 26 October 1989.

12. "Miteinander reden—miteinander handeln," *Volksarmee*, No. 45 (1989).

13. As cited in Knabe, *Unter der Flagge des Gegners*, pp. 113–114.

14. Krenz estimated the crowd to have been 200,000. The 300,000 number is from "Hunderttausende fordern in Leipzig und Schwerin Bürgerrechte und Reformen," *FAZ*, 31 October 1989. For Krenz's comments see Krenz, *Wenn Mauern Fallen*, p. 221.

15. See "Beschluß des Staatsrates der Deutschen Demokratischen Republik über eine Amnestie vom 27. Oktober 1989," *ND*, 28/29 October 1989.

16. Goertemaker, *Unifying Germany*, p. 118.

17. Schabowski, *Das Politbüro*, p. 123.

18. Krenz, *Wenn Mauern Fallen*, p. 221.

19. Goertemaker, *Unifying Germany*, p. 88.

20. Modrow, *Aufbruch und Ende*, p. 24.

21. Hertle, *Chronik des Mauerfalls*, p. 109.

22. Hannes Bahrmann and Christoph Links, eds., *Wir sind das Volk: Die DDR zwischen 7. Oktober and 17. Dezember 1989; Eine Chronik*, p. 83, as cited in Goertemaker, *Unifying Germany*, p. 89.

23. The West Germans were concerned for two reasons. First, they feared the economic burden of hundreds of thousands of East Germans moving to the West. More important, Bonn did not want to do anything that would further destabilize the country. If the demonstrations continued to escalate and if many of the GDR's most important citizens continued to move to the West, West German officials worried that the country could collapse, with all kinds of negative implications for the future for both inter-German relations and East-West ties.

24. The speech is contained in "In großer Offenheit haben wir über alles gesprochen," *ND*, 1 November 1989.

25. Krenz, *Wenn Mauern Fallen*, p. 225.

26. Ibid., p. 151.

27. Teltschik, *329 Tage*, p. 24.

28. Krenz, *Wenn Mauern Fallen*, p. 227.

29. Goertemaker, *Unifying Germany*, p. 86. For Kohl's discussion of this speech, see Kohl, *Ich wollte Deutschlands Einheit*, pp. 118–119.

30. Arnold, *Die ersten hundert Tage des Hans Modrow*, p. 109.

31. The speech is contained in "In gemeinsamer Verantwortung vor unserem Volk schützen wir das sozialistische Vaterland," *Volksarmee*, No. 44 (1989). The quote is from Krenz, *Wenn Mauren Fallen*, p. 220.

32. This is not the place to go into the details of the Schabowski-Krenz debate over whether or not this piece of paper should have been read. Schabowski continues to this day to insist that he was only doing what Krenz told him to do, while Krenz claims that he had no idea that Schabowski would announce it publicly. See Schabowski, *Das Politbüro*, pp. 136–140; and Krenz, *Wenn Mauern Fallen*, pp. 181–182. The best and most complete discussion of the events of November 9 and the following days is contained in Hertle, *Chronik des Mauerfalls*.

33. Krenz, *Wenn Mauern Fallen*, p. 185.

34. Jarausch, *The Rush to German Unity*, p. 63.

35. Hoffmann, *Das letzte Kommando*, p. 27. General Goldbach, who was also present, took a similar line noting that "Someone came in from the Secretariat and stated that something was going on and that the chief of the Border Troops was needed on the telephone. . . . Otherwise, we knew nothing." Goldbach, tape 5 in Eike.

36. Keßler, *Zur Sache und zur Person*, pp. 308–309.

37. "Vor Ort Blutvergießen verhindert," in Koop and Schlößer, eds., *Erbe NVA*, p. 217; and Hertle, *Chronik des Mauerfalls*, pp. 184–185.

38. Streletz, tape 10 in Eike.

39. Reeb, "Wandel durch Annäherung," p. 182.

40. Stechbarth, tape 35 in Eike. Keßler stated that he called Stechbarth and told him "in all clarity" that while these troops should be ready to back up the border troops, "the use of weapons was specifically forbidden." Keßler, *Zur Sache und zur Person*, p. 311.

41. Weber, "Gläubigkeit, Opportunismus und späete Zweifel," in Backerra, ed., *NVA: ein Rückblick für die Zukunft*, p. 61.

42. Hertle, *Chronik des Mauerfalls*, pp. 220–225.

43. Stechbarth, tape 35 in Eike.

44. As quoted in Hertle, *Chronik des Mauerfalls*, p. 262.

45. See Hertle's excellent analysis of this situation in *Chronik des Mauerfalls*, pp. 252–263.

46. As quoted in Hans-Hermann Hertle, "Der Fall der Mauer aus der Sicht der NVA und der Grenztruppen der DDR," *Berliner Arbeitshefte*, No. 99 (August 1995), p. 12.

47. Keßler, *Zur Sache und zur Person*, p. 312.

48. Martin Kutz, "Demokratisierung der NVA? Die Verspätete Reform 1989/90," in Detlef Bald, ed., *Die Nationale Volksarmee* (Baden-Baden: Nomos, 1992), p. 93.

49. Hoffmann, *Das letzte Kommando*, p. 31.

50. Ibid., p. 30.

51. "Nationale Volksarmee in einer neuen Entwicklungsetappe," *ND*, 11/12 December 1989.

52. Several officers noted that they had not had any contact with Keßler and therefore could not evaluate his role.

53. Hoffmann, *Das letzte Kommando*, pp. 34–35. Hoffmann also stated that he was selected by Keßler to be his successor. Theodor Hoffmann, tape 16 in Eike.

54. Hoffmann, *Das letzte Kommando*, p. 40.

55. "Staatspolitische Arbeit konsequent von der Parteiarbeit trennen," *Volksarmee*, No. 48 (1989).

56. Teltschik, *329 Tage*, pp. 21, 27. Two hours later Kohl telephoned Gorbachev to make the same point: the FRG had no interest in instability in the GDR and would do everything possible to avoid exacerbating the situation. Kohl, *Ich wollte Deutschlands Einheit*, pp. 140, 141.

57. Keithly, *Collapse of German Communism*, p. 194.

58. See "Politbüro: Für Dialog am 'Runden Tisch,'" *ND*, 23 November 1989.

59. "Krenz will die 'führende Rolle' der SED streichen. Überarbeitung und Ergänzung der Verfassung," *FAZ*, 25 November 1989.

60. "Seiters rechnet mit Volkskammerwahlen nicht vor Herbst 1990," *FAZ*, 23 November 1989.

61. "DDR-CDU für eine deutsche Konföderation," *FAZ*, 24 November 1989.

62. The first quote is from Modrow, *Aufbruch und Ende*, p. 34; the second is from *ND*, 14 November 1989, as cited in Keithly, *Collapse of East German Communism*, p. 195.

63. Teltschik, *329 Tage*, p. 45.

64. One astute German observer has argued that this was the most important single event in the movement toward reunification. See Hannes Adomeit, *Imperial Overstretch: Germany in Soviet Policy from Stalin to Gorbachev* (Baden-Baden: Nomos, 1998), pp. 438–441.

65. "Zehn Punkte Kohls für einen deutsch-deutschen Weg," *FAZ*, 29 November 1989. For Kohl's comments on this plan see Kohl, *Ich wollte Deutschlands Einheit*, pp. 157–185.

66. Schäuble, *Der Vertrag*, p. 18.

67. Teltschik, *329 Tage*, pp. 52, 63.

68. Hoffmann, *Das Letzte Kommando*, p. 81.

69. "Die Volkskammer streicht die führende Rolle der SED aus der Verfassung," *FAZ*, 2 December 1989, and "Führungsrolle der SED wurde aus der Verfassung der DDR gestrichen," *ND*, 2/3 December 1989.

70. Hoffmann, *Das letzte Kommando*, p. 57. There, Hoffmann argues that NVA officers opposed such an action and that the NVA did not participate in the invasion. "Only a group of liaison officers and communicators were present among allied groups of forces in the area of Prague."

71. "Die Möbel hat Willi Stoph noch abgeholt," *FAZ*, 30 November 1989.

72. Wolf, *Im eigenem Auftrag*, pp. 253ff.

73. "Luxusvilla für den Verteidigungsminister" and "NVA: Militärs auf der Pirsch," both in Koop and Schlößler, eds., *Erbe NVA*, pp. 30, 33–34.

74. Theodor Hoffmann, "Zur nicht-vollendeten Militärreform der DDR," in Bald, ed., *Die Nationale Volksarmee*, p. 108.

75. Rothe, *Jahre im Frieden*, p. 220.

76. Hoffmann, *Das letzte Kommando*, p. 49.

77. Ibid., p. 50.

78. Keithly, *Collapse of East German Communism*, p. 196.

79. Hoffmann, *Das letzte Kommando*, pp. 41, 51.

80. Ibid., pp. 55–56, 58, 61.

81. Ibid., p. 82.

82. Ibid., p. 56.

83. "Heinz Keßler Reports on Army's Deployment in the Economy," *BBC Summary of World Broadcasts*, 11 November 1989.

84. "19,100 Soldaten arbeiten in der Volkswirtschaft," *ND*, 14 December 1994.

85. Hoffmann, *Das letzte Kommando*, p. 57.

86. Hagena, "Die radikale Wende der Nationalen Volksarmee," p. 206. General Hagena based his comments on a visit to the Friedrich Engels Military Academy, where this issue was discussed in some detail. For the text of the military reform plan put before the committee under Süß's leadership, see "Quo vadis - NVA," *Volksarmee*, No. 1 (1990).

87. Hoffmann, "Zur nicht-vollendeten Militärreform der DDR," p. 111.

Chapter 4

1. "East German Party Admits Errors," *St. Louis Post-Dispatch*, 13 December 1989.

2. Gysi, *Einspruch!*, p. 23.

3. Ibid., p. 25.

4. Keithly, *The Collapse of East German Communism*, p. 216.

5. Hoffmann, *Das letzte Kommando*, p. 79.

6. Ibid.

7. Teltschik, *329 Tage*, p. 70.

8. "Stoltenberg bietet der DDR Gespräche über Verteidigungspolitik an," *FAZ*, 8 December 1996.

9. "Kontakte zur Volksarmee?" *FAZ*, 27 December 1989.

10. Hoffmann, "Zur Nicht-vollendeten Militärreform der DDR," p. 113.

11. Arnold, *Die ersten hundert Tage des Hans Modrow*, p. 9.

12. "Aufruf der Nationalen Volksarmee und Grenztruppen," *ND*, 7 December 1989.

13. Hoffmann, *Das Letzte Kommando*, p. 59.

14. Ilse Spittmann, "Deutschland einig Vaterland," *Deutschland Archiv*, No. 2 (February 1990), p. 187.

15. "Gorbatschow auf ZK-Plenum der KPdSU: Die Sowjetunion wird die DDR nicht im Stich lassen," *ND*, 11 December 1989.

16. Hans Modrow, *Aufbruch und Ende*, p. 61.

17. Hoffmann, *Das letzte Kommando*, p. 67.

18. Ibid., p. 69.

19. "East Germany Replaces Honecker-Era Chiefs," *Reuters*, 29 December 1989.

20. "Auch in der Nationalen Volksarmee hat die Umgestaltung begonnen," *FAZ*, 2 January 1990.

21. I am indebted to Colonel Hans-Werner Weber for this observation. E-mail to the author from Colonel Weber dated 28 April 1998.

22. Hoffmann, *Das letzte Kommando*, p. 69.

23. See H. Süß, "Aspekte der Militärreform in der DDR," *Militärwesen*, No. 1 (1990), pp. 22–25. For a copy of the draft doctrine, see "Entwurf der Militärdoktrin der Deutschen Demokratischen Republik," *Militärwesen*, No. 1 (1990), pp. 18–21. By this time, this formerly secret military journal had become available to anyone who took the effort to obtain a copy. See also "Quo vadis NVA?" p. 6.

24. Hoffmann, *Das letzte Kommando*, p. 99.

25. Karl-Heinz Marschner, "Dienen bis zum Ende," in Dieter Farwick, ed., *Ein Staat, Eine Armee, Von der NVA zur Bundeswehr* (Bonn: Report Verlag, 1992), p. 229.

26. "Round Table Session," *BBC*, 28 February 1990.

27. Hoffmann, *Das letzte Kommando*, p. 70.

28. See "Beim Wort Genommen," *Volksarmee*, No. 48 (1989), p. 5.

29. "Welche Konturen sollte die Militärreform haben?" *Volksarmee*, No. 47 (1989), p. 6.

30. As cited in Hoffmann, *Das letzte Kommando*, p. 77.

31. "Staatspolitische Arbeit konsequent von der Parteiarbeit trennen," *Volksarmee*, No. 48 (1989), p. 3.

32. See "Die Volksarmee—unpolitisch?" and "Parteipolitische Arbeit verbieten," both in *Volksarmee*, No. 3 (1990).

33. Theodor Hoffmann, "Ja zur Erneurung zum Wehrdienst zur soldatischen Pflichterfüllung," *Volksarmee*, No. 4 (1990).

34. Reeb, "Wandel durch Annäherung," p. 184.

35. Ibid.

36. "Parteimitgliedschaft in der Armee?" *Volksarmee*, No. 7 (1990).

37. "Civilian Role for East Germany's National Volksarmee Extended," *Jane's Defense Weekly*, 23 December 1989, p. 1382.

38. Paul Heider, "Die NVA im Herbst 1989," *Utopie*, No. 54 (April 1995), p. 55.

39. "Brauchen wir noch die Armee?" *ND*, 28 December 1989.

40. Streletz, tape 10 in Eike.

41. Hoffmann, *Das letzte Kommando*, p. 177.

42. See "Vorläufiges Aktionsprogram des Verbandes der Berufssoldaten der DDR (VBS)," *Volksarmee*, No. 5 (1990).

43. Hoffmann, *Das letzte Kommando*, p. 123.

44. "Wir wollen einen Verband der Berufssoldaten," *Volksarmee*, No. 52 (1989), p. 2.

45. "Brauchen Wir noch die Armee."

46. Hoffmann, *Das letzte Kommando*, p. 91.

47. Hoffmann, tape 16 in Eike.

48. "East German Defense Minister Acts on Army Protests," *Reuters*, 2 January 1990.

49. For Hoffmann's comments on the TV coverage, see Hoffmann, *Das letzte Kommando*, p. 95. The article referred to is "Verteidigungsminister bei Soldaten in Beelitz," *ND*, 3 January 1990.

50. Hoffmann, *Das letzte Kommando*, p. 96.

51. "East Germany Shortens Army Service to Defuse Unrest," *Reuters*, 4 January 1990.

52. As quoted in Hoffmann, *Das letzte Kommando*, p. 104.

53. Weber, "Gläubigkeit, Opportunismus und späte Zweifel," p. 62.

54. "Opposition Parties to Force Alliance against Communists," *The Times* (London), 5 January 1990.

55. "Bedrohliche Ungewißheit," *Der Spiegel*, 22 January 1990, p. 131.

56. These figures are taken from Hoffmann, *Das letzte Kommando*, p. 112.

57. Ibid., p. 143

58. Ibid., p. 122.

59. Ibid., p. 125.

60. As cited in Arnold, *Die ersten hundert Tage des Hans Modrow*, p. 75.

61. Hoffmann, *Das letzte Kommando*, pp. 126–127.

62. As cited in Goertemaker, *Unifying Germany*, p. 130.

63. Teltschik, *329 Tage*, p. 114.

64. "Gorbatschow hat 'prinzipiell' nichts gegen eine Vereinigung der beiden deutschen Staaten," *FAZ*, 31 January 1990.

65. As cited in Goertemaker, *Unifying Germany*, p. 131.

66. Zelnikow and Rice, *Germany Unified and Europe Transformed*, p. 158.

67. See Spittmann, "Deutschland einig Vaterland," p. 189.

68. Teltschik, *329 Tage*, pp. 110–111.

69. Ibid., p. 114.

70. The creation of this working group is discussed in Goertemaker, *Unifying Germany*, p. 132.

71. Hoffmann, *Das letzte Kommando*, p. 145.

72. Ibid., pp. 117, 121.

73. Ibid., p. 121.

74. Ibid., pp. 163, 173.

75. Ibid., pp. 194–195.

76. Ibid., p. 147.

77. Manfred Werther, tape 32 in Eike.

78. "East Germany Says Desertions, Bad Morale Damage Army Readiness," *Reuters*, 28 February 1990.

79. Cited in Hagena, "Die radikale Wende der Nationalen Volksarmee," p. 206.

80. Hoffmann, *Das letzte Kommando*, p. 185.

81. Ibid., p. 178.

82. See "Wie ohne Wehrpflicht weiter?" *ND*, 9 March 1990.

83. "East German Elite Soldiers Protest Conditions," *Reuters*, 15 March 1990.

84. "Brauchen Wir Noch die Armee?"

85. The author was a member of the American delegation to these talks and, since the French spelling of the various countries was utilized in the placement of delegations, he had an opportunity to both watch interactions between the two German delegations and to discuss NVA-related problems in depth with Grätz and his colleagues. It was clear that the East Germans were far more interested in contacts than was the case for the West Germans, although Admiral Wellershoff and his colleagues were always exremely polite. It was also clear that the East Germans were very depressed about the situation in the GDR. For example, in response to a question concerning his future, General Grätz replied, "Who knows? I don't even know if I will have a job next week."

86. Hoffmann, *Das letzte Kommando*, p. 158.

87. Ibid., p. 155.

88. See the interview with Weiskirch, in "NVA und Bundeswehr sollten aktiv mitwirken am Zusammenwachsen," *Volksarmee*, No. 9 (1990).

89. Hoffmann, "Zur nicht-vollendeten Militärreform der DDR," p. 113.

90. Hoffmann, *Das letzte Kommando*, p. 193.

91. Hans-Joachim Reeb, "Eingliederung ehemaliger NVA-Berufssoldaten in die Bundeswehr," *Deutschland Archiv* 8 (August 1992): 850.

92. "Hans Modrow unterbreitete Konzept 'Für Deutschland, einig Vaterland,'" *ND*, 2 February 1990.

93. Modrow, *Aufbruch und Ende*, pp. 119–124.

94. Teltschik, *329 Tage*, p. 124.

95. "Events Overtaking Gradualist Approach to German Unification," *Reuters*, 2 February 1990.

96. Goertemaker, *Unifying Germany*, p. 134.

97. Teltschik, *329 Tage*, p. 132.

98. On February 5 the SED-PDS changed its name to PDS eliminating the old SED in an attempt to gain greater legitimacy among voters. See "Die 'SED' ist weg - die PDS is eine neue Partei," *ND*, 5 February 1990.

99. Eppelmann, *Wendewege*, p. 16.

100. "Warsaw Pact—Endgame: In Eastern Europe, the Military Alliance Is Dead," *Washington Post*, 4 February 1990.

101. "Vierter Runder Tisch beriet militärpolitische Leitsätze," *ND*, 8 February 1990.

102. "East German Soldiers Job-Hunting in West German Army," *Reuters*, 15 March 1990.

103. As cited in Schäuble, *Der Vertrag*, p. 29.

104. "VA-Exklusivinterview mit dem Ministerpräsidenten der DDR, Dr. Hans Modrow," *Volksarmee*, No. 7 (1990).

105. Teltschik, *329 Tage*, p. 140.

106. Goertemaker, *Unifying Germany*, pp. 164, 166.

107. For Genscher's statement, see "Ausdehnung der NATO nach Osten wird es nicht geben," *ND*, 10/11 February 1990. For reference to Bahr's statement, see Hoffmann, *Das letzte Kommando*, p. 152.

108. Teltschik, *329 Tage*, p. 145.

109. Hoffmann, *Das letzte Kommando*, p. 153.

110. "Minister Visits Defense Ministry, Discusses Future Role of Army," *BBC*, 21 February 1990.

111. Hoffmann, *Das letzte Kommando*, p. 154.

112. "Minister Eppelmann in Strausberg," *Volksarmee*, No. 8 (1990).

113. Teltschik, *329 Tage*, pp. 151–152. The logic behind this arrangement was simple: Stoltenberg's position vis-à-vis Kohl was not very strong. And besides, "Kohl wanted quick unification, and while he was sensitive to defense concerns, he was not willing to be diverted or delayed from reaching his goal by the Defense Ministry." Stephen F. Szabo, *The Diplomacy of German Unification*, (New York: St. Martin's Press, 1992), p. 29.

114. "Bonn Will Only Discuss United German Army After Elections," *Reuters*, 22 February 1990.

115. Hoffmann, *Das letzte Kommando*, p. 98.

Chapter 5

1. Modrow, *Aufbruch und Ende*, p. 89.
2. See Goertemaker's discussion of these events, Goertemaker, *Unifying Germany*, pp. 127–128.
3. "Upheaval in the East: Kohl Is Reported Intent on Slowing Unity with the East," *New York Times*, 20 March 1990.
4. Biographical data on Eppelmann are taken from, Eduard Glöckner, "Der Pazifist als Wehrminister: Rainer Eppelmann," *EW,* No 6 (1990), p. 326; and "New East German Defence Minister Is Former Draft Dodger," *Reuters*, 12 April 1990.
5. Ablaß, *Zapfenstreich*, p. 17.
6. Material on these three individuals is from Glöckner, "Der Pazifist als Wehrminister," p. 327.
7. Hoffmann, *Das letzte Kommando*, p. 204. Hoffmann's words in German were, "Die letzten Monaten hatten mich ziemlich mitgenommen, und ich hatte, wie man so sagt, die Nase voll."
8. Eppelmann, *Wendewege*, p. 42.
9. Hoffmann, *Das letzte Kommando*, pp. 205–206.
10. Schabowski, *Der Absturz*, p. 302.
11. Hoffmann, *Das letzte Kommando*, p. 203.
12. Ibid., p. 202.
13. Eppelmann, *Wendewege*, p. 47; Ablaß, *Zapfenstreich*, pp. 44–45; and "FRG-GDR Relations: GDR Defense Minister on Military Aspects of German Unification," *BBC*, 4 May 1990.
14. Ablaß, *Zapfenstreich*, p. 36.
15. Eppelmann, *Wendewege*, p. 77.
16. Ibid., pp. 20–21.
17. Ibid., p. 76.
18. Modrow, *Aufbruch und Ende*, pp. 122–123.
19. Teltschik, *329 Tage*, pp. 179–181.
20. Ibid., p. 194.
21. Goertemaker, *Unifying Germany*, p. 172.
22. Teltschik, *329 Tage*, p. 185.
23. Eppelmann, *Wendewege*, p. 23.
24. "East German Leader Flies to Moscow for Talks on German Unification," *UPI*, 28 April 1990.
25. As cited in Hoffmann, *Das letzte Kommando*, p. 221.
26. "East Germany, Soviets Differ on NATO Role," *UPI*, 29 April 1990.
27. "Stabschefs gegen NATO-Mitgliedschaft," *ND*, 14 April 1990.
28. Hoffmann, *Das letzte Kommando*, p. 219.
29. As cited in ibid., p. 238.
30. Ibid. This statement was also published in *ND*, 14 May 1990. Hoffmann reports other senior Soviet generals took a similar line during the visit. See Hoffmann, *Das letzte Kommando*, p. 239.
31. "East German Elite Soldiers Protest Conditions," *Reuters*, 15 March 1990.

32. "Die Abrechnung," *Volksarmee*, No. 13 (1990).

33. See "Former East German Defence Minister Faces Possible Charges," *Reuters*, 19 January 1990; "Former GDR Defence Minister Arrested," *BBC*, 27 January 1990; and "East Germany Drops Graft Inquiry against Ex-Defence Minister," *Reuter Library Report*, 17 May 1990.

34. Hoffmann, *Das letzte Kommando*, p. 197.

35. Ibid., p. 323.

36. Ibid., p. 179.

37. Ibid., p. 173.

38. Hagena, "Die radikale Wende der Nationalen Volksarmee," pp. 208–209.

39. Jörg Schönbohm, "Vorwort," in Backerra, ed., *NVA: Ein Rückblick für die Zukunft*, p. 6.

40. "East German Army Demoralized by Changes," *Christian Science Monitor*, 10 April 1990.

41. "E. Germany Plans Defense Cuts, May Consider Disbanding Forces," *Reuters*, 3 April 1990.

42. "Eppelmann bezweifelt gemeinsames Heer," *FAZ*, 17 April 1990.

43. "East German Army Short-Staffed But Combat Ready, Says Minister," *Reuters*, 9 April 1990.

44. Teltschik, *329 Tage*, p. 198.

45. Hoffmann, *Das letzte Kommando*, p. 203.

46. "GDR Defence Minister Receives Warsaw Treaty C-in-C," *BBC*, 24 April 1990.

47. "Gysi: Wehrpflicht nach 1990 abschaffen," *ND*, 23 April 1990.

48. Teltschik, *329 Tage*, p. 198.

49. For a discussion of this point, see Reeb, "Wandel Durch Annäherung," p. 183.

50. "Eppelmann: Wehrpflicht ein Stück Demokratie," *ND*, 23 April 1990.

51. For a copy of the letter see "Verschwörung in der NVA?" in Backerra, ed., *NVA: Ein Rückblick für die Zukunft*, pp. 65–66.

52. "Wegen Verstoßes gegen Verfassung entlassen," in Backerra, ed., *NVA: Ein Rückblick für die Zukunft*, p. 66.

53. Reeb, "Eingliederung ehemaliger NVA-Berufssoldaten in die Bundeswehr," p. 847.

54. "Sorgen der Grenzsoldaten," *ND*, 25 June 1990.

55. Held, Friedrich, and Pietsch, "Politische Bildung und Erziehung in der Nationalen Volksarmee," p. 220.

56. Paul Heider, "Die NVA im Herbst 1989," p. 57.

57. Eppelmann, *Wendewege*, p. 81.

58. "Few Jobs Await East German Soldiers As Country Fades Away, *Reuters*, 27 June 1990.

59. As reported in "NVA-Angehörige in die Fremdelegion?" *ND*, 6 August 1990.

60. Hoffmann, *Das letzte Kommando*, p. 232.

61. See the discussion in "Werter Herr Minister: So Fing es an: Bewer-

bungen von Offizieren der NVA," in Paul Klein and Rolf Zimmermann, eds., *Beispielhaft? Eine Zwischenbilanz zur Eingliederung der Nationalen Volksarmee in die Bundeswehr* (Baden-Baden: Nomos, 1993), p. 70.

62. Berlin Army Fails to Inspire New Conscripts," *The Times* (London), 30 May 1990.

63. "Defence Minister Says East German Army Unable to Fight," *Reuters*, 17 May 1990.

64. Ablaß, *Zapfenstreich*, p. 93.

65. "NVA sagt ab," *ND*, 19 July 1990.

66. Hoffmann, *Das letzte Kommando*, p. 294.

67. Ibid., pp. 258–259. See also "East Germany to Trim Army, End Standing Combat Stance," *Reuters*, 6 June 1990.

68. Ablaß, *Zapfenstreich*, p. 132.

69. "1400 Grenzsoldaten aus Dienst entlassen," *ND*, 28/29 July 1990; and "Die DDR hat nach 27 Jahren die Militärgerichtsbarkeit abgeschafft," *FAZ*, 17 July 1990.

70. "NVA entläßt: Frauen zurerst," *ND*, 5 September 1990.

71. "Noch 88,000 NVA-Soldaten im Dienst," *Süddeutsche Zeitung*, 8 November 1990.

72. "Leaders to Decide Warsaw Pact's Fate in Post-Cold War Era," *Reuters*, 7 June 1990.

73. "Warsaw Pact Vows End to Old Structure, Moves to Democracy," *Reuters*, 7 June 1990. See also "Warsaw Pact Summit Urges Transformation; Leaders Endorse Cooperation with NATO," *Washington Post*, 8 June 1990.

74. For a discussion of this last defense minister's meeting, see "Solemn Ministers Gather to Wind Up Warsaw Pact," *Reuters*, 13 June 1990.

75. "Die DDR verläßt das östliche Militärbüdnis," *FAZ*, 25 September 1990.

76. Lothar W. Breene-Wegner, "Kameraden oder Bösewichte?" *Truppenpraxis*, No. 5 (1990), p. 443.

77. Teltschik, *329 Tage*, p. 214.

78. "Eppelmann: Blockfreies Europa ist notwendig," *ND*, 16/17 June 1990.

79. "East German Minister Calls for 1992 Unification," *UPI*, 15 June 1990.

80. "Defense Minister Says Date of Reunification Less Important Than Conditions," *BBC*, 22 June 1990.

81. As cited in Goertemaker, *Unifying Germany*, p. 153.

82. Eppelmann, *Wendewege*, p. 99.

83. "Verteidigungsminister vereinbaren enge Zusammenarbeit," *FAZ*, 28 April 1990.

84. Eppelmann, *Wendewege*, p. 106.

85. Hoffmann, *Das letzte Kommando*, p. 256.

86. "Für Stoltenberg ist die Verkleinerung der Bundeswehr 'kein Tabu' mehr," *FAZ*, 11 April 1990.

87. For a discussion of the meeting, see "Beziehungen von NVA und Bundeswehr," *ND*, 29 May 1990.

88. "Stoltenberg Favors Single German Military," *Xinhua General Overseas News Service*, 13 June 1990.

89. As cited in Hoffmann, *Das letzte Kommando*, pp. 264, 273.

90. "Unter NVA-Generälen?" *FAZ*, 16 July 1990.

91. "Bereitschaft zu kameradschaftlichem Umgang," *FAZ*, 23 July 1990. A similar position is taken in "Weiter in Feindbildern gedacht," *FAZ*, 15 August 1990.

92. "NVA-Führung—Kommunisten reinsten Wassers," *FAZ*, 10 July 1990.

93. "Von der NVA zur Bundeswehr," *FAZ*, 24 July 1990.

94. "Auflösen—ohne Rest," *FAZ*, 25 July 1990.

95. Werner von Schewen, tape 27, in Eike.

96. For Kohl's description of this event, see Helmut Kohl, *Ich wollte Deutschlands Einheit*, pp. 421–444.

97. "Soviets Agree to Germany in NATO," *Los Angeles Times*, 17 July 1990.

98. Teltschik, *329 Tage*, pp. 316–336.

99. "Soviets Agree to Germany in NATO."

100. Eppelmann, *Wendewege*, p. 115.

101. "East German Foreign Minister Accuses Kohl of Arrogance," *Reuters*, 21 July 1990.

102. Hoffmann, *Das letzte Kommando*, p. 296.

103. Goldbach, "Die Nationale Volksarmee," pp. 137–138.

104. Streletz, tape 11 in Eike.

105. See Goertemaker, *Unifying Germany*, p. 199.

106. "Warsaw to Study Proposal for Joint Polish-German Army Units," *Reuters*, 23 May 1990; Hoffmann, *Das letzte Kommando*, p. 250; and Ablaß, *Zapfenstreich*, p. 67. Despite opposition to Eppelmann's proposal, it is worth noting that the idea did not go away. For example, in 1995, the Polish defense minister, Zbigniew Okonski, stated that "The idea of forming a Polish-German military unit modeled after a French-German brigade is being seriously considered." "A Strong Army—a Safe State," *Polska Zbrojna*, 26 October 1995, in *FBIS EEU*, 3 November 1995, p. 46. While such ideas were eventually overtaken by NATO's Partnership for Peace arrangement, the fact is that Eppelmann was ahead of his time.

107. "Auf Bitte Eppelmanns: Egon Bahr berät NVA," *ND*, 6 July 1990.

108. See the interview with Bahr in Hoffmann, *Das letzte Kommando*, pp. 329–330.

109. For a copy of the old oath, see "Wie soll ein neuer Fahneneid lauten," *Volksarmee*, No. 52 (1989). For a discussion of the new oath, see "East German Soldiers Swear New Oath, Drop Communist Allegiance," *Reuters*, 20 July 1990.

110. "Antworten an Eppelmann zur Vereidigung am 20. Juli," *ND*, 21/22 July 1990.

111. Eppelmann, *Wendewege*, p. 118.

112. "Most East German Troops Facing Unemployment After Unification," *New York Times*, 23 July 1990.

113. Knabe, *Unter der Flagge des Gegners*, p. 119. When asked about the new oath, Ablaß argued that Eppelmann was doing nothing more than carrying out the will of the democratically elected Parliament. After all, there was a major difference between the old oath and the new one that those joining the NVA at that time were following. Ablaß, tape 4 in Eike.

114. "Merkwürdiges um die Sicherheitspolitik," *ND*, 11 July 1990.

115. Jarausch, *The Rush to German Unity*, p. 171.

116. Hoffmann, *Das letzte Kommando*, p. 301.

117. Ibid., p. 274.

118. Ibid., pp. 290–291.

119. Ibid., pp. 285, 286.

120. See "Staatssekretär soll zurücktreten," *ND*, 24 July 1990; and Hoffmann, *Das letzte Kommando*, p. 276.

121. Hoffmann, *Das letzte Kommando*, pp. 286, 301.

122. "Per 'Sensebefehl' werden ältere Offiziere in Pension geschickt," *Die Welt*, 11 September 1990.

123. Knabe, *Unter der Flagge des Gegners*, p. 120.

124. As noted in Hoffmann, *Das letzte Kommando*, p. 307.

125. Günther Pöschel, "Seefahrt macht frei! Leider nicht immer . . . Über die Volksmarine der NVA," in Backerra, ed., *NVA: Ein Rückblick für die Zukunft*, pp. 176–177.

126. "Ausführung des Chefs der Nationalen Volksarmee auf der letzten Kommandeurstagung der NVA am 12. September 1990," in Hoffmann, *Das letzte Kommando*, pp. 332–334.

127. Hermann Hagena, "NVA-Soldaten in der Bundeswehr: Integration— nicht Reseverwertung," *EW*, No. 10 (1990), p. 568; and Jörg Schönbohm, "Deutsche kommen zu Deutschen," in Farwick, *Ein Staat, Eine Armee*, p. 39.

128. Ablaß, *Zapfenstreich*, pp. 178–179.

129. Eppelmann, *Wendewege*, p. 161.

130. The term *Ossi* (Easterner) is an uncomplimentary form of address used by many in what was West Germany to refer to East Germans.

Chapter 6

1. While these discussions were supposed to be private, they were soon in the press, much to the unhappiness of Kohl. Teltschik, *329 Tage*, p. 293. For a press report on this meeting, see "Behind German Unity Pact: Personal Diplomacy from Maine to Moscow," *Washington Post*, 22 July 1990.

2. Schäuble, *Der Vertrag*, pp. 200–201.

3. G. Hubatschek, "Der steinige Weg zur Wiedervereinigung," in Farwick, ed., *Ein Staat, Eine Armee*, p. 27.

4. "Schönbohm befehligt zentrales Kommando, *FAZ*, 28 August 1990.

5. Ablaß, *Zapfenstreich*, p. 163.

6. Edgar Trost, "Probleme der Personalauswahl," in Farwick, ed., *Ein Staat, Eine Armee*, pp. 170–205.

7. Schönbohm, *Zwei Armeen und ein Vaterland*, pp. 31–32.

8. "NVA: An Army Conversion," *International Defense Review* 23, No. 10 (1 October 1990): 1093.

9. Trost, "Probleme der Personalauswahl," p. 176.

10. Hans Peter von Kirchbach, Manfred Meyers, and Victor Vogt, *Abenteuer Einheit* (Frankfurt am Main: Report Verlag, 1992), p. 48.

11. Hisso von Selle, "Going from East to West: the 9th Panzer Division Artillery," *Field Artillery*, June 1993, p. 28.

12. Friedrich Steinseifer, "Zusammenfügen und verkleinern," *Truppenpraxis*, No. 1 (1991), p. 19.

13. Schönbohm, *Zwei Armeen und ein Vaterland*, p. 47.

14. Von Selle, "Going from East to West," p. 28.

15. Schönbohm, *Zwei Armeen und ein Vaterland*, p. 33.

16. Steinseifer, "Zusammenfügen und verkleinern," pp. 19–20.

17. The term *Wessi* is a somewhat unflattering term used by East Germans to describe West Germans.

18. "Die NVA wird auf 50 000 Mann reduziert," *FAZ*, 11 September 1990.

19. Trost, "Probleme der Auswahl," p. 192.

20. Schönbohm, *Zwei Armeen und ein Vaterland*, p. 33. Emphasis in the original.

21. Cited in Trost, "Probleme der Auswahl," p. 184.

22. Steinseifer, "Zusammenfügen und verkleinern," p. 21.

23. For the legal document setting up these categories as well as noting the responsibilities of former NVA personnel in the Bundeswehr, see "Die NVA im Einigungsvertrag," *EW*, No. 10 (1990), pp. 572–573. See also, Hagena, "NVA-Soldaten in der Bundeswehr, p. 568.

24. Von Selle, "Going from East to West," p. 29.

25. Herbert König, "Bericht aus einer anderen Welt," *Truppenpraxis*, No. 3 (1992), p. 234.

26. "Das Dienstverhältnis der Soldaten der Volksarmee soll ruhen," *FAZ*, 29 August 1990.

27. Von Selle, "Going from East to West," p. 28.

28. "Soldaten dürfen nicht auf der Straße stehen," *FAZ*, 30 November 1990.

29. Schönbohm, *Zwei Armeen und ein Vaterland*, p. 33.

30. Hoffmann, *Das letzte Kommando*, p. 301.

31. "Soldiers Still Leaving NVA," *BBC*, 13 September 1990.

32. "Soldaten dürfen nicht auf der Straße stehen."

33. Schönbohm, "Deutsche kommen zu Deutschen," p. 43.

34. Schönbohm, *Zwei Armee und ein Vaterland*, pp. 39–40.

35. "Die Bundeswehr im beigetretenen Teil Deutschlands," *Soldat und Technik*, No. 11 (1990), p. 780.

36. Schönbohm, *Zwei Armeen und ein Vaterland*, p. 51.

37. "Die Einheit auch in der Bundeswehr gestalten," *Soldat und Technik*, No. 11 (1990), p. 776.

38. Schönbohm, *Zwei Armeen und ein Vaterland*, p. 92.

39. Wolfgang Gülich, "Der Prozeß der deutsch-deutschen militärischen Vereinigung aus der Sicht eines Brigadekommandeurs in den neuen Bundesländern—Versuch einer ersten Bewertung," in Klein and Zimmermann, *Beispielhaft?*, pp. 24–25.

40. "Schönbohm klagt: Uns fehlen Unteroffiziere," *Die Welt*, 24 December 1990.

41. "Bonn: NVA-Bestände als Golfhilfe für die USA," *Die Welt*, 22/23 September 1990.

42. Hans Peter von Kirchbach, Die Kasernen," in von Kirchbach, Meyers, and Vogt, *Abenteuer Einheit*, pp. 98–99.

43. "Noch 88 000 NVA—Soldaten im Dienst," *Süddeutsche Zeitung*, 8 November 1990.

44. Schönbohm, *Zwei Armeen und ein Vaterland*, p. 84.

45. Von Schewen, tape 27 in Eike.

46. "East German Army Full of Surprises," *The San Francisco Chronicle*, 14 December 1990.

47. "GDR Defense Ministry Donates Army Trucks, Equipment to Third World," *Inter Press Service*, 1 September 1990.

48. "Bonn: NVA-Bestände also Golfhilfe für die USA."

49. Steinseifer, "Zusammenfügen und verkleinern," p. 23.

50. "Germany Disposes East's Assets; UN Gets Chunk of Communist Regime's Military Goods," *Defense News*, 13 March 1995.

51. "Bonn Braces for Absorption of East Germany's Army," *Los Angeles Times*, 30 September 1990.

52. Günter Holzweißig, "Auflösen - Ohne Rest?" *Deutschland Archiv*, No. 10 (1990).

53. Knabe, *Unter der Flagge des Gegners*, pp. 103–104. The first comment was from a former NVA colonel, the second from a commander.

54. Horst Prayon, "Die 'Feinde' von einst sollen Kameraden werden," *EW*, No. 11 (1990).

55. Günther Gilleßen, "Die Armee die dabeistand," *FAZ*, 10 November 1990.

56. "Wir müßen unsere Feldwebel neu backen," *Die Welt*, 1 December 1990.

57. Hoffmann, *Kommando Ostsee*, pp. 212–213.

58. Von Schewen, tape 27 in Eike.

59. Rüdiger Volk and Torsten Squarr, "Die innere Zustand der NVA," in Farwick, ed., *Ein Staat, Eine Armee*, p. 257. Another source claims that a unit had to be able to leave its base combat-ready within one hour. See König, "Bericht aus einer anderen Welt," p. 235. Regardless of which source is more accurate, the fact is that no Western army could have matched this reaction time. It could only be attained if everything were subordinated to combat readiness. According to the former head of East Germany's ground forces, the Soviet military was at a 100 percent level of combat readiness. While this is probably true, the political benefits from such a highly prepared military within the Warsaw Pact and in East German—Russian relations is also significant. See Stechbarth, tape 35 in Eike.

60. Frau. Dr. Pietsch, tape 14 in Eike.

61. Karl-Heinz Marschner, "Dienen bis zum Ende," p. 208.

62. Schönbohm, "Deutsche kommen zu Deutschen," p. 37.

63. Dieter Farwick, "Einige Antworten," in Farwick, ed., *Ein Staat, Eine Armee*, p. 305.

64. Von Kirchbach, Meyers and Vogt, *Abenteuer Einheit*, pp. 85, 93–94, 97.

65. Breene-Wegener, "Kameraden oder Bösewichte?" p. 440.

66. König, "Bericht aus einer anderen Welt," p. 236.

67. Breene-Wegener, "Kameraden oder Bösewichte?" p. 442.

68. "Zur Einleitung," in Backerra, ed., *NVA: Ein Rückblick für die Zukunft*, p. 14.

69. Weber, "Gläubigkeit, Opportunismus und späte Zweifel," p. 58.

70. Prayon, "Die Feinde von einst sollen Kameraden werden," p. 637.

71. Reeb, "Wandel durch Annäherung," p. 181.

72. Paul Klein, Ekerhard Lippert, and Georg-Maria Meyer, "Zur sozialen Befindlichkeit von Offizieren und Unterofizieren aus der ehemaligen Nationalen Volksarmee," in Klein and Zimmermann, eds., *Beispielhaft?*, p. 56.

73. "Wir dienen demselben Vaterland," *Truppenpraxis*, No. 4 (1991), p. 337.

74. Gilleßen, "Die Armee die dabeistand,"

75. Von Kirchbach, Meyers and Vogt, "Personalfragen," *Abenteuer Einheit*, p. 79.

76. Von Selle, "Going from East to West," p. 30.

77. Klein, Lippert, and Meyer, "Zur sozialen Befindlichkeit," p. 54.

78. "Wert militärischer Tugenden entscheidet sich am wofür," *Die Welt*, 12 October 1990.

79. "Schatten der Vergangenheit," in von Kirchbach, Meyers, and Vogt, *Abenteuer Einheit*, p. 132.

80. Reeb, "Eingliederung ehemaliger NVA-Berufssoldaten in die Bundeswehr," p. 848.

81. König, "Bericht aus einer anderen Welt," p. 238.

82. Held, Friedrich, and Pietsch, "Politische Bildung und Erziehung in der NVA," p. 227.

83. Marschner, "Dienen bis zum Ende," p. 210.

84. Klaus-Jürgen Engelien and Hans-Joachim Reeb, "Wer bist du—Kamerad?" *Truppenpraxis*, No. 6 (1990), p. 652.

85. *Economist*, 22 August 92, p. 37.

86. Bernhard Ickenroth, "Der einstige 'Klassenfeind' in der Kaderschmiede für Politoffiziere der NVA," *Europäische Sicherheit*, No. 5 (1991), p. 283.

87. "Schönbohm klagt: Uns fehlen Unteroffiziere," *Die Welt*, 24 December 1990.

88. Von Kirchbach, Meyers, and Vogt, *Abenteuer Einheit*, p. 36

89. Von Selle, "Going from East to West," pp. 30–31.

Chapter 7

1. Von Kirchbach, Meyers, and Vogt, *Abenteuer Einheit*, p. 125.

2. Halvor Adrian, "Suche nach Halt in einer fremden Welt," *Truppenpraxis*, No. 6 (1992), p. 545.

3. Engelien and Reeb, "Wer bist du Kamerad?" p. 651.

4. Sabine Collmer, *et al.*, *Einheit auf Befehl?* (Opladen: Westdeutscher Verlag, 1994), p. 147.

5. The military figures were provided to the author by Colonel Weber and

differ slightly from those provided by Volk and Squarr, "Der innere Zustand der NVA," p. 247.

6. Klein, Lippert, and Mayer, "Zur sozialen Befindlichkeit," p. 52.

7. Marschner, "Dienen bis zum Ende," p. 217.

8. Sabine Collmer and Georg-Maria Meyer, "Früher 'Zur Fahne,' Heute 'Zum Bund': Soziale Deutungsmuster von wehrpflichtigen Soldaten aus den neuen Bundesländern," in Klein and Zimmermann, eds., *Beispielhaft?* p. 42.

9. Dirk Sommer, "Zwischen Hoffen und Zagen," *Truppenpraxis*, No. 3 (1991), p. 302.

10. See "Meine Mutter dachte, ich sei desertiert," *FAZ*, 23 March 1991.

11. Koop and Schlößer, eds., *Erbe NVA*, p. 250.

12. "Wir müßen unsere Feldwebel neu backen," *Die Welt*, 1 December 1990.

13. Schönbohm, *Zwei Armeen und ein Vaterland*, p. 130.

14. Von Kirchbach, Meyers, and Vogt, *Abenteuer Einheit*, p. 34.

15. Sommer, "Zwischen Hoffen und Zagen," p. 302.

16. Collmer and Meyer, "Früher 'zur Fahne,' Heute 'Zum Bund,' " p. 42.

17. Klein, Lippert, and Mayer, "Zur sozialen Befindlichkeit," *Beispielhaft?* p. 58.

18. Wolfgang Fechner, "Der Wehrbeauftragte gewinnt Vertrauen," *Europäische Sicherheit*, No. 3 (1991), p. 173.

19. "Wir dienen demselben Vaterland," *Truppenpraxis*, No. 4 (1991), p. 336.

20. Von Selle, "Going from East to West," p. 29.

21. Von Kirchbach, Meyers, and Vogt, *Abenteuer Einheit*.

22. Reeb, "Eingliederung ehemaliger NVA-Berufssoldaten in die Bundeswehr," p. 850.

23. Adrian, "Suche nach Halt in einer fremden Welt," p. 546.

24. Von Kirchbach, Meyers, and Vogt, "Das Vorkommando," *Abenteuer Einheit*, p. 34.

25. Klein, Lippert, and Mayer, "Zur sozialen Befindlichkeit," p. 58.

26. Von Kirchbach, Meyers, and Vogt, "Personalfragen," *Abenteuer Einheit*, p. 80.

27. Klein, Lippert, and Mayer, "Zur sozialen Befindlichkeit," p. 55.

28. Hermann Hagena, "Die ungleiche Aufteilung von 'Ossis' und 'Wessis,' " *Europäische Sicherheit*, No. 3 (1991), p. 170.

29. "Wir dienen demselben Vaterland," p. 332.

30. Hans Peter von Kirchbach, *Reflections on the Growing Together of the German Armed Forces: The Eggesin Garrison as an Example for the Unification of the Two Armies* (Carlisle Barracks, Pa.: Strategic Studies Institute, 1992), p. 3.

31. Klein, Lippert, and Mayer, "Zur sozialen Befindlichkeit," p. 56.

32. Trost, "Probleme der Personalauswahl," p. 187.

33. See Hans Peter von Kirchbach, "Die Einheit leben," in Farwick, ed., *Ein Staat, Eine Armee*, pp. 149–150. This was a battle that Schönbohm would fight throughout his six-month tenure in Kommando-Ost, finding ways to countermand the orders issued by bureaucrats in Bonn who had little understanding of the situation on the ground in the former GDR. See, for example, his discussion with the Bundeswehr's inspector general in Schönbohm, *Zwei Armeen und ein Vaterland*, p. 81.

34. Von Kirchbach, "Die Einheit leben," p. 149.

35. "Wir dienen demselben Vaterland," p. 338.

36. Schönbohm, *Zwei Armeen und ein Vaterland*, p. 90.

37. Ibid., p. 134.

38. Ibid., p. 206.

39. "Start bei der NVA—Ende beim 'Bund,'" in Koop and Schlößler, eds., *Erbe NVA*, p. 13.

40. Friedrich Holtzendorff, "Das Risiko und the Chance der einstigen NVA-Soldaten," *EW,* No. 10 (1990), p. 564.

41. Reeb, "Eingliederung ehemaliger NVA-Berufssoldaten in die Bundeswehr," p. 853.

42. "Wir dienen demselben Vaterland," p. 333.

43. Reeb, "Eingliederung ehemaliger NVA-Berufssoldaten in die Bundeswehr," p. 854.

44. "Wir dienen demselben Vaterland," p. 333.

45. Prayon, "Die 'Feinde' von einst sollen Kameraden werden," p. 636.

46. "Wir dienen demselben Vaterland," p. 333.

47. Reeb, "Eingliederung ehemaliger NVA-Berufssoldaten in die Bundeswehr," p. 856.

48. Herbert König, "Ein schwerer und schmerzhafter Prozeß," *Truppenpraxis*, No. 5 (1991), p. 489.

49. König, "Bericht aus einer anderen Welt," p. 234.

50. Ibid.

51. Reeb, "Eingliederung ehemaliger NVA-Berufssoldaten in die Bundeswehr," p. 856.

52. Schönbohm, *Zwei Armeen und ein Vaterland*, p. 80.

53. Von Kirchbach, *Reflections on the Growing Together of the German Armed Forces*, p. 7.

54. Schönbohm, *Zwei Armeen und ein Vaterland*, p. 76.

55. Ibid., p. 87.

56. Ibid., p. 89.

57. Werner von Schewen, "Abschied von der heilen Welt," *Truppenpraxis*, No. 6 (1991), p. 611.

58. Reeb, "Eingliederung ehemaliger NVA-Berufssoldaten in die Bundeswehr," p. 855.

59. Ibid.

60. Schönbohm, *Zwei Armeen und ein Vaterland*, p. 136.

61. Reeb, "Eingliederung ehemaliger NVA-Berufssoldaten in die Bundeswehr," p. 852.

62. Von Schewen, "Abschied von der heilen Welt," p. 611.

63. Schönbohm, *Zwei Armeen und ein Vaterland*, p. 249.

64. Reeb, "Eingliederung ehemaliger NVA-Berufssoldaten in die Bundeswehr," p. 852.

65. "Mehr Einrichtungen in den Osten," *FAZ*, 1 June 1991.

66. Josef Heinrichs, "Jeder bekam seine Chance," *Truppenpraxis*, No. 5 (1993), p. 553; and *White Paper 1994* (Bonn: Federal Ministry of Defense, 1994), p. 16. Heinrich used the figure 3,100.

67. Goldbach, tape 5, in Eike.

68. "Wir dienen demselben Vaterland," p. 334.

69. Von Kirchbach, *Reflections on the Growing Together of the German Armed Forces*, p. 14.

70. Schönbohm, *Zwei Armeen und ein Vaterland*, p. 179.

71. Von Schewen, "Abschied von der heilen Welt," p. 609.

72. Heinrichs, "Jeder bekam seine Chance," p. 554.

73. *White Paper 1994*, p. 16.

74. Von Schewen, "Abschied von der heilen Welt," p. 610.

75. Schönbohm, *Zwei Armeen und ein Vaterland*, p. 181.

76. Ein wt-Sonderseminar, "Das Heer auf dem Weg in das Jahr 2000," *Wehrtechnik*, February 1992, p. 23; and "Wir dienen demselben Vaterland," p. 334.

77. "Wir dienen demselben Vaterland," p. 332.

78. Bernard Fleckenstein, *Germany after Unification: Converging and Conflicting Views* (Stausberg: Sozialwissenschaftliches Institut der Bundeswehr, 1996), p. 11.

79. Ibid., p. 12.

80. Federal Ministry of Defense, Fue S I 4-Az24–03–00, *Sachstandsbericht an den Unterausschuß 'Streitkräftefragen in den neuen Bundesländern' des Verteidigungsausschusses des Deutschen Bundestages* (10 May 1996) p. 7, as cited in Fleckenstein, *Germany after Unification*, p. 13.

81. "Wir dienen demselben Vaterland," p. 336.

82. Schönbohm, *Zwei Armeen und ein Vaterland*, p. 138.

83. Ibid., pp. 142, 155, 162.

84. "Bald Pfarrer in ostdeutschen Kasernen," *FAZ*, 8 December 1990.

85. Fleckenstein, *Germany after Unification*, p. 11.

86. "East German Forces Assigned to NATO," *NATO Review*, March 1995, p. 18.

87. Paul Klein and Werner Kriesel, "Offiziersbewerber (1992) aus den alten und neuen Bundesländern: Ein empirischer Vergleich," in Klein and Zimmermann, eds., *Beispielhaft*, p. 101.

88. Vera Gaserow, "Ausbildung in Stiefeln," *Die Zeit*, 30 July 1993.

89. "Der Bosnien-Einsatz der Bundeswehr birgt unkalkulierbare Risiken; Seit Wochen trainieren deutsche Soldaten für ihre Friedenmission," *Focus Magazin*, 29 January 1996.

90. "Bundeswehr-Entlassung bestätigt Hoppe täuschte arglistig," *Süddeutsche Zeitung*, 28 December 1995.

91. G. Hubatschek, "Der steinige Weg zur Wiedervereinigung," in Farwick, ed., *Ein Staat, Eine Armee*, p. 28.

92. Knabe, *Unter der Flagge des Gegners*, p. 123.

Chapter 8

1. All direct quotes in this chapter are taken from the answers given to the questions in the questionnaire at the end of this book.

2. This is not to suggest that regular officers were not irritated at having to put up with political work and political officers. In the first instance, it took away time from regular military exercises, while in the second, it often meant putting up with individuals who lacked the skills of a line officer. As a Russian admiral who was in charge of the Northern Fleet's submarines put it to this author several years ago, "They are a nuisance—they can't even stand watch."

Index

About the Author

Dale R. Herspring is Professor and Head of the Department of Political Science at Kansas State University. A former Foreign Service Officer with the Department of State, he is the author of numerous books and articles. His most recent book is *Russian Civil-Military Relations* (Indiana University Press). He is currently working on a book to be entitled, *Chaplains, Political Commissars, and Political Officers: From Cromwell to the End of the Cold War.*